Female Suicide Bombers

Female Suicide Bombers

ROSEMARIE SKAINE

McFarland & Company, Inc., Publishers
Jefferson, North Carolina, and London

LIBRARY OF CONGRESS CATALOGUING-IN-PUBLICATION DATA

Skaine, Rosemarie.
    Female suicide bombers / Rosemarie Skaine.
        p.   cm.
    Includes bibliographical references and index.

    ISBN 0-7864-2615-2 (softcover : 50# alkaline paper) ∞

    1. Suicide Bombings.   2. Women suicide bombers.
3. Terrorism.   I. Title
HV6431.S556   2006
303.6'25 — dc22   2006001511

British Library cataloguing data are available

On the cover: (top) Suicide bomber Dareen Abu Aisheh in
2002 *(AP Photograph/Nasser Ishtayeh/HO); (bottom)* Israeli
forensics team investigating a 2002 suicide bombing in Jerusalem
(AP Photograph/Jerome Delay)

Manufactured in the United States of America

McFarland & Company, Inc., Publishers
  Box 611, Jefferson, North Carolina 28640
    www.mcfarlandpub.com

Acknowledgments

With warmth and gratitude I thank Max Gross, dean of the School of Intelligence Studies at the Joint Military Intelligence College in Washington, D.C., for recommending students who have extensively researched female suicide bombers and for his support of my writing in general. For interviews I thank Heather A. Andrews, author of *Veiled Jihad: The Threat of Female Islamic Suicide Terrorists*, master of science, strategic intelligence thesis, the Joint Military Intelligence College, July 2005, and Lisa Kruger, author of *Gender and Terrorism: Motivations of Female Terrorists*, master of science, strategic intelligence thesis, the Joint Military Intelligence College, 2005.

I express my deep appreciation and regard to Rear Admiral D.M. Williams, Jr., USN (Ret.), former commander of the Naval Investigative Service Command, for his interview and for his mentoring over time. His expertise and guidance were very helpful.

I am grateful to Hanley J. Harding, Jr., nuclear security specialist and founding board member of Aurora Protection Specialists of Boca Raton, Florida, for his interview and generous support of my work overall.

I appreciate the contribution and support of Jennifer Hardwick, senior director at the Terrorism Research Center, Inc., in northern Virginia.

For sources I am grateful to the Center for Special Studies at the Intelligence and Terrorism Information Center near Gelilot, north of Tel Aviv; Gillian McIllwaine, ESRC project secretary at the Center for the Study of Terrorism and Political Violence at the University of St. Andrews in St. Andrews, Scotland; and Sheryl Mendez, New York bureau editor of photography at *U.S. News and World Report*.

Acknowledgments

For generous assistance in locating and processing images of female suicide bombers, thanks to Jorge Jaramillo, licensing agent for the Associated Press.

I am indebted to the following people for their help in special ways: Erin Solaro, journalist and author of a forthcoming book with the working title, *Beyond GI Jane: American Women, the War on Terror and the New Civic Feminism*; Diane Brandt of Cedar Falls, Iowa, longtime friend; and Paulette Mouchet, a family member.

For tirelessly assisting with editing and proofreading I thank James C. Skaine, professor emeritus for communication studies at the University of Northern Iowa in Cedar Falls.

Richard L. and Nancy L. Craft Kuehner and William V. and Carolyn E. Guenther Kuehner provided ongoing support of my work.

Robert Kramer, professor emeritus for the Center for Social and Behavioral Research and Department of Sociology, Anthropology, and Criminology at the University of Northern Iowa, advanced the book through his expertise in technology.

Cass Paley, my friend of yesteryear, came and gave without taking.

To John R. Brownell, J.D.,
for his work in justice and peace

Table of Contents

Preface

At each moment of its history ... each society has a definite
aptitude for suicide.

Emile Durkheim[1]

Combatants in armed conflicts throughout history have wanted the
world to accept their definition of their cause and actions and their
definition of the opponent's cause and actions.

One side speaks of liberation and liberating, the other of unjustified
aggression and terrorism. The current Palestinian-Israeli conflict provides many familiar examples of this battle over definitions.

The use of females as suicide bombers is a relatively recent happening, and they are more frequently becoming the weapon of choice. Some
female suicide bombers left video, audio or written statements before
they killed themselves. Many left nothing. It is chilling that so many
cannot share their thoughts or reasons for killing themselves.[2] For most
of them, we can only ascribe motives because our interpretation of the
bomber's suicide "becomes an *ex post facto* reconstruction of her life history."[3] Information gained from the women who attempted suicide and
women who considered it but did not do it helps us understand those
who were successful in their bombing.

The motives of suicide bombers are interrelated with the social conditions under which the death occurs. The bomber's inclination to suicide is most easily understood, as Durkheim stated, "by relation to the
collective inclination, and this collective inclination is itself a determined
reflection of the structure of the society in which the individual lives."[4]
The collective conscience comprises the totality of beliefs and practices,

1

of folkways and mores. And from this collective conscience, each individual conscience draws its moral sustenance. When a society is in crisis, the adjustment of an individual to common beliefs is upset and anomie or breakdown or absence of social norms and values appears and is manifested through suicide. Life histories of some suicide bombers and attempted suicides interrelate with sociological variables.[5]

Personal motives such as acquiring honor for herself or family or both are sometimes attributed to female suicide bombers. Or, as in the case of Chechen Black Widows, revenge for loss of family members to the Russian military may be the motive. In this case, suicide may be totally or in part what Durkheim labels anomie. Robert A. Pape's research indicates that less than one-third of the attackers represent anomie.[6]

Elements other than societal influences bring pressure to bear. In one case, a female bomber may have had a love relationship that went wrong. In another case, a woman's brother had committed a crime, and to save his life, she gave her life in a suicide bombing. In Lisa Ling's documentary "Female Suicide Bombers: Dying to Kill," the question was raised: Does she really want to commit suicide?[7]

Motives inspired by social conditions such as honor to her country are also attributed to female suicide bombers. Suicide bombers seek harmony with the society in which they live and adopt the ways of thought and action around them.[8] The bombers are so tightly integrated into their society that they commit suicide. Durkheim labels this type of suicide altruistic and notes that this explanation also applies to those individuals who seek to be martyrs.[9] Modern theorists compare Durkheim's altruistic martyr theory to the terrorist attack of September 11. Those who commit altruistic suicide do so because they feel that it is their duty.[10] Durkheim allows for the overlapping of types of suicide. For example, anomie may be associated with altruism: "One and the same crisis may ruin a person's life, disturb the equilibrium between him [her] and his [her] surroundings, and, at the same time, drive his [her] altruistic disposition to a state which incites him [her] to suicide."[11] Durkheim believed that suicide could not be explained by its form alone but that suicide must be related to social concomitants.[12]

Pape points out that in team suicide, not all members of a squad are motivated purely by altruism. Rather, the motives are mixed, but altruistic suicide is probably necessary for the attack to occur. Single-person missions may be motivated by altruism.[13] Pape concludes that suicide terrorism is not usually an act in which an individual is seeking relief from a painful existence but rather the attacker is acting out of altruism wherein there are "high levels of social integration and respect for community values."[14] It is conceivable that attackers are motivated by more than one type of suicide, but the role of altruism is much more significant, according to Pape.[15]

An ethics of form is needed in the examination of the female suicide bomber. Effort is made to present women empathetically and in more than strictly historical terms.[16] To achieve this goal, I present the female suicide bomber in the context of the power of the society in which she lives, of the terrorist group of which she is a member and of her society as a part of the larger global community.

Bombers work as parts of organizations, rarely as individuals. These organizations and their roles in the bombing must be understood. Some experts believe that we should view suicide bombers as guided missiles, carefully prepared and launched by some larger, organized group, instead of picturing them as driven to kill themselves and others out of a spontaneous surge of emotion.

Understanding the female suicide bomber should aid global societies in the struggle to protect and defend themselves against the attacks. Chapter 1 discusses the long tradition of suicide attackers and martyrdom and modern suicide bombing. It defines suicide bombing and discusses its scope and its multiple causes, including the interrelationship of society and religion. The role of religion symbolically embodies society itself. Religion's power is through representations. God, for example, is societally transfigured and symbolically expressed.[17] Society is the source of the sacred and it is society that defines what is sacred and what is profane.[18] Organized terror is examined including the scope of training and use of the Internet. The al-Qaeda network and Iraqi insurgents, including their female participants, are examined.

Chapter 2 describes the scope of women bombers. It asks what happens when women kill and examines Western societal biases that tend to favor women not killing. Reasons women bomb are presented. The analysis of Palestinian and Chechen women stresses that individual women are shaped by social facts.[19] The reasons some Chechen women perform the death act may be different from those of their Arab sisters while other Chechen women may commit suicide for the same reasons as do Arab women.

Imminent is a new stage of fear.[20] The fear includes the loss of human rights for the women. It also includes fear of Russian acts of terror in their society. This chapter includes organizations known to enlist women and explores the reasons terrorists consider women bombers the "weapon of choice."[21] Methods of recruitment are examined, including methods of male and female handlers.

Chapter 3, "Freedom Fighters or Terrorists?" discusses the bomber in both roles. Military strategic responses are explored, and the question is raised as to why women are used as bombers. The chapter continues the discussion of Western societal biases that tend to favor women not killing and touches on the legal realities that terrorism involves. International law and terrorism as well as U.S. domestic security and foreign policy are examined.

Chapter 4, "Middle East Conflicts in Lebanon and Turkey," discusses the nature of these conflicts and describes the relevant organizations, the Syrian Socialist Nationalist Party (SSNP/PPS) and the Kurdistan Workers Party (PKK). This chapter highlights individual female bombers.

Chapter 5 discusses the nature of the conflict in Sri Lanka, the relevant organization, the Liberation Tigers of Tamil Eelam (LTTE), and activity of the female unit, Black Tigresses. The lives and missions of LTTE female bombers are examined.

Chapter 6 discusses the nature of the Chechen-Russian conflict, the relevant organization, the Chechen Rebels, and activity of the female unit, the Black Widows. The roles of women in the sieges of the Russian Dubrovka House of Culture and Beslan School No. 1 are presented as are the specific missions of certain female bombers.

Chapter 7 discusses the nature of the Palestinian-Israeli conflict and the relevant organizations: the al-Aqsa Martyrs Brigade, Palestinian Nationalists, the Palestinian Islamic Jihad (PIJ), and Hamas. The link between Palestinian terrorism and Islamic fundamentalism is explored. The scope of female bombers is presented and aspects of the lives of some are examined. One section is dedicated to the bombers whose missions were not completed.

Chapter 8 discusses the effects of terror, primarily on U.S. policy, and the prospect for new policy approaches. Continued human rights watch and continued global intervention are advocated. Research indicates that use of female and male suicide bombers will continue and that use of female suicide bombers will increase.[22] The United States' role is to provide leadership, diplomatically, economically, informationally and militarily, to combat this problem.

Chapter 9 presents thoughts on why it is important to examine the tactics of the female bombers as women in war. The evolution of weaponry and the role of women in these attacks are explored.

1

The Phenomenon of Suicide Bombing

[W]hat has to do with war, must be assigned to women also, and they must be used in the same ways.

— Plato[1]

"Tuesday, September 11, 2001, dawned temperate and nearly cloudless in the eastern United States.... For those heading to an airport, weather conditions could not have been better for a safe and pleasant journey,"[2] begins the *9/11 Commission Report*. Among the travelers were Mohamed Atta and Abdul Aziz al Omari, hijackers of American Airlines flight 11 that crashed into the north tower of the World Trade Center. Other hijackers on three other aircraft were also boarding for flights. Two planes crashed into the World Trade Center, one into the Pentagon, and one into the Pennsylvania countryside. More than 2,800 people were killed.[3] These attacks were the first by suicide bombers within the U.S.

The United States has not yet had a female suicide bomber attack, but its military in Iraq encountered one in April 2003. Female bombers were still being used in Iraq in 2005.[4] Scholars and advocates in the field are certain that female bombers will be employed in the United States. Heather A. Andrews, author of *Veiled Jihad: The Threat of Female Islamic Suicide Terrorists*, writes, "Women could very well be the perpetrators of the next 9/11."[5] Jennifer Hardwick, senior director of the Terrorism Research Center Inc. in the Washington, D.C., area, identifies a trend for her audiences: "My most pressing concern is that the U.S. is completely unprepared for suicide bombings, especially by a woman."[6] Further, Lisa Kruger, author of *Gender and Terrorism: Motivations of Female Terrorists*, writes: "International terrorism is on the forefront of the U.S. national security agenda and threat analysis requires information regarding terrorist motivations, intent, capability, and effectiveness. Without accurate information, good analysis is not possible and results in flawed anti-terrorism policy."[7] Based on post–9/11 research, the United States needs to include the possibility of a female suicide bomber attack on the scale of 9/11.

The Long Tradition of Suicide Attackers and Martyrdom

Suicide attackers and martyrdom have existed for centuries. In the first century the Jewish Sicaris used suicide attackers. In the 11th century, the Moslem Hashishiyun and the Ismalis-Nizari, Muslim fighters, used it. In the 18th century Asians did.[8] In every case, Muslims used the suicide attacks to fight Western predominance and colonial rule.[9] Zedalis explains that the Assassins, a Muslim sect, adopted the strategy to advance the cause of Islam. The fighters viewed their deaths as acts of martyrdom for the glory of God. The difference between the Assassins and today's suicide bombers is that the Assassins murdered specific individuals rather than random targets. Robert A. Pape notes that today's forms of suicide bombing include exploding car bombs or suicide vests near busy places, while earlier instances were "mainly suicide missions rather than suicide attacks, and were much less common than they are now."[10]

Early Christendom and Islam had their share of martyrs. Christoph Reuter notes that the city squares of Beirut and Damascus are called "Martyrs' Square." In modern times, however, the ideal martyr "is equipped with weapons and technologies of unprecedented destructive power."[11]

Two thousand years ago the Jewish Sicarians in the imperial Roman world entered battle with the goal of dying. The medieval Crusades had their assassins. In the eighteenth century, Muslims rebelled against Western colonial power on the Malabar coast of southwest India, in northern

Sumatra and in the southern Philippine Islands. Religious duty and personal heroism motivated these groups, Reuter explains. In the twentieth century, suicide attacks were used by the Japanese kamikaze pilots in World War II.

Modern Suicide Bombing

In the 1980s, Hezbollah used suicide attacks as tactics in the civil war in Lebanon.[12] The suicide attack on the U.S. Marine barracks in Beirut, Lebanon, on October 23, 1983, caused casualties that were among the first in the war on terrorism for the United States, said Marine Lieutenant General Jan C. Huly.[13] Sgt. Melvin Lopez Jr. describes the attack:

> In the early morning hours of 23 October 1983, a truck loaded with explosives crashed through the security perimeter of the United States Marine Corps Barracks in Beirut, Lebanon. In the explosion that followed, 241 U.S. military personnel were killed and 80 seriously wounded.[14]

The troops were part of a multinational force sent after war broke out in 1982. Fifty-eight French nationals were also killed. The attack prompted the withdrawal of all American and French forces from Lebanon. Suicide bombers directed their efforts against the Israeli Defense Force in southern Lebanon during the Lebanese civil war. Israel withdrew in May 2000.[15]

After the Hezbollah used the tactic, other groups adopted suicide bombings: Chechen rebels in 2000,[16] the Tamil Tigers in Sri Lanka in 1987, the Palestinian Islamist group Hamas in Israel in 1994, the Kurdistan Workers Party in Turkey in 1996, and al-Qaeda with the 1998 bombings of the U.S. embassies in Kenya and Tanzania and other attacks. Religious and secular Palestinian terrorist groups employed it extensively in the second Palestinian intifada (uprising) that began in 2000.[17]

The suicide terror attack against the United States on September 11, 2001, catapulted suicide bombing into a global threat.[18]

Definition

Boaz Ganor, director of the International Policy Institute for Counter Terrorism (ICT), defines suicide terrorism as "the operational method in which the very act of the attack is dependent upon the death of the perpetrator. [Aimed at] striking a blow to public moral[e]."[19] Ganor recognizes the differences in theoretical and operational definitions of terrorism:

> When dealing with terrorism and guerrilla warfare, implications of defining our terms tend to transcend the boundaries of theoretical discussions. In the struggle against terrorism, the problem of definition is a crucial element in the attempt to coordinate international collaboration, based on the currently accepted rules of traditional warfare.[20]

I agree with Ganor's definition of terrorism. When I began my research for this book, a friend and expert on terrorism said to me: "Gender importance of a bomber is largely a Western concept. Militarily, a bomber is a bomber." I believe that whatever the gender or motivation of the bomber, the end result sought is the same, death. And gender is but one element of the complex phenomenon of suicide bombing. If we are to understand it fully, we must understand also the societal roles of men and women. All of the societies in which women have participated in suicide bombing are patriarchal.[21]

In addition to a sound definition, we must consider the role of terrorist organizations. Clara Beyler of ICT explains that an organization benefits from the success of the suicide attack in two ways: first, the goal of slaughtering human beings, and, second, the ability to get attention and have the media focus on the group's nationalistic or religious cause. Suicide bombing provides an additional focus to terrorism. The emphasis is not only on the victims, but also on the perpetrators. Beyler adds that the relationship of terrorism to female suicide bombing is unexpected.

> One of the most surprising developments has been the way in which suicide terrorism has opened the stage for the entry of female

combatants, who are increasingly involved in what was once a male-dominated arena.[22]

Preston Taran believes the West should not use terms that detract from the heroic acts of the shaheed, or martyr. The act of martyrdom "is a complex act on the part of an individual, who needless to say is under tremendous personal and spiritual stress."[23] Raphael Israeli, a former intelligence officer in the Israeli army and professor of Islamic and Middle Eastern history at Hebrew University in Jerusalem, believes the Western label "suicide bomber" is a misnomer. The label implies a disposition toward madness and an Islamic frame of reference and diagnosis is necessary to comprehend this "unparalleled mode of self sacrifice."[24]

I agree with these authors because, whatever the label, whatever the definition, such bombing is a military strategy that causes the loss of not only the bomber's life but the lives of unsuspecting others. Acceptable terms are attacker, fighter, bomber, soldier, combatant.

The Scope of Suicide Bombing

By 2001, male and female bombers had been used by 17 terror organizations in 14 countries. From 1980 to 2001, suicide bombing accounted for 3 percent of terrorist incidents, but caused half of the total deaths, even when the fatalities from 9/11 are excluded.[25]

Suicide bombing attacks are increasing. Since the 1983 attack on the U.S. barracks in Beirut, Lebanon, about 188 attacks have occurred in ten countries: Lebanon, Israel, Sri Lanka, India, Pakistan, Afghanistan, Yemen, Turkey, Russia and the United States. Robert A. Pape presents these figures:

> The rate has increased from 31 in the 1980s, to 104 in the 1990s, to 53 in 2000–2001 alone. The rise of suicide terrorism is especially remarkable, given that the total number of terrorist incidents worldwide fell during the period, from a peak of 666 in 1987 to a low of 274 in 1998, with 348 in 2001.[26]

From 2000 to 2003, more than 300 suicide attacks killed more than 5,300 people in 17 countries and wounded many thousands more.[27]

Pape's database contains 315 suicide attacks from 1980 through 2003. More troublesome, he says, is that the attacks are climbing from an average of three a year in the 1980s to ten a year in the 1990s to more than 40 in 2001 and 2002, and almost 50 in 2003. Pape believes that most worrying of all is the intensely deadly nature of the act. He found that from 1980 through 2003, 3 percent of all terrorist incidents were suicide attacks but that this accounted for 48 percent of all deaths, making the average suicide terrorist attack 12 times more deadly than any other form of terrorism, even with the exclusion of the casualties of 9/11.[28]

Defining the scope of suicide bombing is fraught with difficulties. Sources differ. Reports are sometimes initially withheld, as was the case in U.S. State Department's 2004 country-by-country report, *Patterns of Global Terrorism*. This report has been issued every year since 1986, accompanied by statistical tables. When released, the report showed an increase in terrorism incidents around the world in 2004. Even though the document was reported to have been altered to strip it of its pessimistic statistics, the 2004 edition showed a big increase, from 172 significant terrorist attacks in 2003 to 655 in 2004. Much of the increase took place in Iraq and contradicted Pentagon claims that the insurgency was waning.[29]

Motivations of Bombers

The table of contents of the 2005 At Issue series, *What Motivates Suicide Bombers*, suggests multiple causes of suicide bombing. Two of the essays discuss the pros and cons of Islam and identify despair and hopelessness as motivations to bomb. Other essays explore the promise of an afterlife, American imperialism, nationalism, anti–Semitism and television as motives.[30]

At least 70 percent of the 300 attacks from 2000 to 2003 were religiously motivated, with more than 100 attacks by al-Qaeda or affiliates acting in al-Qaeda's name.[31] Scott Atran identifies this trend along with the increased prominence of suicide terrorism in recent years.

In 2002, the Palestinian Authority broadened the religious significance of martyrdom through poetry. It presented martyrdom as a Christian ideal as well an Islamic ideal that is incumbent upon every Moslem, according to Itamar Marcus of the Palestinian Media Watch. The following poem glorifying martyrdom was read and displayed on the screen of a Palestinian Authority television program, "The Beat of the Words." Marcus writes, "The poem promises that the Martyr, in Afterlife will, together with the Koran, 'carry a Cross.'"[32]

The Winds of Revolution[33]

Why do you kill my dream,
And not let me die as a Martyr?
My death will strengthen me,
And melt the iron for me.
I do not die to end,
Because in my death — is life,
In my death — is a hymn.
I am, my friend, a revolution in a human body,
A determined volcano.
I will carry my soul on my shoulder,
And in the Afterlife I will carry
A Cross and a Koran.

Religion symbolically embodies society itself. It is power greater than individual people. It gives energy, asks for sacrifice and suppresses selfish tendency. Religion's power is through representations. God, for example, is societally transfigured and symbolically expressed.[34] Thus, society is the source of the sacred. Society defines what is sacred and what is profane.[35]

In his analysis of Islam and terrorism, Peter David, political editor of *The Economist*, describes the relationship between the sacred and the society. People who believe that Islam advocates terrorism may do so not on the basis of the Koran but do so because "it is difficult to divorce Islam from terrorism, especially when terrorists themselves say they are acting in the name of Islam."[36] This difficulty was apparent to the terrorists training in Afghanistan before 9/11. The Taliban and al-Qaeda were successful in hijacking Islam by proclaiming their reforms were in the name of Islam. The Taliban and al-Qaeda "were neither representative of Afghanistan nor Islam, the world of Islam refused to heed the call to join the Taliban and bin Laden in a *jihad* against the infidel U.S. and its allies. Even Pakistan, the birthplace of the Taliban and their most consistent supporter, quickly repudiated the terrorist acts of 11 September, supported the USA and withdrew its support from the Taliban."[37]

As do others who write on suicide bombing, David recalls the horror of the September 11 suicide attacks on the United States. He reasons that because the 9/11 terrorists cited Islam as the inspiration for their attack, Islam has clearly been a motivating factor of terrorists. He says arguments can be found for and against terrorism but that the 19 men who took part in the 9/11 attacks produced big consequences, including the subsequent U.S. military actions in Afghanistan and Iraq. He concludes that it is not Islam, the faith, that provides the answer, but the "history, sociology and politics of Islam are undoubtedly a part of it."[38]

Some reason that nationalism motivates suicide bombers. Robert A. Pape argues "Contrary to popular perception, suicide bombers are not overwhelmingly motivated by religion, despair or the promise of an afterlife, but by nationalism.... The use of suicide terrorism is ... a strategic method aimed toward securing nationalist goals."[39] In a 2005 interview with Reuters, Pape said:

> Islamic fundamentalism is not the primary driver of suicide terrorism. Nearly all suicide terrorist attacks are committed for a secular strategic goal — to compel modern democracies to withdraw military forces from territory the terrorists view as their homeland.[40]

He believes that these reasons account for the surge in suicide attacks in Iraq and around the world.

Pape notes the Tamil Tigers of Sri Lanka (LTTE), a secular terrorist group, are not motivated by religion. The LTTE was responsible for 75 of the 186 terrorist attacks from 1980 to 2001. Among Islamic suicide attacks, secular groups represent about a third.[41]

The promise of an afterlife is another reason that motivates suicide bombers. Raphael Israeli believes suicide bombers become martyrs to access heavenly paradise. In paradise, a martyr can drink wine without a resulting hangover and is married to 72 beautiful virgins.[42] With the advent of women bombers, the afterlife concept needed to be re-examined. For instance, what would be an afterlife substitute reward of virgins for the female bomber? Certainly, all other aspects of the promise outlined by Raphael Israeli are applicable to women — the exaltation of position, jewels, fine silk, alcohol and the assurance that their relatives will also be in paradise.

In an earlier work, Israeli explains that the deputy director of the authoritative Al-Azhar University, Sheikh 'Abd al-Fattah Jam'an replied, in part, "Some are women who acceded to Paradise from this world and are obedient Muslims who observe the words of Allah: 'We created them especially and have made them virgins, loving and equal in age.'"[43]

In addition, Israeli provides the connection of an afterlife with Islam. Through an examination of songs, Israeli writes that one can discover the "three elements of the Islamikaze makeup: first, delegitimization of the enemy (the desecrators of al-Aqsa, who are cursed by Allah); second, the call for jihad, which binds all Muslim fighters, more so the fundamentalists who are not waiting for the established community or regime to launch it; and third, luring the predisposed to be a suicide bomber and to go to their death without fear and with great rewards awaiting the strong of heart."[44]

Raphael Israeli explains that a passage in the Koran links self-sacrifice and daring in battle with paradise. The prophet Muhammad motivated his followers not to fear battle by describing the next world as a better one. The tradition involves the angels Munkir and Nakir, who question all deceased Muslims before they enter Paradise. Martyrs bypass this interrogation, enter heaven directly, and are spared the trials on resurrection day. A hadith specifically says, in part, the *shahid* (male martyr) will be pardoned by Allah, admitted to paradise, marry beautiful women and be spared the tomb and will not be submitted to judgment.[45] For the female martyr, marrying beautiful women is not generally an attraction of paradise, but being recreated as a virgin in paradise is.

American imperialism is given as the reason for the suicide bombing of some groups. Osama bin Laden, the founder of al-Qaeda, is the mastermind of terrorist attacks, including the September 11, 2001, assaults. Bin Laden holds the American imperialism premise. He believes the United States has insulted Islam in three basic ways, through the establishment of military bases in the Holy Land of Saudi Arabia, seeking to destroy Iraq and other Arab nations in order to gain access to Middle Eastern oil, and unrelenting support of Israel. He considers the actions of the United States as a declaration of war on God, putting the United States in partnership with the devil. This view justifies holy war and the belief that every Muslim must kill Americans to "restore honor and dignity to the Middle East and to Islam."[46] In 1998, on the basis of al-Qaeda's justification, bin Laden issued a *fatwah* (edict) to all Muslims to kill the Americans and their allies, civilian and military.

Hanley J. Harding, Jr., director of operations and programs development for Aurora Protection Specialists, writes "'holy wars' are not 'merely' for religious purposes, they are very much a quest for political expansion."[47] Harding believes the fundamentalist movement "is publicly fueled by Islamic fundamentalism, while being privately driven by money and the quest for political power."[48] He explains:

> The Holy Qur'an codifies the justification for the expansion of Islam, at any cost, but wherever there is terrorism, it is ultimately supported by money. And it is not money merely sufficient for buying weapons and supplies for the faithful ... it is money for paying the faithful to remain faithful to the terrorist political aims and goals, even if it is only money for the families of suicide bombers. The money flows in very large sums so the faithful will keep joining up and keep at their "holy" work ... the well-paid "holy" work of terrorism.[49]

Harding writes that terrorists do not care whom they kill while striking their targets. He explains:

> The small civilian cells of fundamentalist terrorism operate on a much smaller [than a massive global scale], striving mightily to create as much death and destruction as they can, not only for "the cause" but for the sheer egotistical gratification of having accomplished a successful and spectacular act of terrorism. So, we have heavy social and religious reinforcement, money and personal gratification ... all very compelling forces to keep terrorists at their work.[50]

Anti-Semitism is the basis for suicide bombings on Israel, because some Arab groups believe the Jews are devils and in the name of God, they need to be killed, writes Fiamma Nirenstein, author and Italian journalist based in Jerusalem, Israel. She states: "Anti-Semitic propaganda abounds in the Arab world. Middle Eastern schools, television and radio stations, newspapers, and government agencies all go to great lengths to demonize Jews in order to create a common enemy for the Arab world to unite against."[51] Yet Israel is expected to live with the very people who attempt to annihilate them, she laments.

Nirenstein believes that the misrepresentation of Israel by Arab world media produces suicide bombers because there are few if any countervailing sources. Israel is seen as "a malignant force embodying every possible negative attribute — aggressor, usurper, sinner, occupier, corrupter, infidel, murderer, barbarian."[52] Examples reflecting these attitudes are seen in television promotions urging children to martyr themselves and in Arab popular culture's hit song "I Hate Israel." The Arab schools teach that Israel is evil and that evil should be rooted out. Nirenstein concludes that many world leaders do not recognize that grievances against Israel have nothing to do with dividing territory and political authority but "with the entire Zionist project, with the very existence of a Jewish state in the Middle East."[53]

Those who believe that Islam does not stand behind suicide bombing hold that Islam is a peaceful religion. President George W. Bush said that Islam is a peaceful religion that does not condone terrorism. He said, "These acts of violence against innocents violate the fundamental tenets of the Islamic faith."[54]

On CNN's *Larry King Live*, Muslim scholar Dr. Maher Hathout, a retired physician and senior adviser to the Muslim Public Affairs Council, explained that to commit suicide is not in the Koran. The idea that suicide is a religious idea is coming from the misuse of Islam to prey on others. He said:

> The only thing that is inexcusable in Islam is suicide. There's no excuse for it. So suicide is completely prohibited, and the suicide to kill others is even worse. It is totally unacceptable.... They highlight certain stories and bring them to the forefront to play on the ignorant and the gullible, and to lead them to death.[55]

Preston Taran states that suicide is forbidden in Islam. Individuals are not permitted to kill themselves, but martyrdom is not suicide. He explains:

> However, one who gives up his life to the cause of Allah is not considered to have committed suicide. This act is considered sacrificial, and a noble performance. Although the individual's life is given up, it is not a suicide, for it is done not for self-fulfillment but to the glory of Allah. It is not suicide to know one will die in the act of defending your God, your people and your religious beliefs.[56]

Daniel Pipes, director of the Middle East Forum and board member of the U.S. Institute of Peace, reasons that many suicide bombers hold militant beliefs and are motivated by a revolutionary activism. He maintains that because these types of bombers are well educated, middle-class people with jobs and families, they are free to engage in bombings. They are not the children of poverty and despair. Pipes asks a provocative question: Could militant Islam result from wealth rather than poverty? "Militant Islam results more from success than failure,"[57] he concludes. Pipes believes that Westerners have a ways to go in understanding Islam. Islamists see wealth as a means to an end, that end being power. Only when Westerners put economics into perspective and appreciate the religious, cultural and political dimensions will the causes of militant Islam be understood.[58]

The Training of Bombers

Terrorists may consider online training and indoctrination safer than training camps. These commodities are available from web sites with names such as "Jihad On Line, Thunderbolts of Right and The Tip of the Camel's Hump (an Islamic equivalent to the moral high ground)."[59] Further, some online "training manuals published by al-Qa'ida comprise a syllabus of seven courses; Shari'ah and Jihad (holy law and holy war), Explosives, Light Arms, Assassinations, Hand-To-Hand Combat, Intelligence Gathering On Targets and Communications."

U.S. intelligence agencies and terrorism specialists conclude that the global jihad movement has become web-directed. Al-Qaeda and its offshoots are building a massive library of training materials, a shift from their earlier emphasis of solo communication. Jihadists are safer in cyberspace because they do not have face armies or police forces. Crossing borders with false documents ceases to be a problem. According to Gabriel Weimann at the University of Haifa in Israel, eight years ago he found 12 terror-related web sites. Today, he tracks more than 4,500.[60]

Internet use began with al-Qaeda's fixed sites. Realizing these sites were too vulnerable, groups turned to posting on jihadist bulletin boards and sites that offered free upload services where files could be stored. Realizing emails can be intercepted, terrorists have taken to using "dead drop." This method involves opening an account on a free public email service such as Hotmail, writing a draft message, saving it as a draft, then transmitting the email account name and password during discussion on a relatively secure message board. The intended recipient then opens the email account to read the draft. No message was sent, so risk of interception is reduced. Finally, adopting encryption wherever possible helps keep groups such as al-Qaeda ahead of their electronic pursuers.[61]

In September 2004, cyber-jihadists introduced a cyber magazine, *Al-Khansaa*, named after a female poet who converted to Islam during the time of Muhammad. It promotes a distorted brand of women's liberation. The first editorial praised the example set by two female suicide bombers:

> We stand shoulder to shoulder with our men, supporting them, helping them, and backing them up. We educate their sons and we prepare ourselves. We will stand covered by our veils and wrapped in our robes, weapons in hand, our children in our laps, with the Koran and the Sunna of the Prophet of Allah directing and guiding us. The blood of our husbands and the body parts of our children are the sacrifice by means of which we draw closer to Allah.[62]

Christoph Reuter, international correspondent for the German magazine *Stern*, says the reasons given by men who recruit women, as in the case of the LTTE, have nothing to do with the Western sense of feminism, but with the need to replace the men who are needed for combat duty against the government troops.

Not to be ignored is the concept of creating a sense of community within the organizations. The LTTE's Black Tigresses, for example, have a number of steps women must take to join the suicide squad. According to Pape, the first step is that those who join must be highly motivated to perform their mission. Mental stability is valued over tactical military competence. The second is that attackers are trained in special camps designed only for suicide missions. Each day members engage in physical exercises, arms training and political classes that stress results. The third is that attackers conduct dress rehearsals near the intended location of an attack and study past operations through films of actual suicide missions. Pape wrote that only one known example exists of a Black Tiger withdrawing from a mission. From 1980 to 2001, Pape found the Black Tigresses and Tigers performed 76 suicide attacks.[63]

In his analysis of suicide terrorism, Scott Atran concludes:

> Support and recruitment for suicide terrorism occur not under conditions of political repression, poverty, and unemployment or illiteracy as such but when converging political, economic, and social trends produce diminishing opportunities relative to expectations, thus generating frustrations that radical organizations can exploit. For this purpose, relative deprivation is more significant than absolute deprivation.[64]

Atran's analysis reflects Durkheim's theory of altruistic suicide. In seeking to live in harmony with the society in which they are so tightly integrated, those who commit altruistic suicide do so because they feel that it is their duty.[65]

Organized Terror

Scott Atran maintains that those who conceive terrorism belong to an intellectually elite group with enough material wealth to pursue personal advancement but that they choose for themselves a life of struggle and sacrifice. They often require of their followers a greater commitment.

Atran writes these leaders are not irrational but are "Using religious sentiments for political or economic purposes."[66]

Atran explains that cell loyalties are culturally contrived, mimic and temporarily override genetically based fidelities to kin while obtaining the belief in sacrifice. The cells are small, representing a tight brotherhood. The Harkat ul-Mujahedeen is a Pakistani affiliate of the World Islamic Front for Jihad against the Jews and Crusaders, the umbrella organization formed by bin Laden in 1998. Recruits are required to take The Oath to Jihad, which affirms that, by their sacrifice, they help secure the future of their family of fictive kin. It states "Each [martyr] has a special place — among them are brothers, just as there are sons and those even more dear."[67]

It is critical to understand how the leaders turn ordinary desires into a "craving" for the mission to the benefit of the organization.[68] Atran maintains that for a nation to understand and deflect suicide terrorism, there must be a concentration on the organization's structure, indoctrination methods, and ideological appeal more than on personality attributes of the recruits.

Each society depends on communal support, but the reasons for support differ. The Palestinians, for example, combine a sense of historical injustice with personal loss and humiliation by Israeli occupation while al-Qaeda and Jemaah Islamiyah are more ideologically driven.[69]

Robert A. Pape provides an example of the importance of the sense of community within the LTTE. Female LTTE fighter Nandini explained in a 1995 interview that the strength and honor of the Black Tigers is the use of their very lives as missiles along with a determination and purpose that is unmatched by conventional weaponry. Nandini gives further insight into the benefits of community and the practice of choosing death over capture: "If I am captured and I give up ten names of people in the movement, they'll capture and torture those ten to get a hundred names, and after capturing a hundred people they can capture a thousand people, and so on."[70] This method, she maintains, would destroy the movement. If she gave up her life by taking cyanide, for example, she is protecting not only the movement but the lives of those people the enemy would capture.

Christoph Reuter argues it is necessary to focus on specifics of the movements for an accurate analysis. This focus shows that individual bombings are very different from each other.[71] Eight organizations that use female suicide bombers are discussed in Chapter 2 and in detail in chapters 4 through 7. A discussion follows on the al-Qaeda Network and Iraqi insurgency.

The Al-Qaeda Network and Iraqi Insurgents

Osama bin Laden's organization, al-Qaeda, was responsible for the suicide bombings against the U.S. embassies in Nairobi, Kenya, and Dar-es-Salaam, Tanzania. Two hundred twenty-four people were killed and about 5000 wounded. Two suicide bombers affiliated with al-Qaeda blew themselves up in a boat in Aden harbor next to the USS *Cole*. Seventeen U.S. sailors were killed.[72]

The most notable suicide attacks of the al-Qaeda network are the September 11 attacks on the United States. The suicide attacks by al-Qaeda in Saudi Arabia in the spring of 2003 came with a drastic reduction in the U.S. military and civilian presence in the country.[73]

Osama bin Ladin established al-Qaeda in 1988 with Arabs who fought in Afghanistan against the Soviet Union. The group helped finance, recruit, transport, and train Sunni Islamic extremists for the Afghan resistance. Their purpose is to unite Muslims to overthrow regimes that are not Islamic and to throw out Westerners and non–Muslims from countries. Their ultimate goal is to establish Islamic leadership and governance throughout the world.[74]

In February 1998, al-Qaeda issued a statement under the banner of the World Islamic Front for Jihad Against the Jews and Crusaders. They said "it was the duty of all Muslims to kill U.S. citizens, civilian and military, and their allies everywhere."[75]

In June 2001 al-Qaeda merged with al-Jihad, the Egyptian Islamic Jihad, and renamed itself Qa'idat al-Jihad. In late 2004 al-Qaeda merged with Abu Mus'ab al-Zarqawi's organization in Iraq, and al-Zarqawi's group changed its name to Qa'idat al-Jihad fi Bilad al-Rafidayn, which means al-Qaeda in the Land of the Two Rivers.[76]

Al-Qaeda's strength is difficult to assess, says the U.S. State Department. However, it estimates that the organization numbers several thousand and is worldwide. It is an umbrella for many Sunni Islamic extremist groups, including some members of Gama'a al-Islamiyya, the Islamic Movement of Uzbekistan, and the Harakat ul-Mujahidin. Since the U.S. invaded Afghanistan, al-Qaeda has moved in small groups across South Asia, Southeast Asia, the Middle East and Africa.[77]

Al-Qaeda is among the insurgent groups in Iraq as the Qa'idat al-Jihad fi Bilad al-Rafidayn (QJBR). Other names include: al-Zarqawi Network, al-Qaeda in Iraq, al-Qaeda of Jihad Organization in the Land of The Two Rivers and Jama'at al-Tawhid wa'al-Jihad.[78]

The Jordanian Palestinian Abu Mus'ab al-Zarqawi (Ahmad Fadhil Nazzal al-Khalaylah, a.k.a. Abu Ahmad, Abu Azraq) established cells in Iraq soon after the start of the U.S.-led coalition invasion of Iraq. The group formalized in April 2004 to bring together jihadists and other insurgents in Iraq fighting against U.S. and coalition forces. Zarqawi and his group helped finance, recruit, transport, and train Sunni Islamic extremists for the Iraqi resistance. In October 2004 the group merged with al-Qaeda. Their immediate goal is to expel the coalition and establish an Islamic state in Iraq. Their longer-term goal is to proliferate jihad from Iraq into "Greater Syria," that is, Syria, Lebanon, Israel, and Jordan, according to the U.S. State Department.

Jabin T. Jacob, research officer at the Institute of Peace and Conflict Studies in New Delhi, India, writes "The suicide bomber phenomenon had a faster genesis in American-occupied Iraq, in comparison to the Palestinians who adopted this tactic in the mid–1990s after several decades of Israeli occupation."[79] Jacob questions whether religious reasons alone cause suicide attacks in a secular country such as Iraq. In an unequal fight, suicide bombing has become the Iraqi resistance's ultimate weapon.

Conclusion

Examining women within their total context is essential, but to fully understand the phenomenon of suicide bombing, a closer look at participation of women bombers is necessary, for indeed, the U.S. military is experiencing the women's attacks in Iraq. For a nation, a better understanding of women attackers and their methods is critical to a sound defense. Plato understood well that gender assignment had nothing to do with equality or feminism but with what was considered just and the best defense. For, he observed, such a state could not exist until "philosophers became kings, and kings became philosophers."[80]

2

The Female Suicide Bomber in Society

[T]o be ready for the increasing threat of women terrorists, we must recognize women as rational actors as opposed to emotional reactors of violence.

— Lisa Kruger
Graduate, Joint Military Intelligence College[1]

According to the Council on Foreign Relations, women have performed about one-third of the Liberation Tigers of Tamil Eelam's (LTTE) suicide attacks and two-thirds of the attacks by the Kurdistan Workers Party (PKK). These organizations and others, including the Syrian Socialist Nationalist Party, have used pregnant women to get past security checks on the way to their targets.[2]

Over 30 female suicide bombers carried out attacks against the Russians since 1999, Kim Murphy writes in the *Los Angles Times*.[3] Raphael Israeli reports that about a dozen cases of Palestinian women who participated in the Islamikaze (a term coined by Israeli) attacks against Israelis were recorded and documented.[4]

Robert A. Pape's survey represents 462 suicide terrorist attackers from 1980 to the end of 2003. The survey identified the gender of 381, and of those 59, or 15 percent, were female. Pape identified the proportion of female attackers in some groups:[5]

al-Qaeda	none [Note: after 2003, al-Qaeda used female attackers]
Palestinians	6 (5 percent)
Lebanese Hezbollah	6 (16 percent)
Tamil Tigers	23 (20 percent)
Chechens	14 (60 percent)
PKK	10 (71 percent)

Pape's survey identified the age of 261 attackers from the same five groups. The percentage of males and females from 15 to 18 years was similar, 13 percent and 14 percent, but females were less likely to be in their late teens and early twenties and more likely to be in their mid-twenties and older.[6]

Is it possible to provide a profile of the typical female bomber? Clara Beyler of the International Center for Terrorism, concludes from her research that it is difficult to make accurate generalizations because female suicide bombing is too recent, the attacks too few, not enough research has been undertaken and the sample size is too small.[7]

Pape is not sure. He says the sizable increase in suicide terrorism over the last 20 years "suggests that there may not be a single profile."[8] He does report a shift in some characteristics of the suicide terrorists' profile. Suicide bombers now come from a range of lifestyles and have diverse characteristics. The bomber may be college educated or uneducated, married or single, man or woman, socially isolated or integrated, 13 years old or 47. This profile is a departure from earlier studies that described suicide bombers as uneducated, unemployed, socially isolated and single men in their late teens and early 20s.

Jacqueline Rose, a reviewer for the *London Review of Books*, also believes that a suicide assassin profile may not be possible.

> For years, Israeli secret service analysts and social scientists have been trying to build up a typical profile of the suicide "assassin," only to conclude that there isn't one. It may indeed be that your desire to solve the problem is creating it, that burrowing into the psyche of the enemy, far from being an attempt to dignify them with understanding, is a form of evasion that blinds you to your responsibility for the state they are in.[9]

2. The Female Suicide Bomber in Society

Scholars have concluded that certain aspects of profiling are possible. David Lester *et al.* suggest that bombers may share personality traits such as an authoritarian personality and that they may be characterized by risk factors that increase the chance of suicide.[10] Ami Pedahzur *et al.* suggest that Palestinian terrorists from 1993 to 2002 fit the altruistic type of suicide but have some elements of the fatalistic type. These authors label these terrorists under the category of fatalistic altruistic suicide.[11]

The Israel Security Agency reports that women bombers were from the margins of Palestinian society and did not usually fit the accepted profile of the average Palestinian woman.[12] Yoni Fighel, a researcher for the International Center for Terrorism, reports that most of the women are from two extremes of Palestinian society and neither group fits the image of the traditional Palestinian woman. He writes: "Some of them were professional women with education and training far beyond the average, while others were common young women with neither education nor career. These women were united in that they carried a large amount of personal 'baggage.'"[13]

Fighel illustrates the "baggage" concept through the life of 29 year old Hanadi Jaradat, a trainee lawyer from Jenin and the second female suicide bomber for the Islamic Jihad (see Table 7.1). Although there is no evidence to show how Jaradat became an attacker, Fighel believes the loss of two family members in the conflict "was no doubt the trigger — the catalyst — for her final act."[14] Although Jaradat's motives will never be fully known, Fighel writes, "Something went wrong between her return to the West Bank after graduating from law school and June 2003, when two of her family members were killed."[15] According to Fighel, Jaradat may have been facing questions about why she was single. Her status in Palestinian society combined with her emotional predisposition made her "easy prey" for the Palestinian Islamic Jihad's (PIJ) "sharks."

Shaul Kimhi of the International Policy Institute for Counter-Terrorism in Herzliya, Israel, and his colleague Shemuel Even of the Jaffee Center for Strategic Studies at Tel-Aviv University in Tel-Aviv, Israel, conducted a study that found in the Palestinian-Israeli conflict most suicide perpetrators were: ages 17 to 23, 81 percent; from Judea and Samaria, 84 percent; single, 93 percent; high school educated, 51 percent; Moslems, 100 percent.[16]

Palestinian Rahnah Jaradat, center, holding a picture of her daughter Hanadi and accompanied by other relatives, mourns over her death at the family house in the northern West Bank town of Jenin. Hanadi Jaradat, 27, an apprentice lawyer, blew herself up in the Maxim beach restaurant in Haifa, Oct. 4, 2003 (AP Photograph/Mohammed Ballas).

Kimhi and Even report that, after December 2001, Fatah and the National Resistance joined the Hamas and the Islamic Jihad in perpetrating attacks. In addition, women joined in the suicide attacks. By January 2003, 24 women had been captured before committing attacks. By January 2004, seven women had exploded.[17]

Debra D. Zedalis reports in June 2004 that the U.S. Department of Homeland Security profile of bombers applied only to men. Thus, women were not subject to the same scrutiny for visa application or resident alien status.[18]

Kimhi and Even present a typology of suicide terrorists in the Israeli-Palestinian conflict. Their classification suggests four categories of suicide bombers: religious fanatic, exploited, avenger, and nationalist fanatic.

They base their categories on the motive of the suicide bomber and the course the bomber undergoes from recruitment to detonating the bomb. They state that their research suggests some overlap of the four categories, yet it is possible to see a prototype of distinct groups.[19]

Kimhi and Even formulated hypotheses about the dominant personality traits of the prototypes. The religious and social/nationalist types have a steadfast nature. The religious prototype is also goal-focused, believes in a divinely determined fate, is influenced by people she or he reveres and a belief in the afterlife. The social/nationalist prototype is also sure in his or her ways and willing to sacrifice self. The other two prototypes, avenger for suffering and exploited, have much more of a negative view. Kimhi and Even describe bombers motivated by retribution for suffering as hopeless, vengeful and having a tendency to see their lives as worthless. The exploited type is characterized as dependent, anxious, having difficulty resisting pressure and seeking recognition.[20]

Birgit Langenberger, a Ph.D. student in political science at the Graduate Faculty of New School University, suggests that female suicide bombers are not merely instruments of norms, that they have good reasons to act violently. She notes, "Women make use of the non-violence myth, ironically asserting their gender-difference precisely because it enables them to operate undercover behind enemy lines."[21] Langenberger proposes that we are locked in a triple bind in the ways that women and violence are viewed: women's violence is not different from that of men, nor is it an instrument of men, nor is it purely emancipating. She submits that "we make the mistake of taking their speech or action at face value."[22] She leaves us with the question of whether the bombers' actions speak for themselves and carry a promise of emancipation, although Nida Alahmad, also a Ph.D. candidate at New School University, stresses in her response to Langenberger that emancipation is "crucial to understanding of women's political agency and their engagement with political violence."[23]

What Happens When Women Kill

I believe that female bombers can and do have more than one role, but to understand fully the women who martyr themselves, we need to examine what we can of the lives they lived. In so doing, caution is needed in the examination of sources. Belinda Morrissey, author of *When Women Kill*, writes that when women murder, mainstream and feminist legal and media discourses are often read as displaying evidence of trauma. She warns, "The impulse to project on to others impulses and traits that are present in and unacceptable to the self is especially clear in mainstream legal and media discourses."[24]

Morrissey explains that at least two of the primary defense mechanisms, projection and regression, are present. First, women are sometimes vilified by turning them into monsters because it is safer than facing the "savagery at the core of 'the law' and the media."[25] Vilification allows displacement of the offender from her society. It insists on her otherness. Knowledge that she is produced by that society can be avoided. In contrast, regression allows a return to safety and familiarity demonstrated in the use of stock narratives of women who kill, writes Morrissey.

The defense mechanisms of projection and regression reactions to trauma "result in representations of women who kill which deny the human agency of their female protagonists and confirm that female aggression has no place in our culture."[26] As a villain, she is an evil being, not human. Vilification often advances to the mythification of women who kill. Morrissey cites examples from literature, especially Medea, or the evil witch. In mythifying her, she becomes familiar rather than contemporary. These strategies distance the female from her society.

Perhaps most appropriate to the female suicide bomber is Morrissey's concept that "victimism denies agency through invoking victimology theses which insist on the powerlessness of the oppressed. Many portrayals of women who kill depict them as so profoundly victimized that it is difficult to regard them as ever having engaged in an intentional act in their lives."[27]

In my attempt to humanize the women who bomb, where possible I have included some personal aspects. We cannot ignore the role of organizations and handlers, but we can recognize that women, in their own right, are real and do kill. Morrissey insists that relevant to cultural studies is that "representations should be analyzed as representations and not as 'true' reflections of a unitary, pre-existing self."[28]

Western Societal Biases Tend to Favor Women Not Killing

In her review of Belinda Morrissey's book, *When Women Kill: Questions of Agency and Subjectivity*, Tracy L. Conn wrote, "Belinda Morrissey persuasively argued that the media's efforts to rewrite women's violent acts as life-givers, whereas the purposeful termination of life is more commonly attributed to men. This difference was based mainly on the fact that women are seen so."[29]

Rose thinks most will agree that "the story of suicide bombing is a story of people driven to extremes."[30] Ultimately, she believes, "We need to find a language that will allow us to recognize why, in a world of inequality and injustice, people are driven to do things that we hate. Without claiming to know too much. Without condescension."[31] While some female attackers may have personal reasons for participation, I believe capturing what we do know without condescension about the women who perform the bombings is a meaningful step in helping us comprehend why they elect martyrdom.[32] Belinda Morrissey advises that we need to be aware of media and legal discourses.[33] The dialogue perpetuated by media and legal sources sustains the concept that women do not kill, and the myth trickles into all walks of society. This myth persists in spite of existing "facts, information, scholarly work, or academic journals."[34]

Reasons Women Bomb

Women participate in suicide bombing for diverse reasons.

The Pew Global Attitudes Project conducted a series of worldwide public opinion surveys interviewing over 74,000 people in 50 populations, 49 countries and the Palestinian Authority. The opinion gap between men and women is not large. In 14 Muslim countries surveyed men were more likely than women to say suicide bombings and other forms of violence against civilian targets is justifiable.[35] But three-quarters (72 percent) of Lebanese women agree with men that suicide bombing is justifiable. In Jordan, the number of women holding that view narrowly outnumbers men (45 percent to 41 percent). When asked one question about the justifiability of suicide bombing carried out by Palestinians against Israel and a second about these acts carried out against Americans and other Westerners in Iraq, the number of people in all four countries that say violence is justified increased, and in Turkey the number increased considerably.[36]

Stephanie Shemin has a different perspective. She says that as Palestinian women give their lives, in the final analysis, "their quest for equality will be futile, for feminism and nationalism don't go hand in hand in the Arab world."[37] Shemin reminds us that since the beginning of Palestine's struggle for independence, its women have been told that women's rights are subordinate to Palestinian rights. When women participated in the 1987 intifada with the idea that national liberation meant social liberation, women did not realize their ideal. Only five out of 88 members of the Legislative Council are women. Issues such as bride-price and spousal abuse are on the sidelines. Women were not included in the negotiations of the Oslo accords and were not given prominent positions in the political structure created by the Palestinian Authority. In the current intifada, women perform domestic or stereotypical roles, such as nurses. Shemin believes "equality should be fought for with leadership, not explosives."[38]

In Turkey and Sri Lanka, history has allowed women to participate in the act, but in Chechnya and Palestine, using women as suicide bombers is a more recent phenomenon. The involvement of women has not only been allowed, it has been planned. Beyler writes that men may be motivated by religious or national fanaticism which women share, but she notes a difference between men and women suicide attackers:

> [W]omen consider combat as a way to escape the predestined life that is expected of them. When women become human bombs, their intent is to make a statement not only in the name of a country, a religion, a leader, but also in the name of their gender.[39]

Not all women see the role of suicide bomber as liberating. Barbara Victor, former reporter on the Middle East for CBS television and *U.S. News and World Report*, interviewed a Palestinian woman who held her dead child in the midst of the stench of death caused by bombing. The woman said:

> You American women talk constantly of equality. Well, you can take a lesson from us Palestinian women. We die in equal numbers to the men.[40]

Victor poignantly adds, "This tragic concept of women's liberation stayed with me."[41]

Heather A. Andrews, author of *Veiled Jihad: The Threat of Female Islamic Suicide Terrorists*, focuses primarily on female Islamic suicide bombers from Palestine and Chechnya. For comparison purposes, she includes the Liberation Tigers of Tamil Eelam (LTTE) females in her case studies "to illustrate that females living under traditional, patriarchal societies are subject to the same problems, which drives them to commit these acts."[42] Andrews explains:

> I examined the motivations of female bombers on an individual basis, and while each of their stories differed, there were common themes that arose. These female bombers tend to be from traditional, patriarchal societies that restrict them in some manner or the focus of society tends to be on the males. These women set out to prove that they can do the same job as the males and hope to attain equality in death. Some of these women may be indirectly affected by living in a patriarchal society, but they are all affected. Becoming a suicide bomber also allows women to struggle for their emancipation while maintaining their Muslim identity. Women want to prove that the purpose of their lives go beyond having children and living subordinately under male rule. Instead, a woman can take control of her own destiny and accomplish at least one great act.[43]
>
> Prior to their act, they briefly get a glance at a less restricted life as they are treated better by their male counterparts. These women, after all, are aiding in the struggle. They, too, look forward to martyrdom and paradise. Paradise sounds much better than the hell on earth that many females live. In my research, I concluded that there is a catalyst that places immediacy of a female to conduct an attack. This catalyst is usually attributed to a deeply personal event or crisis that has occurred in a woman's life such as the death of a loved one, ultimate humiliation by the enemy to the breaking point, or the need for moral purification.[44]

Lisa Kruger, in her thesis *Gender and Terrorism: Motivations of Female Terrorists*, focuses on gender-biased myths that make it difficult to recognize the actual motivations of women terrorists. The myths are:

Violent women are reluctant victims who are persuaded by men;
Violent women are primarily motivated by personal and emotional reasons;
Violent women are more ruthless than violent men;
Women terrorists have twice as much to fight for due to gender.[45]

Kruger believes these myths exist because "we have limited data on motivations of women terrorists, thus we rely on perceptions and gendered expectations; there is contradiction in reporting; groupthink; the media is obsessed with why or how women are led or forced into violence."[46]

From her research and personal experience in male-dominated arenas such as the martial arts and the military, Kruger reached the following conclusions:

- When a female terrorist strikes, media and journalists tend to point out the gender more than when a male terrorists strikes. The focus is then turned to, "why would a girl do such a thing?" Her role in the larger organization is widely ignored and her motivations are analyzed at the individual level while motivations of male terrorists are analyzed in terms of group, organizational, and political goals.
- The skewed focus on women at the individual level leads journalists to search for personal factors that "caused" her to resort to violence instead of looking into her choice in participating in a wider group cause. In my opinion, when one looks for personal tragedy as a cause for violence, one is bound to find it. Most observers do not place the same degree of emphasis on personal tragedies in male terrorists' lives even though nearly all of them exhibit the same personal sense of loss, death of loved ones, hopelessness, and isolation as women terrorists. In a sense, it makes women seem more selfishly motivated by personal revenge instead of motivated to assist in a group cause.
- The focus on women as personally motivated leads to the perception that women are not capable of rational thought in

choosing violence. Instead, the perception is that women are led to violence. Because of gender stereotypes, it may appear that women are reactive and emotional when it comes to violence. However, centuries of historical examples show women are often proactive and rational in their attempts to gain the asymmetric advantage through surprise.

• In order to effectively deal with women terrorists, it is essential to recognize that like men, women are motivated by political goals, ethnic/nationalistic pride, and a desire to protect loved ones.

• A paradox exists: women are viewed as naturally passive unless they are affected personally. Yet, when they do become violent, they are defined as more ruthless than men. The idea that women are more ruthless arises from cultural myth as well as the notion that if a "pretty, small girl" becomes violent she must be extra ruthless since it's "not in her nature." There is no substantial evidence that women terrorists are more ruthless or more dangerous. Such claims are largely based on perceptions. The term ruthless is subjective and cannot be measured!

• My thesis describes the worldwide participation of women in violent terrorist activities.

• In my opinion, it is dangerous to categorize motivations of women as different from men. Doing so would cause analysts to look for "female-type" motivations and ignore that women can rationalize the use of violence in the same manner as men. We will be caught off guard if we allow ourselves to think that women will use violence only if they are pushed far enough on a personal or emotional level.[47]

Kruger concludes, "One last thought — to be ready for the increasing threat of women terrorists, we must recognize women as rational actors as opposed to emotional reactors of violence."[48]

Why Palestinian Women Perform the Death Act

The relationship between the sacred and society can be seen further in the role of Palestinian women fighters. Individual women are shaped by social facts.[49] Hamas reasons, "Jihad (holy war) is obligatory on every Muslim, male or female."[50] Muslims must override the restrictions on women to defend the land against the invading enemy, according to Raphael Israeli.[51]

Society defines the sacred and the profane and that is the reason there is serious conflict in Islam regarding the status of women, writes Israeli. In very conservative societies like Saudi Arabia, Sudan and Iran, women are to be protected and must abide by strict rules of conduct. In other societies, many Muslim women are emancipated and their freedom resembles that of their Western counterparts. The answer to the contradiction lies in the concept of honor. A man's honor is related to deeds he performs while a woman's honor is related to her behavior and aloofness from the male society. The linkage is in the male's ability to preserve his woman's honor.[52]

This linkage was well demonstrated during the time the Taliban controlled Afghanistan. Nasrine Gross, who has been teaching in Kabul since the overthrow of the Taliban, said that when the Taliban came, they took the authority away from the men to decide whether a woman would wear a chadari, work outside the home, or be educated. The Taliban decided these things, disempowering the men. When men are disempowered, they cannot fight back. The Taliban restricted Afghan women more every day, not to punish the women, but to disempower the men. "The women of Afghanistan are the honor of the men, and when you dishonor the men, you disempower them," Gross says.[53]

We witness society's defining of religion in Muslim societies undergoing revolution. Raphael Israeli writes that the dilemmas regarding women's conduct come to the forefront more acutely in these societies and, by necessity, solutions and compromises are reached.[54]

Palestinian women have participated in the Palestinian national struggle since the outbreak of the first intifada in 1987 and the second in 2000. In spite of the fact that women participated as cabinet members, speakers, members of research centers and in terrorism, they did not believe they were recognized. It wasn't until 1994 that women lobbied for legislation to rectify their lack of recognition. The Palestinian Liberation Organization saw the national struggle as more critical than equality and kept firm control over the organizations that worked for women's equality, according to Israeli. The women were frustrated and the restrictions on them remained which "may have contributed to their turning else-where."[55]

On January 25, 2006, Hamas won a majority in the Palestinian parliament, taking control of the government from Fatah.[56] Hamas addresses the role of women in articles 17 and 18 of its charter. The articles are based on the law of Allah from the Qur'an and Shari'a Law. Article 17 begins:

> The Muslim women have a no lesser role than that of men in the war of liberation; they manufacture men and play a great role in guiding and educating the [new] generation. The enemies have understood that role, therefore they realize that if they can guide and educate [the Muslim women] in a way that would distance them from Islam, they would have won that war.[57]

Article 17 concludes by urging Muslims to "fulfill their duty in confronting the schemes of those saboteurs"[58] and that with Islam as their guide they will wipe out the organizations that are the enemies of humanity and Islam.

Article 18 stresses that the primary role of women is to care for the home and teach Islamic moral concepts to the children. In this way, children will be prepared for the duty of jihad. It recites the importance of both men and women surrendering to Allah and for those men and women who remember Allah, "He has prepared for them forgiveness and a vast reward."[59] Israeli contends that what seems like equality on the face of it is "as hollow as the promises of the PLO and the Palestinian Authority," leaving one path remaining, that of a fighter.[60]

Once the Palestinian clerics united by sanctifying the "Islamikaze" as a legitimate struggle, "they could not exclude women and children from it,"[61] writes Israeli. In addition, the loss of lives gave birth to a new attitude toward including women and children. All that was required was a person willing to be indoctrinated and die for Allah.

The Israel Security Agency believes that the primary motive for the involvement of women in terrorism is personal "alongside the basic nationalistic motive."[62] The Agency perceives a romantic motive on the part of women. Women have romantic links with the militants who recruit them. Some women have a personal distress motive, such as suicidal tendencies due to despair over life or parental opposition to the daughter's marriage.

Hilla Dayan of the Sociology Department of the Cape Town Democracy and Diversity Institute believes that people must recognize the full scope of the political context in cases of female suicide bombers. The causes of female suicide bombing do not stem merely from pervasive sexual abuse and oppression. In addition, an examination of media reports shows that they often depict female and male suicide bombers differently, making unclear the reasons women martyr themselves.[63]

V.G. Julie Rajan, a Ph.D. candidate in comparative literature at Rutgers University, offers two reasons Palestinian women participate in suicide bombing: the unity of the contradictory images of power, the traditional and nontraditional, and the ability to engender unity. Palestinian women rise above the gender norms of their society when they visibly participate in the building of a nation. But unlike male bombers, "women can bring the greatest subversive potential known, from the deepest layers of the unconscious."[64] Rajan writes that the reason women are successful in stirring this consciousness is that they are still associated with traditional female gender norms in domestic life while at the same time they are associated with masculine gender norms of aggression and violence.

Individuals who associate female bombers with motivations of gender oppression will find oppression is not borne by one gender but is born of despair and hopelessness. The Palestinian population finds the Israeli occupation humiliating. They find themselves living in a lawless and violent society. As families face the loss of loved ones, some turn to suicide bombing. Ilene R. Prusher, a writer for the *Christian Science Monitor*, says that more Palestinians at a younger age are becoming bombers. Oppression does not affect just women.[65] Children are particularly vulnerable because while they are feeling a sense of hopelessness, they are indoctrinated into martyrdom. Kenneth R. Timmerman, a writer for *Insight* magazine, gives this example of Yasser Arafat's address in August 2002 to a chanting auditorium full of children:

> Oh, children of Palestine! The colleagues, friends, brothers and sisters of Faris Quda [a 14-year-old who died in the conflict]. The colleagues of this hero represent this immense and fundamental

power that is within, and it shall be victorious, with Allah's will! One of you, a boy or a girl, shall raise the [Palestinian] flag over the walls of Jerusalem, its mosques and its churches.... Onward together to Jerusalem.[66]

Children blend the gender norms in the sense that as a group they represent both genders.

Rajan writes that bomber Reem al-Raiyshi is an example of combining of gender norms. Reem al-Raiyshi committed the death act on January 14, 2004. She was a young mother in her early twenties. She had a son who was three and a daughter who was 18 months (see Table 7.1). Rajan notes that Reem al-Raiyshi challenged the traditional female gender norms of passivity and nonviolence when she said, "I was hoping to be the first woman, where parts of my body can fly everywhere."[67]

Rajan writes that the power of Palestinian female suicide bombers is seen in their ability to generate unity by "blurring borders."[68] Women have risen above the faction groups, religious and secular, that sometimes get in the way of the Palestinian freedom movement. Many of the women have a higher purpose, freedom for Palestine.

Rajan illustrates that the concept of creating unity is underscored in the martyrdom of Dareen Abu Aisheh, the second female suicide bomber. Her beliefs were the same as those of Hamas (see Table 7.1). The Hamas turned down her proposed martyrdom. But "Abu Aisheh was not deterred from her dedication to Palestine,"[69] Rajan explains. Abu Aisheh was able to set aside her compatible beliefs with the Hamas and performed the suicide under the auspices of the secular

Dareen Abu Aisheh, a Palestinian, was the second female suicide bomber (AP photograph/ Nasser Ishtayeh/Ho).

Reem al-Raiyshi, the mother of two, in an image released by Hamas (AP Photograph/ Hamas HO).

al-Aqsa Martyrs Brigade. This ability is immortalized in a picture taken just before her death. She is wearing a Hamas headband, but she dies under the aegis of the al-Aqsa Martyrs Brigade. Rajan concludes that Abu Aisheh symbolically unites the belief systems of the factions, secular and religious, in the name of Palestinian nationalism. This unity "would ultimately endow Palestinian rebel forces with an unprecedented level of power."[70] Rajan believes that the effect of her martyrdom in 2002 is evidenced in the unified support of the January 2004 bomber, Reem al-Raiyshi, sponsored by both the Al-Aqsa Martyrs Brigade and Hamas.

Also significant is the May 19, 2003, attack in Israel. Hiba Da'arma, a Palestinian, blew up at the entrance to a mall in Afulah, killing three civilians and wounding 83, after being stopped by security guards. Beyler writes,

> The Al-Aqsa Martyrs Brigades and the Palestinian Islamic Jihad took responsibility for the attack, marking the first time the PIJ claimed responsibility for an attack conducted by a woman.[71]

Chechen Women Perform the Death Act

In 1991, the Chechen government demanded independence from Russia. In 1992, violence broke out between the Chechen government and citizens who wanted Chechnya to remain part of Russia. In 1994, Russia sent troops against the separatist forces. In 1996, a cease-fire ended the fighting. In 1997, Russian leader Boris Yeltsin and the Chechen leader signed a peace treaty.[72] A second Chechen war began soon after, in 1999.[73]

Initially, Chechen women may have had reasons in addition to those of their Arab sisters. Women are shaped by their personal circumstance. Lisa Ling of *National Geographic* conducted a study that revealed a woman bomber may have an inability to bear children or may be pregnant but vulnerable with no way out.[74]

Since 1999, Chechen women attackers hope to help Chechnya establish an independent Muslim state in the Russian-occupied region, states Kim Murphy. Other reasons are: the women may be seeking revenge because they have lost husbands or children; they have been traumatized by the Russian military, who kidnap and torture Chechen civilians and destroy their homes; and "are drugged and brainwashed into becoming suicide bombers for the Chechen cause."[75] Murphy calls these sentiments a "deep domestic rage."[76]

In December 2003 Abu al-Walid Ghamidi, Chechnya's rebel commander, said that most of the suicide attacks were carried out by women who were wives of martyred mujahedin. The wives themselves, their honor and everything in their lives are being threatened. Robert A. Pape said, "They do not accept being humiliated and living under occupation."[77]

Even if Chechen women have other than personal reasons for becoming suicide bombers, they are far from being freedom fighters with an equal right to die for their beliefs. Viv Groskop writes:

> Chechnya's female martyrs are more likely to be forced, blackmailed or brain-washed to their deaths. Even when they have chosen their mission, it is not because of a religious mission or a political cause, but for personal reasons: to avenge the death of a husband or a brother. More often than not ... they are pawns in a man's game.[78]

Some Chechen women may perform suicide missions for the same reasons that the Arab women do. Imminent, then, is a new stage of fear.[79]

The idea that Chechen women perform attacks in the spirit of national cause just as do their male counterparts is illustrated in the very significant attack in October 2002. About 50 abductors, 18 of them women, dressed in black and wearing explosive belts, took over a crowded Moscow theater. Clara Beyler writes:

> This marked the first time in the history of female suicide terrorism that such a team was established, signaling a shift from an individual action to a group structure. Although large-scale operations occurred in the past, only a small number of women had assumed the role of warriors.[80]

A new stage of fear arrived; Chechen women became part of organized terror. Beyler notes two other attacks in 2003 that were significant. On July 10, 2003, a Chechen female suicide bomber failed to detonate her bomb at a downtown Moscow restaurant, but a bomb expert was killed when he tried to defuse it. Beyler writes that this failed attack may be connected to the July 5 attacks (see Table 6.2). Zarema Muzhikhoyeva was arrested and charged with terrorism and premeditated murder. The importance of her arrest is that it uncovered information about the terror group behind the plot. She had intended to target a McDonald's restaurant. She got lost and entered the closest café, where she tried to detonate the defective bomb and was caught.[81]

Whether Chechen women perform attacks because of personal problems alone is a timely question. The crucial issue is that women, Arab and Chechen alike, have brought about a new profile to suicide bombing as a method of terror. As Pape suggests of all bombers, their profile has clearly changed from earlier times.[82]

Methods of Recruitment

The organizations' efforts at recruitment vary. For example, the Islamic Jihad (PIJ) distributed newsletters at universities in the West Bank and Gaza Strip that praised all of its women as fighters. The newsletter features young women recruits from Gaza who talk about the merging of their traditional homemaker roles with fighter roles. A young leader pointed out that Islam has no restrictions on women becoming bombers. He cites how a woman fought alongside Islam's founder.[83] In some battles Muslim "women took sword and shield and joined active combat, to be later praised by the Prophet." Um-Salamah, the wife of the Prophet, diffused the crisis among the Muslims at the Hudaybiah treaty.[84]

The identification of potential candidates takes place in northern West Bank universities and in towns and villages particularly in the Jenin region. The PIJ has established a well-trained network of operatives, including some highly skilled women. Its first success in recruiting women was Heiba Daragmeh[85] (see Table 7.1).

But there are obstacles to training women as bombers. As examples, rigid social norms do not permit women to be alone with men if they are not family members, and women are not to show their bodies to men even in death. "A woman who blows herself up leaves behind a body likely to be inspected by male police investigators."[86]

In spite of the obstacles, Karla J. Cunningham contends that female involvement in terrorist activity "creates a mutually reinforcing process driving terrorist organizations to recruit women at the same time women's motivations to join these groups increases: contextual pressures impact societal controls over women that may facilitate, if not necessitate, more over political participation up to, and including, political violence; and operational imperatives often make female members highly effective actors for their organizations, inducing leaders toward 'actor innovation' to gain strategic advantage against their adversary."[87]

Cunningham writes that the involvement of women in terrorist organizations resulted out of a need to include new members due to heavy government pressures. Most significant is Cunningham's finding that "regardless of the region, it is clear that women are choosing to participate in politically violent organizations irrespective of their respective organizational leaders' motives for recruiting them."[88]

The Male Handlers

In some instances, the men who handle the women who become suicide martyrs use methods similar to those used for males who become suicide bombers. Raphael Israeli notes that the natural fear of death is innate in everyone and must be overcome. This fear is overcome by making the promise of an afterlife attractive to young people.[89] Yoram Schweitzer found few differences in methods used with respect to gender. He writes:

> Organizational leaders and handlers, who take advantage of their innocence, enthusiasm, loss of focus, and often their personal distress and thirst for revenge, expose women as well as men to intense indoctrination and manipulation.[90]

The men who handle the women who become suicide bombers are to do whatever needs doing to make the suicide happen, writes Christopher Dickey.[91] A psychologist interviewed by Barbara Victor explained,

> When an adolescent boy is humiliated at an Israeli checkpoint, from that moment, a suicide bomber is created. At the same time, if a woman becomes a shahida, one has to look for deeper, more underlying reasons.[92]

Dickey acknowledges that probably men who prepare women for their deaths know instinctively how to find the underlying reasons.

Hanley "Doc" Harding, a nuclear security specialist and founding board member of Aurora Protection Specialists of Boca Raton, Florida, sheds light on the recruitment of suicide bombers, male and female. He writes:

> The Muslim world is psycho-sociologically "layered..." along the analogy of a head of cabbage, or an onion. If one places cupped hands around the "world-cabbage" or "world-onion" and squeezes, the pressure applied to the outside is transmitted toward the center.[93]

The fundamentalist Muslim "leader's" goal is to identify select persons from among the layers, in order to make further use of them. Those identified as suitable are sorted according to mental capacity and emotional malleability/pliability. The sorted and "ear-marked" are forced down, layer-by-layer, toward the center, or "core ideology" of the "leader." By the time they reach this high-pressure "ideological core," the psychological and indoctrinative pressures have assured their permanent psychological molding into a useful set of "tools" for the "leader." Some molding is aimed at creating suitable "sub-leaders" (the organizational "core officer cadre") which are allowed a certain autonomy of action because they can be trusted to follow orders without question. The "soldiers" and "sub-soldiers" are closely controlled by the cadre, as their mental and emotional faculties (and consequent "style" of indoctrination) have imprinted them as suitable for one purpose— cannon-fodder and/or "blind fanatics" (suicidal obedients). Alternatively, the madrassas (local neighborhood religious schools for boys only) are feeder farms for crops of cannon-fodder which have been indoctrinated since childhood according to the wants of the "leaders." The petty clergy who run these local religious schools are pretty much self-deluded into allying themselves and all their efforts to the "leader's" wants. His doctrine is their doctrine. Politics is skillfully blended with religious fanaticism into the highly effective imprinting of an endless supply of financially poor and ignorant boys who will grow into men who might as well have ROMs implanted into their brains. It's not a question of possible latent curiosity as to "what's out there?," but rather a total acceptance of their indoctrinated life as "that's all there is, there ain't no more, don't even bother asking (don't dare ask or you'll burn in hell), that's all there is." It is even whispered that the boys' meager diets are subtly and carefully "managed" and even supplemented / augmented with certain medicinal herbs which stultify brain cells and render the mind even more pliable. A close historical study of the Muslim religion reveals its "political breakaway" from Judaism policy. The Muslim religious dogma and doctrine is well structured around — and closely interwoven with — a core of political power and iron-fisted control.[94]

Do these imprinted actually believe in the cause into which they have been inducted (many, without even realizing that they have, in fact, been selected for induction, even though they were/are under the delusion that they were accepted as volunteers to the cause)? In a fashion, yes, they "believe," but that belief is in large part not because of voluntarism but, rather, the carefully nurtured indoctrination/motivation process to which they have been both subtly and overtly subjected. The psychology of such subjugation has been perfected over thousands of years.[95]

The sorted are now sent back "up" through the layers, until they are embedded into the layer of society in which they will prove most useful to the "leader's needs."[96]

Now, the women, ah yes, the women (more often teenagers, actually). They are a new resource from the "new school" of female patriots who "wish to join" their male counterparts, shoulder-to-shoulder, in the jihad. And so, the leader is "allowing" them to participate, as exemplary women, fighting for the "cause." Such a privilege! Since females are forbidden to attend the madrassas, a plethora of other psychological ploys is used on them — the special honor and privilege of being in the "female elite" among the men; the chance of "being in on" a "special secret"; and all the sundry other psychological tantalizers which have been quickly adapted and perfected to lure the female psyche into the doctrine of "the cause."[97]

Reports of disgust with Fatah handlers indicate that the handlers are not always successful. Fatah operatives Tauriya Hamamra, 25, and Arin Ahmed, 20, are two young women who backed out of suicide missions and were taken into custody by Israeli security forces (see Table 7.2). Four months after volunteering for martyrdom, Hamamra, a devout Muslim from northern Samaria, felt her operators were "making a business out of the blood of shaheeds." Hamamra said she feared "Allah ... would not accept me as a shaheed" if she blew herself up among "babies, women [and] sick people.... I began ... to imagine my family sitting in a restaurant and someone coming in and blowing them up."[98] She said it was against her religious beliefs to follow orders to "dress like an Israeli woman ... go with my hair loose, with sunglasses and make-up and tight clothes."[99]

Hamamra's objections to the outlook of the handlers made her have second thoughts. The handlers would insist the attack come off even when there were not many people around. She stated:

> What was important for them was to succeed in perpetrating an attack, whether there were casualties or not, and then they would be able to pat themselves on the back.... I felt they were making a

business out of the blood of shaheeds, that all they cared about was that people would say they managed to pull off an attack.[100]

Arin Ahmed, from Bethlehem, backed out of suicide missions twice. Her first unsuccessful attack was a strike in Rishon LeZion. Handlers convinced her to try another in Jerusalem's pedestrian mall, but she again backed off.[101]

The Role of a Female Handler Black Fatima

Black Fatima, a Chechen rebel, is female and middle-aged. She has a hooked nose and dark hair, according to Kim Murphy.[102] Tom Parfitt, in Moscow, states "photofits of her show a middle-aged woman wearing dark glasses. Police say that she is aged about 40, about 5 feet 5 inches tall, with dyed blonde hair."[103] People who attended a Russian pop festival spotted Black Fatima at the concert where 14 music fans were killed by two female suicide bombers in 2003. Black Fatima is believed to have planned to guide the bombers to their target by mobile phone. The Moscow police captured female bomber Zarema Muzhikhoyeva, who disclosed the full scale of Black Fatima's involvement as the Moscow-based ringleader of the suicide bombing operation. Black Fatima, or Lyuba, directed Muzhikhoyeva's attack.[104]

Black Fatima is the recruiter for women shahidas, martyrs for Chechnya, who become Black Widows. She will appear at the homes of would-be attackers and has discussions behind closed doors. After the prospective suicide bomber disappears with the Black Fatima, the parents often are not informed why. They learn later either from members of the terrorist group or by recognizing their daughters on television footage.[105]

The methods of the Black Fatima were discovered through interviews with Black Widows in Russian custody who were not successful in carrying out their attacks.

Organized Terror

Organized terror organizations use suicide bombing to promote martyrdom and self-sacrifice as a last resort against more powerful enemies.

Suicide bombing brings acknowledgment of their plight. Debra D. Zedalis of the U.S. Army War College found that terror organizations claim it is their only effective weapon against the wealth, weapons, persons and political power of their more powerful enemies.[106]

Robert A. Pape contends that suicide bombers are not irrational but are part of a strategic effort to accomplish specific political goals. In many cases, the attacks are politically timed.[107] V.G. Julie Rajan illustrates how the strong political impact of the suicide mission of Palestinian female bomber Andaleeb Takafka's lay in her timing, noting that it coincided with Israel's incursions into occupied cities in the West Bank and with U.S. Secretary of State Colin Powell's visit to the Middle East.[108]

Heather A. Andrews believes that female bombers have an immense psychological effect on the larger struggle in which their organization is involved:

> Female suicide bombers create fear in an organization's target audience because it now means that all aspects of a society are now involved in the struggle and anyone could be a suicide bomber. Organizations have taken advantage of the fact that terrorism is still very male-centric along with gender biases that even the West is subject to. Women are supposed to be the givers of life, not the takers. Such biases make it easier for women to penetrate security. The shortage of female security personnel also makes a female bomber more potent because male security personnel are more reluctant to search women. In traditional societies in particular, by touching a women, her honor, as well as that of her family, is offended. Women can also feign pregnancy while disguising a bomb underneath their clothes. This method is especially effective for women who wear a jilbab or sari.[109]
>
> Another thought of mine is that organizations with societal prejudices might be inclined to see females are more expendable that male members. Females often do not have operational experience and as suicide bombers, they do not have to be trained to the same extent as a soldier or someone who is going to conduct a more difficult operation. Alas, some of the positions taken by members of a patriarchal society include the fact that women are not valued as much as men, and their lives can be expended rather than a male who can aid the struggle in another way.[110]

Yoram Schweitzer writes that the use of female bombers in the past signified secular terrorism, but the line between secular and religious "has become increasingly blurred."[111] The use of female suicide bombers violates religious principles and social norms that do not allow women into male activities because to do so would require women to be in close contact with men to whom they are not married. Fundamentalist terrorist organizations are willing to use women regardless of religion and tradition because they are aware of the tactical advantages. Women are perceived as innocent and nonviolent. Schweitzer writes that the use of women bombers could be "possibly opening a Pandora's Box of demands by women for rights and freedoms currently denied Them."[112]

Organizations Known to Enlist Women

In June 2004, Zedalis identified eight organizations known to enlist female suicide bombers.[113] In addition, reports indicate Iraqi insurgents have had females commit the death act,[114] and Hezbollah, an umbrella organization, has made use of female suicide bombers.[115] The organizations are:

1. Hezbollah
2. Syrian Socialist Nationalist Party (SSNP/PPS)
3. Liberation Tigers of Tamil Eelam (LTTE)
4. Kurdistan Workers Party (PKK)
5. Chechen rebels
6. Al-Aqsa Martyrs
7. Palestinian Islamic Jihad (PIJ)
8. Hamas
9. Al-Qaeda network
10. Iraqi insurgents

Hezbollah

Pape identified six women the Hezbollah used as attackers in Lebanon from 1982 to 1986. One of the women, Norma Hassan, was a Christian high school teacher. Pape presents photographs of four of the six female attackers. He writes, "Many are dressed in Western clothes, with stylish haircuts and even makeup, hardly projecting an image of Islamic fundamentalism."

Syrian Socialist Nationalist Party (SSNP/PPS)

The Syrian Socialist Nationalist Party (SSNP/PPS) holds the distinction of having a woman commit the first suicide attack. The PPS stands for the Syrian name Populaire Syrian. (See Table 4.1.) Mehaydali was in her late teens and known to her admirers as "The Bride of the South."[116] In 1985, the SSNP/PPS sent her to blow herself up near vehicles transporting Israeli soldiers in Lebanon. Schweitzer explains the significance of the first female suicide bomber is that her attack "paved the way for several other Lebanese women acting on behalf of other secular terrorist organizations."[117]

According to Clara Beyler, "of the 12 suicide attacks conducted by the SSNP, women took part in five. Of the suicide bombings conducted by the PKK in Turkey, 66 percent (14 out of 21 suicide attacks) were carried out by women (this number includes both successful and thwarted attacks)."[118]

Liberation Tigers of Tamil Eelam (LTTE)

Exact strength is unknown, but the LTTE is estimated to have 8,000 to 10,000 armed combatants in Sri Lanka, with a core of 3,000 to 6,000 trained fighters and 4,000 women.[119] Its attempted assassination of Chandrika Kumaratunga, president of Sri Lanka, in 1993 was perpetrated by a female suicide bomber.[120] (See Table 5.1.)

The members of the LTTE suicide unit, "The Black Tigers," are men and women. Every member carries a cyanide capsule around his or her neck to take if captured. The purpose of the capsule is to keep the LTTE's secrets.[121] The female suicide bomber unit is known as the Black Tigresses. Its members are highly trained to perform only one mission that insures their death and the deaths of others, according to Robert A. Pape. Cunningham writes that the role of female Tigresses is modeled after women's participation in the Indian National Army during the war with Britain in the 1940s. This war included female suicide bombers.[122]

Christoph Reuter reports that of the estimated 10,000 active Tigers, one-third are women and girls. That number rises to about 60 percent among the subset of suicide commandos.[123] Reuter explains that the emancipation of Tamil women in the political context of Sri Lanka led to equal rights and military duties in the struggle for Tamil independence, and "female units have been included in battles since 1984, and Tamil Tiger training camps for women have been in place since 1987, with the first woman commanding a rebel unit in 1990."[124]

The high proportion of women in bombing missions is due to the fact that many Tamil men have died or emigrated. The men available are used in combat against the government troops. Men are more suitable because they can go greater distances carrying heavier weapons. Women are more suited to carrying bombs hidden under their clothing, appearing pregnant.[125] The Tigers invented the suicide belt.[126] The exploding belt was originally designed for the female body.[127] Robert A. Pape writes that the Tamil Tigers is the world's most prolific suicide terrorist organization.[128]

The most famous LTTE female bomber is Thenmuli Rajaratnam, known as Dhanu.[129] Four of her brothers were killed in conflict; her home was looted and she was gang-raped. Dhanu belonged to the LTTE from the mid–1980s and trained to be a Black Tigress in the late 1980s. She was the first to use a suicide belt. On May 21, 1991, she killed India's Prime Minster Rajiv Gandhi and herself by detonating an explosive vest after bowing down at Ghandi's feet during an election rally.[130]

Kurdistan Workers Party, or Party Karkeren Kurdistan (PKK)

Like the Tamils, the Party Karkeren Kurdistan (PKK) has a substantial number of women in its suicide brigade. Earlier women fought in the guerilla war to liberate their country and themselves. Traditional and extremely conservative Kurdistan society allowed only limited roles for women of looking after children, the household and the animals. Girls were sold to their husbands, who practiced bigamy and intermarriage. While the law allows primary school education for girls, many women are illiterate.[131]

Equal rights are not permitted in Kurdistan society, but the PKK grants equal rights for women. Women receive the same training and fight alongside the men. The PKK leader, Abdullah Őcalan, repeatedly claimed that he did not order women to carry out the attacks, but Reuter provides evidence to the contrary.

> The most famous case is that of seventeen-year-old Leyla Kaplan, a PKK recruit who blew herself up in November 1996 in front of the headquarters of the police special forces in the South Turkish capital of Adana, killing three policeman. Another female PKK combatant, Turkan Adiyaman, had previously been asked to volunteer. After she refused, she was shot in front of Leyla Kaplan, as an example of the fate that befalls shirkers.[132]

Zedalis reports that the first female PKK suicide bombing took place in June 1996 (see Table 4.2) and may also be the first instance of an apparently pregnant bomber. The attack killed six Turkish soldiers; the bomber's name is unknown.[133]

Chechen Rebels

Most significant is that Yoram Schweitzer believes that it is possible that "the growth in the number of Chechen female suicide bombers signals the beginning of a change in the position of fundamentalist Islamic organizations with respect to the involvement of women in suicide attacks."[134]

The Beslan Middle School No. 1 attack was a sophisticated strike. A shredded black belt and bloodied camouflage utility vest were found in the hall next to the cafeteria where a female suicide bomber detonated herself. Thirty-two attackers with one known female succeeded in killing over 350 people. It is believed that autonomous groups connected with al-Qaeda were responsible.[135] (See Table 6.1.) Women attackers are known as Black Widows, a term coined by the Russians when they first arrived on the scene.[136] Shamil Basayev first organized the Black Widows in 2000.[137]

Al-Aqsa Martyrs Brigade, Palestinian Nationalists

The shootings and suicide bombings by the al-Aqsa Martyrs Brigade includes including female suicide bombings. In January 2002, a female terrorist, Wafa Idris, carried out a suicide attack in Jerusalem that killed an elderly man and wounded about 40 people.[138] Idris's attack made the al-Aqsa the first Palestinian terrorist group to use a female suicide bomber.[139] Idris was a paramedic who detonated a 22-pound body bomb filled with nails and metal objects in a shopping district.[140] (See Table 7.1 and photo in Chapter 7.)

Palestinian Islamic Jihad (PIJ)

Palestinian Islamic Jihad's first female suicide bomber was a 19-year-old student, Hiba Daraghmeh. In May 2003, she detonated a bomb in a shopping mall and killed three people. In October 2003 the second PIJ female bomber struck. Hanadi Jaradat was a 29-year-old lawyer. She killed 21 Israeli and Arab men, women, and children in a popular restaurant.[141] (See Table 7.1.)

Hamas

The Hamas publicizes its use of women for suicide attacks. On January 14, 2004, the first female Hamas bomber, 22-year-old Reem al-Reyashi, killed four Israeli soldiers at a checkpoint with a ten-pound bomb with ball bearings and screws. Al-Reyashi was the first mother in Israel to perform a suicide attack. She left behind a husband, a 3-year-old son, and a 1-year-old daughter.[142] (See Table 7.1.) Significantly, her attack was seen as a joint operation between the Hamas and the al-Aqsa Martyrs' Brigade and marked a policy shift. The Israeli Foreign Ministry said that the attack was a good example of cooperation between Palestinian groups.[143]

Al-Qaeda Network

Zedalis reported that a "first" yet to strike is the first female suicide bomber representing al-Qaeda.[144] But in 2004, one of the 33 attackers at the Beslan School No. 1 attack in Chechnya was female and autonomous groups with an al-Qaeda connection were suspected of carrying out the attack.[145] (See Table 6.1.) In addition, in 2003, Pakistani police grew alarmed when their intelligence suggested Islamist militants were preparing to deploy female suicide bombers against the government.[146]

According to Mia Bloom, in 2002, Indian security forces went on high alert to guard against possible female suicide bomber attacks. The Pakistan-based Islamic organizations associated with al-Qaeda, Jaish-e-Mohamed and Laskar-e-Tayyaba, were thought responsible. In March 2003, *Asharq Al-Awsat* published an interview with a woman, Um Osama, who said she was the leader of the women Mujahadeen of al-Qaeda. The network said it organized female suicide bomber squads from Afghans, Arabs, Chechens and others. Their purpose was to target the United States.[147]

Bloom lists other events that suggest al-Qaeda's employment of women bombers. Near the time of the U.S. invasion of Iraq, on March 29, 2003, two women, Waddad Jamil Jassem and Nour Qaddour al-Shanbari, attacked coalition forces by suicide car bomb attack.[148] One was pregnant at the time. In a video, Waddad Jamil Jassem said, "I have devoted myself [to] Jihad for the sake of God and against the American, British, and Israeli infidels and to defend the soil of our precious and dear country." In a separate video, the other woman, not identified by Bloom, but most likely Nour Qaddour al-Shanbari, said, "We say to our leader and holy war comrade, the hero commander Saddam Hussein that you have sisters that you and history will boast about."[149]

Iraqi Insurgents

The BBC has reported Iraqi women committing suicide bombing. On April 3, 2003, two female suicide bombers killed three coalition soldiers at a checkpoint northwest of Baghdad near the Haditha Dam and about 80 miles from the Iraq-Syria border. Iraq's official news agency reported that a pregnant woman ran from the car just before the explosion, dying in the blast, as did the female driver of the vehicle.[150]

The Arabic television network al-Jazeera broadcast separate videotapes of two Iraqi women. One bomber identified herself as "martyrdom-seeker Nour Qaddour al-Shanbari." She placed her hand on a copy of the Koran and vowed "to defend Iraq and take revenge from the enemies of the Islamic nation." The second woman, Waddad Jamil Jassem, said: "I have devoted myself to jihad for the sake of God and against the American, British and Israeli infidels."[151] Six months after the two women attacked, a female with an explosives belt was captured. She attempted to enter the Green Zone, the heavily protected headquarters of the U.S. in Baghdad.[152]

Nour Qaddour al-Shanbari was one of two women responsible for a suicide bombing at a checkpoint in Iraq (AP Photograph/AL-Jazeera via APTN).

In September 2005, a female suicide bomber blew herself up outside an army recruitment center in Tal Afar, a northern Iraqi town.[153] The explosion killed eight and wounded 57. Dressed in men's clothing, she detonated a belt of explosives that sprayed metal balls. Al-Qaeda in Mesopotamia, the terrorist group led by the Jordanian militant, Abu Musab al-Zarqawi, claimed responsibility for the attack.[154]

The al-Qaeda statement said the bombing was carried out by "a blessed sister from the al-Baraa bin Malek martyrdom brigade.... [and] May God accept our sister among the martyrs."[155] The statement did not provide clues to the bomber's identity.

On November 9, 2005, 38-year-old Muriel Degauque from Charleroi, Belgium, attacked an American patrol in the town of Baquba,

Iraq, north of Baghdad. No soldiers were killed, and one was slightly wounded. Degauque, a convert to Islam from Catholicism, is the first Western woman to carry out a suicide bombing in Iraq.[156]

Gender confusion has occurred in cases of Iraq bombings. An unidentified female dressed like a man detonated herself in Tal Afar on September 28, 2005. Five civilians were killed and over 30 were injured. She is thought to be the first woman bomber for al-Qaeda in Iraq.[157] In October 2005, al-Qaeda in Iraq claimed that a female bomber accompanying her husband detonated in an attack on an American patrol in Mosul.[158] On November 5, 2005, guerrillas disguised as women killed six and wounded 10 at a police checkpoint in Buhriz, 35 miles north of Baghdad.[159] On December 6, 2005, reports indicated that two females bombed Baghdad's police academy in a classroom filled with students. Thirty-six police officers were killed and 72 people were wounded, including an American contractor.[160] The U.S. military, however, later reported the bombers were men.

Examples Elsewhere: Jordan and Egypt

On November 9, 2005, 35-year-old Sajida Mubarak Atrous al-Rishawi from Ramadi, Iraq, participated in an attack on the Radisson SAS, Grand Hyatt and Days Inn hotels in Amman, Jordan. The woman was thought to have been in the Radisson. Fifty-seven people were killed. Al-Rishawi, who survived the attack, was the wife of one of the bombers in Jordan and was the sister of an al-Qaeda leader, one of Abu Musab al-Zarqawi's lieutenants, who had been slain in western Iraq.[161] In a statement, al-Zarqawi said that the female "was the venerable sister of Umm Omaira" and was the wife of Abu Omaira. "She chose to accompany her husband to his martyrdom."[162] If this is true, this attack would be the first known case of a husband and wife suicide bomber team.

On April 30, 2005, veiled females Negat Yousri and Iman Ibrahim Khamees opened fire at a bus on Salah Salem highway in Cairo. Although the actual bombing was by a male, this attack was the first by women in Egypt. Negat, the male bomber's sister, then shot and wounded her companion, Iman, the male bomber's girlfriend, and committed suicide. Khamees died in hospital of her wounds. Seven were wounded.[163]

Yoram Schweitzer writes that organizations have a variety of reasons for using women in suicide bombing, "but all deceptively used the innocent appearance of a "pregnant" woman in order to by-pass the heavy security arrangements while approaching their targets. All of them dwell on women's desire to prove their abilities and devotion to the organization and to their supreme leader. In several cases, especially in P.P.S. [Syrian Socialist Nationalist Party] there were romantic feelings involved."[164] Noteworthy is that the female suicide bomber who blew herself up outside an army recruitment center in Tal Afar was dressed as a male. Her reasons or her identity have not been disclosed. Methods used, such as dress, need more evaluation.

3

Freedom Fighters or Terrorists?

There are no suicide bombers. They are freedom fighters.
— Leila Khaled, former hijacker
and central committee member,
Popular Front for the Liberation of Palestine[1]

Leila Khaled, as a known and self-confessed terrorist who has never changed her views, is an affront to all decent-minded citizens.

— Neville Nagler, director general,
Board of Deputies of British Jews[2]

The suicide bomber is used as a tactical act of warfare. Analyses that focus on the bombers themselves, their histories and psychologies often ignore the fact that suicide bombers do not act on their own. Most attacks are arranged by organizations with political agendas. These organizations carefully screen possible suicide bombers because it is important that they have the ability to carry through. Suicide bombers have to be ready to die for a cause they believe to be just, such as liberating or defending their homeland. The introduction to the *At Issue* series that examines what motivates the suicide bomber says that experts say it is important to recognize that: "[L]ike other soldiers, suicide bombers are following orders, participating in a warfare campaign intended to overwhelm an enemy and rack up military victories."[3] Thus, the acts of the suicide bombers are not random or mindless.

Bombers as Freedom Fighters

Leila Khaled hijacked two planes, one in 1969 and the other in 1970, after stuffing hand grenades into her bra. She was captured in London after the second hijacking was thwarted in mid-flight. She was later released in exchange for more than 300 passengers on other captured airliners. She now lives in Amman, Jordan.[4] In 1969 Khaled hijacked a TWA aircraft which was diverted to Damascus. She escaped after she was put on the same bus as the victims. The next year she attempted to hijack an El Al flight. The plane made an emergency landing at Heathrow. She was put in jail for 28 days before she was freed in exchange for a hostage. She was charged but not put on trial.[5] The first hijacking touched off the 1970 Black September war between Jordan and the Palestine Liberation Organization inside Jordan.[6] Khaled became the interna-

tional pin-up of armed struggle. Then she underwent cosmetic surgery so she could do it again. Thirty years after her attacks, she describes herself as a woman at war.[7] Khaled and Dalal al-Mughrabi are categorized as forerunners of the female suicide mission era.[8] (See Tables 4.1 and 7.1.)

In the twenty-first century, Leila Khaled is a respected central committee member of and powerful symbol for the Popular Front for the Liberation of Palestine. In 2002, she spoke before a student meeting at the School for Oriental and African Studies in London.[9] In an interview with the *Telegraph*, she said:

Leila Khaled, who successfully hijacked a TWA airliner to Damascus, Syria, in 1969, totes a submachine gun at a Palestinian refugee camp in Lebanon in November 1970 (AP Photograph/Eddie Adams).

> All Palestinian factions are freedom fighters. We are glorifying life because we want peace,

but when we are always the targets of the Israelis I don't think we are going to meet them with flowers. We continue our struggle by all means including armed struggle.[10]

Khaled's appearance in London illustrates the dichotomy that exists between the perceptions of suicide bombing. While Khaled saw herself as a freedom fighter, some British officials and group leaders saw her as a terrorist. *Telegraph* reported that Andrew Dismore, member of Parliament for Hendon, wrote to David Blunkett, the Home Secretary. Dismore said, "I asked Mr. Blunkett whether we will now be taking action against her for the 1970 hijack. I just think it's a nonsense. What on earth is British justice about when we are allowing the hijacker who put people in fear of their lives to wander round making speeches with impunity."[11]

Neville Nagler, director general of the Board of Deputies of British Jews, also wrote a letter to the Home Secretary. Nagler said: "Leila Khaled, as a known and self-confessed terrorist who has never changed her views, is an affront to all decent-minded citizens. She should never have been allowed into the country. We would request that she be expelled."

Bombers as Terrorists

Suicide terrorism is defined by Boaz Ganor, director of the International Policy Institute for Counter Terrorism, as "the operational method in which the very act of the attack is dependent upon the death of the perpetrator." Even more importantly, he says, suicide terrorism is aimed at "striking a blow to public morale."[12]

Thus, the definition that terrorism is "a synthesis of war and theater" makes sense when Debra D. Zedalis writes that "this descriptor aptly applies to female suicide bombing."[13] She lists four major reasons suicide bombers, male or female, are used:

1. It is a simple and low-cost operation (requiring no escape route or rescue mission).

2. It increases the likelihood of mass casualties and extensive damage (since the bomber can choose the exact time, location, and circumstances of the attack).

3. There is no fear that interrogated terrorists will surrender important information (because their deaths are certain).

4. It has an immense impact on the public and the media (because it precipitates an overwhelming sense of helplessness).[14]

Zedalis adds that the infliction of fear and anxiety on the entire population produces a negative psychological effect. Christoph Reuter echoes:

> Suicide attacks affect us profoundly and powerfully. They remind us that there are people who consider their struggle — whatever the cause — to be more important than their own lives. They stir up fear in us; they pull the rug out from under our feet. For there is no way to retaliate against attackers who strike, not merely in order to kill people, but to die at the same stroke. They annihilate the entire logic of power, since no credible threat can be made against someone who has no desire to survive.[15]

Thus female bombers accentuate the goals of terrorism.

Why Women Are Used as Bombers

Women have always been allowed to serve in U.S. military intelligence. Although considered a noncombatant role, intelligence takes a great deal of bravery and skill.[16] Among the early reasons for use of female bombers may have been like those in intelligence, that women were not suspects. After continued use of women as bombers, societies should be becoming disabused of this reason. However, as late as 2004, the Israel Security Agency reported that women were seen as arousing less suspicion than men.[17] And Zedalis includes stereotyping of women in her four reasons terrorists use female suicide bombers as the "weapon of choice."

1. Tactical advantage: stealthier attack, element of surprise, hesitancy to search women, female stereotype (e.g., nonviolent).

2. Increased number of combatants.

3. Increased publicity (greater publicity = larger number of recruits).

4. Psychological effect.[18]

Zedalis explains that a woman without arousing suspicion can move about among the people and then attack. The element of surprise has shock value. In the case of Palestinian bombers, Zedalis adds another reason: They are designed to embarrass the Israeli government and to demonstrate Palestine's desperation in that women rather than men are fighting. Zedalis concludes, "Suicide bombers provide the low-cost, low-technology, low-risk weapon that maximizes target destruction and instills fear — women are even more effective with their increased accessibility and media shock value."[19]

Karla J. Cunningham includes in the use of the term "terrorism" women's involvement in politically violent organizations and movements.[20] She suggests that even a cursory look at history provides many examples of women's participation: Sigenobu Fusako, founder and leader of the Japanese Red Army; Ulrike Meinhof, West German Baader-Meinhof Gang; Ashraf Rabi, Iran 1974; women in Indian National Army in the 1940s; Algerian Resistance Movement's use of the veil in the 1950s; Ku Klux Klan; Third Reich; Joan of Arc; and the Russian Revolution. Cunningham writes:

> Importantly, the "invisibility" of women both within terrorist organizations, and particularly their assumed invisibility within many of the societies that experience terrorism, makes women an attractive actor for these organizations, an advantage that female members also acknowledge. This invisibility also makes scholarly inquiry of the phenomenon more difficult and may lull observers into the false assumption that women are insignificant actors within terrorist organizations.[21]

Amy Caiazza, study director of the Washington-based Institute for Women's Policy Research, gives another reason women are dangerous and lethal fighters:

> Soldiers don't want to shoot their mother or their wife. There's this ingrained sexism in men that they're going to hesitate a second before they kill a woman. Women have been able to exploit that stereotype and become very dangerous and very lethal fighters.[22]

The Israel Security Agency reported that women terrorists are disguised to allow them to blend in on the Israeli street. They were given an overall Western appearance, "including by wearing non-traditional clothing such as short clothes, pregnancy outfits and modern hairstyles."[23] In most cases, the women were from the margins of Palestinian society and did not usually fit the profile of the average Palestinian woman. The main reason women were involved in terrorism was personal, but this motive existed alongside the nationalistic motive. Personal motives consisted of romantic links with their recruiters, personal distress such as despair over life and parental opposition to the daughter's marriage. Women are used in terrorism mostly as suicide bombers or intended suicide bombers. Women have served as assistants in planning and perpetration of terrorist activity.[24]

Legal Realities and Terrorism

International law and the United States' (or any country's) foreign policy and domestic security involve legal realities and terrorism. Whether suicide bombers are perceived as freedom fighters or as terrorists, they are in violation of international and domestic laws. Some states argue that those nations that say they are protecting themselves are themselves, in some cases, in violation of international law, according to Matthew Lippman. Global law is undergoing change as it attempts to grapple with what it defines as terrorism. It is not uncommon for a cultural lag to exist in the law, for it is both a social product and a social force.

International Law and Terrorism

According to Matthew Lippman, terrorism in the twentieth and twenty-first centuries is a "new clerical culture of death and destruction."[25] The 9/11 suicide attack on the United States changed three aircraft and their 200,000 pounds of jet fuel into weapons of mass destruction and represented a new brutal variation of terrorism which threatened the safety and security of the worldwide community. He writes:

> Terrorist suicide bombings which possess a transnational dimension contravene the International Convention for the Suppression

of Terrorist Bombings and other instruments. This Bombing Convention requires signatory States to penalize and to punish individuals delivering, placing, discharging or detonating an explosive or other lethal device in, into or against a place of public use, a State or government facility, a public transportation system or an infrastructure facility. These acts are to be criminalized when committed with the intent to cause death, or serious injury or to cause extensive destruction in those instances in which this destruction results in or is likely to result in major economic loss.[26]

Lippman concludes the "global society is witnessing a new world order based on the struggle against terrorism."[27]

Richard A. Falk agrees that a new world order is occurring. He advocates, "It is more important than ever that a renewed, and understandable, preoccupation with the security of states since the events of September 11, 2001, be persuasively reconciled with respect for international law."[28] He writes that the attacks of 9/11 understandably required adjustments in international law to meet the challenge of terrorism. But "the generalized dismissal of legal guidelines for the use of force in foreign policy is unjustified, as is the generalized contention that 'security' lies beyond the reach of law."[29] The U.S. action that it could protect its security without a "permission slip"[30] sent a destructive signal to the international society that the most dominant state in the world said, in effect, that "international law is irrelevant when it comes to shaping security policy as a matter of foreign policy."[31]

Another example of the lack of understanding of international law was the case of Israeli society building its wall, according to Falk. The wall was built to provide security and to protect Israeli society against the mortal harm inflicted by suicide bombings. This purpose "is not the end of the argument as to the character of permissible action by a sovereign state, especially when it is operating outside its territorial boundaries. The Court made clear here that if this security wall had been located on Israeli territory rather than occupied Palestinian territory, it would not have been illegal."[32] Due to the wall's illegal location, it caused severe harm to be "inflicted upon the scope of the Palestinian right of self-determination, as well as the suffering ... to those Palestinians trapped on the structure's west side, that is, the Israeli side."[33]

Wayne N. Renke writes, "We have to fight the terrorists as if there were no rules, and preserve our open society as if there were no terrorists."[34] Renke suggests that the "presumption of normal process" may be refuted only if strict criteria are met:

1. The nation must face a severe and extraordinary risk or threat.

2. Normal process must be inadequate to reduce the risk.

3. The means adopted to reduce or eliminate the risk must have a reasonable chance of success; that is, the means should be carefully focused and the risks posed to others must be as small as is reasonably possible.

4. The expected benefits of an operation must be balanced against the foreseeable costs of the operation.

5. The process for authorizing the military operations should be appropriate.

6. In a democracy, there must be provision for openness, transparency, and public accountability.[35]

Renke concludes that terrorism presents society with a seriousness, a need to act now against it and to avoid "looping disengaged debate."[36] This proaction will ensure successful policies especially if policies are to restrict any long-standing civil liberties, according to Renke.

But does the new type of terrorism mean that the United States needs to revise laws or to respect the laws that it has. The United Nations has a long history of combating terrorism. In 1937, the League of Nations detailed the Convention for the Prevention and Punishment of Terrorism. Since then, the United Nations and regional intergovernmental organizations have dealt with terrorism from a legal and political perspective.[37]

Twelve universal legal instruments related to terrorism have been adopted from 1963 to 1999.[38] The 12 have major terms that relate to acts aboard and hijacking of aircraft, internationally protected persons, taking of hostages, protection of nuclear material, unlawful acts in airports, on ships or fixed platforms on shore, the making of plastic explosives, and suppression of terrorist bombing and financing. In addition, most of the conventions provide that parties must establish criminal jurisdiction over offenders, for example, the state(s) where the offense takes place, or, in some cases, the state of nationality of the perpetrator or victim. These provisions established there should be "no safe haven for terrorists."[39] Many states, however, are not party to or are not implementing these legal instruments.[40]

A supplement added to the 1994 Declaration on Measures to Eliminate International Terrorism established an Ad Hoc Committee to prepare draft conventions on the suppression of terrorist bombing and nuclear terrorism. "In part, it emphasized not to extend political asylum to terrorists and urged States to promptly extradite or subject to trial terrorists and those involved in the financing, planning or incitement of terrorism."[41]

According to Lippman, "there is little doubt that [the Convention for the Suppression of Terrorist Bombings] prohibited the planning and executing of suicide bombings."[42] Further, writes Lippman, it "significantly negated claims of religious justification for suicide bombing,"[43] because, in part, the convention required that state parties adopt domestic legislation criminally condemning acts within the convention, specifically "where they were intended or calculated to provoke a state of terror in the general public, in a group of persons or in particular persons." Such acts were "under no circumstances justifiable by considerations of a political, philosophical, ideological, racial, ethnic, religious or other similar nature" and were to be punished by penalties which reflected the "grave nature of this criminal conduct."[44]

In spite of the many U.N. actions against terrorism, the acts of war are so complex that international law continues to evolve. On July 13, 2005, the United States moved to strengthen U.N. sanctions against al-Qaeda and the Taliban. The U.S. circulated a draft resolution that would spell out in greater detail which terrorist suspects could be punished. Current U.N. sanctions require all 191 U.N. member states to ban travel and freeze assets associated with Osama bin Laden's terror network and the former Taliban rulers and to freeze their financial assets.[45]

The resolution includes a detailed list of who should fall under the sanctions, such as those parties who helped finance, plan or otherwise support al-Qaeda, bin Laden, the Taliban "or any cell, affiliate, splinter group or derivative thereof." The definition is designed to help close loopholes that the U.S. believes have allowed some terror suspects to go unpunished.[46]

Each country and, in some cases, areas, that is party to the United Nations and other international legal instruments strives to bring its laws parallel. The countries that have legal instruments as of 2003 are Australia, Canada, France, India, Israel, Japan, Pakistan, United Kingdom and the United States, according to *Jurist*, the Legal Education Network, University of Pittsburgh School of Law.[47]

Regional conventions include, "Regional Arab Convention for the Suppression of Terrorism (League of Arab States, 1998), Convention of the Organization of the Islamic Conference on Combating International Terrorism (1999); European Convention on the Suppression of Terrorism (PDF; 1977); OAS Convention to Prevent and Punish Acts of Terrorism Taking the Form of Crimes against Persons and Related Extortion that are of International Significance (Organization of American States; PDF 1971); SSARC Regional Convention on Suppression of Terrorism (PDF; South Asian Association for Regional Cooperation, 1987)."[48]

Since the London bombings, the European Union, a 25-nation bloc, spurred legal activity in July 2005 by agreeing to speed up measures to cut off funding for terrorist groups. Following the September 11 attacks on the United States and the March 2004 Madrid bombings, the EU took action to combat money laundering and banking secrecy that help the illegal moving of money.[49]

Although United Nations officials say more than $90 million belonging to suspects who are linked to al-Qaeda or the Afghan Taliban have been frozen, banks are nearly powerless to identify terrorists solely on the basis of their financial activity.[50]

The scope of legal activity indicates that much of the world views the suicide bomber as a terrorist rather than a freedom fighter. But that does not diminish the lack of understanding that exists between the West and Islam. United Nations Secretary-General Kofi Annan announced the launch of an initiative, co-sponsored by Spain and Turkey, which aims to overcome hostile perceptions that sow discord and foster violence. The initiative, Alliance of Civilizations, came about because "Events of recent years have heightened the sense of a widening gap and lack of mutual understanding between Islamic and Western societies — an environment that has been exploited and exacerbated by extremists in all societies."[51]

With regard to international law on terrorism, I asked retired Rear Admiral D.M. Williams, Jr., a former commander of the Naval Investigative Service Command, currently renamed as the Naval Criminal Investigative Service, whether the United Nations can be effective with its charter and resolutions. He replied:

> The other day when people were criticizing John Bolton as President Bush's nominee to be the U.S. ambassador to the United Nations, John McCain said, "The United Nations is an organization that has three countries, Syria is one of them, that are involved with terrorism that are on the U.N.'s Human Rights Commission." That is absurd. In that circumstance, when the United Nations is charged with human rights responsibility, those are the people who would produce draft texts of human rights resolutions. That is one reason you would not get any kind of agreement because they are not going to produce anything that is going to stop what they are doing from a diplomacy standpoint.[52]

International instruments are lawful guides for regions and countries to use in formulating their laws.

Military Strategic Responses

Some believe that when women commit such deadly acts, it signifies how desperate a political crisis is. Even President George W. Bush noted the Ayat Akhras attack as symbolic of the severity of the conflict between the Israelis and the Palestinians. (See Table 7.1.) He said, "When an 18-year-old Palestinian girl is induced to blow herself up and in the process kills a 17-year-old Israeli girl, the future itself is dying."[53] But such acknowledgment is also a recognition that human life is taken on both sides of war. So, how does a country like the United States in conflict look upon the concept of gender and upon the concept of freedom fighter versus terrorist?

One answer is that these ideological concepts may hinder agreement. Williams states:

> I don't think the United States should be doing anything that particularly addresses women in terms of diplomacy, if that is what you are asking. I make no distinction based on gender. It is very,

very difficult to achieve any kind of international agreement on these issues. When I was in graduate school in the University of London, studying armed conflict, the professor would always say that one man's terrorist is another man's freedom fighter. You see a lot of that, which inhibits trying to achieve some kind of agreement.

In the Munich Olympics hostage situation in 1972, much of the terrorist activity ended up being associated with the cause of the Palestinians, so a political debate ensued about the correctness of the cause which tried to get people to focus not on the correctness or lack thereof of the cause, but on the total absence of any correctness of any terrorist activity. That is where the difficulty lies.

Trying to get states to agree just to extradite terrorists to be tried by another sovereign state has in the past been very difficult, if not impossible. People who commit such acts or are responsible for such acts, would go to a location where the sympathies of the people there would not permit them to be extradited. I don't want that to sound like they are not acting on principle, because, in some cases, you would see people trying to extradite somebody and the other country would say, "As a matter of principle, we are not going to do this for any number of reasons." There are a number of states that won't extradite people to the United States because the United States has the death penalty and, for terrorist acts if there are multiple homicides involved, that is what you would expect the sentence of a U.S. court to be if the person ultimately ended up being convicted. There are ancillary issues that are involved, but, principally, when you start talking about terrorism, the difficulty in achieving agreement is that people look at, or have a tendency to look at, the underlying purpose for engaging in that conduct. If they have some sympathy with that underlying purpose then they tend to reflect more on that than on the conduct.

The United States and other countries in the international community tried for years to reach agreement about extraditing people who hijacked airliners. It was virtually impossible to do so. Occasionally, there is a case like the Libyans who were turned over for trial, but those cases tend to be the exceptions that prove the rule than anything else. Sometimes countries cannot find people. The United States has been grappling with this problem for as long as I can remember. Certainly, my entire life in the military we were trying to deal with what the response should be. Trying to find the terrorists and try them is one course of action, but you have to adopt a policy to have any chance of success. That is akin to what [George W.] Bush adopted which is you have to go root them out where they are. We need to enlist the support of Pakistan and other countries where traditionally terrorists have been. In Afghanistan, for years terrorists were trained there. In Sudan, terrorist training camps have been there for a long time. So you have to stop that at the roots.[54]

The nature of war has changed. Philip Bobbitt writes that one has but to examine the Iraq example. War is no longer modeled after World War II or even the Persian Gulf War. The goals of the leaders are also different from leaders of past wars.[55] Ray Youngblut, a World War II veteran, echoes Bobbitt when he comments on current military conflicts, "We don't know who we're mad at."[56] On what basis, then, does the military proceed in combating terrorism? Williams explains:

> Yes. A lot of innocent, obviously innocent, people get killed as the result of the actions of the suicide bombers, but a lot of people also get hurt, inconvenienced and are subjected to very intrusive results. People who are not like that, who are trying to prevent some kind of terrorist act, find it a difficult problem to deal with, whether it is females or males.[57]
>
> The problems that are presented for military organizations are not things that would surprise people if they sat down and followed them out for awhile because the military functions as part of a state. The state is taking action. In the case of terrorists, for the most part, that frequently is not the case. They may be acting independently or if they are acting on behalf of some state, hat is difficult if not impossible to prove. Having said that, the military functions on a body of rules that relates to targeting discretion. You are only allowed to attack military objectives. You don't attack churches. You don't attack hospitals. You don't attack civilians. If you look at the object of terrorist attacks, they are precisely the opposite of that. Indiscriminate killing is their touchstone and hallmark. Innocent civilians, children are killed. They don't really care. You can cite any number of examples of that from international wars; the bombing of airliners, the bombing of the World Trade Center, the IRA killing of Lord Mountbatten. All of those involved incidents of where the people being attacked are civilians that have no connection to combat.[58]

There was a story on *60 Minutes* the other night about West Point and the lessons they were teaching there. They had a captain who had just returned from Iraq who had graduated from West Point several years earlier. He was describing the circumstances and used the term "Wal-Mart combat operations." What he was describing was — you are in a Wal-Mart trying to stock the shelves conducting combat operations. So who do you kill? The very success of the terrorists depends on disguising who they are. In most cases, they are suicide bombers so they can get a bomb in place. So the killing is going to be indiscriminate. It is most probably going to be directed at civilians, at the general populace. But it is designed to create fear, terror and have people stop what they are doing. The problem it creates for military people is discerning who the enemy is and the possibility that innocent people may be killed. I cite, for example, the Italian security officer who had negotiated the release of the Italian journalist and was headed to the airport. The [U.S.] military people believed that it was a suicide bomber and so they attacked the car. But I was talking about the fact that they had rules of engagement which governed their conduct, that described for them whom they are authorized to shoot at, who they are not, what they are authorized to attack, what they are not, how they respond to a particular situation. They are trained on it all the time. Terrorists and suicide bombers are the exact opposite. They have no such rules. The only rule is: there are none. When you start putting women into that equation and if you are in a situation like the Middle East where most of the women are Moslem and they would wear more outer clothing than women in other cultures, it exacerbates that problem.[59]

The problem you have if you are an institutional entity trying to deal with it is not unlike what you see when you get to an airport today. How do you deal with that? How do you sort the wheat from the chaff? We end up giving up a lot of freedoms that we have in order to get on an airplane to take up somewhere, to make sure that it is safe to do that, so it affects us all in our everyday activities. For military people, the problem that it presents dramatically to them, particularly in a hostile environment, is how do you distinguish the terrorist from somebody who is going to church or to the mosque or to wherever? So that is why I say that kind of thought process is not remarkable if you spend some time giving any thought to it at all.[60]

Thus, the military in the United States acts at the direction of the state. It is not concerned with ideological issues. State policy, then, should be modeled after international principles. The United Nations struggles to address the issues for all of humanity. The problem is that all countries do not participate or agree. In the case of the United States, much controversy abounds from within and out of the country.

Conclusion

Although Leila Khaled was a hijacker whom Neville Nagler, a British citizen of Jewish ethnicity, saw as a terrorist, Khaled perceived herself a freedom fighter. From the perspectives of two worlds, both descriptions are true. Much is necessarily made of terminology in determination of policy, but could suicide bombing be, as one young Islamist male said on CNN Headline News, "just plain wrong"?[61] At any rate, President George W. Bush has added to the terminology discussion. Bush proclaimed that the United States is waging a global war on terror after 9/11. According to Jim Hoagland, "His initial use of the phrase and the concept rallied a dazed nation against a movement of killers who had been picking off Americans and others without retribution."[62] In 2005, President Bush declared we are in "a global struggle against violent extremism."[63] Joint Chiefs Chairman Gen. Richard Myers said that the military "objected to the use of the term 'war on terrorism' before, because if you call it a war, then you think of people in uniform as being the solution" whereas the answer may entail agents "more diplomatic, more economic, more political than ... military."[64] Perceptions in all parts of the world will continue to vary, and suicide bombing for some is a tactic of war. But the United States' strategy will be determined by how present and future leaders perceive suicide bombing and how they direct the country.

4

Middle East Conflicts in Lebanon and Turkey

"To liberate the south from the occupation of the Zionist terrorists ... who are not like us."

— Sana Youssef Mhaydali
first suicide bomber
SSNP/PPS member[1]

The Lebanon Civil War

The Lebanese Civil War (1975–1990) had its origin in the conflicts and political compromises of Lebanon's colonial period, Christian and Muslim interreligious strife, and proximity to Syria and Israel. The situation was exacerbated by the nation's changing demographic trends. Palestinian refugees made Lebanon their home after Israel became a state in 1948. Between 350,000 and 400,000 Palestinian refugees remain in Lebanon.[2]

The war began in April 1975. The early fighting was primarily in south Lebanon, occupied first by the Palestine Liberation Organization, and later by Israel.[3] Syria and Israel had significant involvement in the war. Israel invaded Lebanon the first time in 1978, in the Litani Operation, but withdrew under pressure from U.S. President Jimmy Carter. Israel gave arms and paid the salaries of South Lebanese Army (SLA) soldiers. In 1982 Israel invaded, in Operation Peace for Galilee. They drove out the Palestine Liberation Organization (PLO) and when a bomb killed Lebanon's president, Bahir Gemayel, Christian militiamen massacred 900

Palestinian civilians at the Shabra and Shatilla refugee camps. Israel was attempting to build up militarily and to defend itself by using forces in neighboring nations, according to David B. Doroquez.[4]

Hezbollah, or Party of God, was founded in 1982 in response to the Israeli invasion. Hezbollah is considered a Lebanese umbrella organization composed of Islamic Shiite groups and organizations that appear to be loosely organized. It included members of the 1980s coalition of groups known as Islamic Jihad. It has close ties to Iran and Syria. Its bitter foe is Israel. It opposes the West. Hezbollah's goal is to create a Muslim fundamentalist state similar to Iran.[5]

Hezbollah is a significant force in Lebanon's politics and a major provider of social services. It operates schools, hospitals, and agricultural services for thousands of Lebanese Shiites. It also runs the al-Manar satellite television channel and broadcast station.[6] Hezbollah's base is in Lebanon's Shiite-dominated areas, parts of Beirut, southern Lebanon, and the Bekaa Valley. Cells operate in Europe, Africa, South America, and North America.

Hezbollah has several thousand members and is responsible for almost 200 attacks since 1982 that have killed over 800 people.[7] Robert A. Pape writes Hezbollah are Islamic fundamentalists "driving suicide terrorism."[8] The group is proud of its attacks that forced Israeli and Western military to leave the country.[9] Hezbollah's major attacks include:

1. a series of kidnappings of Westerners in Lebanon, including several Americans, in the 1980s;

2. the suicide truck bombings that killed more than 200 U.S. Marines at their barracks in Beirut, Lebanon, in 1983;

3. the 1985 hijacking of TWA flight 847, which featured the famous footage of the plane's pilot leaning out of the cockpit with a gun to his head; and

4. two major 1990s attacks on Jewish targets in Argentina — the 1992 bombing of the Israeli Embassy (killing 29) and the 1994 bombing of a Jewish community center (killing 95).[10]

"Hezbollah in Lebanon ... incorporated suicide bombings as an effective terrorist tactic, after receiving training from the Iranian Revolutionary

Guard," Heather A. Andrews writes.[11] Hezbollah's first attack was the American embassy in Beirut in April 1983, followed by assaults on the U.S. Marine headquarters and the French Multinational Force in October 1983. These two attacks resulted in 300 killed and dozens wounded. The attack on the Marine headquarters "made an indelible impression on world public opinion and terror organizations alike."[12] Yoram Schweitzer says that after Western forces withdrew from Lebanon, Hezbollah targeted its suicide activities against Israeli Defense Forces and South Lebanese Army posts.

Andrews credits the modern form of suicide bombing as originating in Iran out the Shiite preoccupation with martyrdom, in the 1980s followed by the export of suicide terrorism to Hezbollah, spreading throughout the Middle East and into Sri Lanka and Chechnya. She says, "Thanks to globalization, this tactic has now reached all parts of the world."[13]

Syrian Socialist Nationalist Party (SSNP/PPS)

The Syrian Socialist Nationalist Party (SSNP/PPS) is sometimes referred to as the Syrian National Party (SNP)or the Parti Populaire Syrien (PPS). It "was an important landmark in the ecumenical movement of Syrian nationalism."[14] The group is a secular pro–Syrian Lebanese organization.[15]

Syria is one of seven countries that the U.S. State Department has on its list of state sponsored terrorism[16] but has not been directly involved in terrorist operations since 1986.[17] Syria supports Hezbollah and several other terrorist groups that either are headquartered in Syria or maintain offices there: Popular Front for the Liberation of Palestine-General Command, Palestinian Islamic Jihad, Hamas, and from 1980 to 1998, the Kurdistan Workers' Party.[18]

The SSNP conducted 12 suicide attacks and women took part in five. This number includes both successful and unsuccessful missions.[19] According to Beyler, the SSNP did not proclaim fatwas or edicts at the time. She writes:

> Supposedly, a female member of Hizballah ... conducted the last
> suicide bombing of the period before Israel left South Lebanon

and, at the time, the spiritual leader of the Hizballah, Fadllallah, did not make any statement. It is only in 2002 that he ... approved of female suicide bombers.[20]

Robert A. Pape provides new information about the years 1982 to 1986. Six of the 37 attackers were women. Ideological affiliation revealed that most were associated with groups that opposed Islamic fundamentalism, including three of the Christian faith.[21] Many details remain unknown about some of the early female attackers affiliated with the Syrian Socialist Nationalist Party, but insight can be gained from known information about some of the attackers. (See Table 4.1.)

Table 4.1
Female Suicide Bomber Missions
Hezbollah–Israeli/Lebanese Conflict, 1969–1987

Date	August 29, 1969, and September 6, 1970
Name/Home	Leila Khaled (or Khalid) /—
Age/Status	25 /—
Organization	Popular Front for the Liberation of Palestine
Place of Attack	Rome-Athens flight TWA #840
	Amsterdam-New York flight El Al #219
Casualties	0
Details	Hijacked two planes after stuffing hand grenades into her bra. In first hijacking, plane was blown up, but no one was killed.[a] In second hijacking, plane was overtaken and landed safely at Heathrow Airport near London. She was captured in London after the second hijacking was foiled in mid-flight. She was later released in exchange for more than 300 passengers on other captured airliners.[b]

Date	March 11, 1978
Name/Home	Dalal al-Mughrabi /—
Age/Status	19/—
Organization	Fatah
Place of Attack	Israeli bus on the road between Tel Aviv and Haifa
Casualties	39 killed, 72 wounded

*Notes to the Tables may be found on pages 192–197.

Details   Led a group of 11 attackers (including a second woman) to hijack a bus; nine victims were attackers and two were captured.[c] They landed at the beach of Kibbutz Ma'agan Michael, killing an American photographer and a taxi driver. They hijacked a bus that included many children on a day trip to the north. They forced the driver to return to Tel Aviv on the coastal highway while firing on passing cars.

A shoot-out occurred when the bus approached a blockade near Tel Aviv. The attackers got out of the bus to fire missiles. The bus exploded and most passengers were either burned alive or killed by gunfire.

Date	April 9, 1985
Name/Home	Sana Youssef Mehaydali a.k.a. Sana'a Mehaidl a.k.a. Khyadali Sana /—
Age/Status	17 (some say 16) / first suicide attack by a woman
Organization	Syrian Social Nationalist Party SSNP/PPS
Place of Attack	Occupied southern Lebanon near Jezzine
Casualties	2 killed, 2 wounded
Details	First suicide bomber for SSNP/PPS. Sana Youssef Mehaydali drove a Peugeot car into IDF convoy. Soldiers were killed or injured. Reason given: "avenge the oppressive enemy." Known to her admirers as "the Bride of the South." She explained her motive to liberate the south from the Zionist terrorists' occupation.[d] Attack is ascribable to the Shiite sphere; there is often talk about the "Shiite girl" or "Muslim girl." Secular organization is also clear.[e]

Date	May 9, 1985[f]
Name/Home	Wafaa Nour E'Din /—
Age/Status	23 / widow
Organization	—
Place of Attack	Lebanon
Casualties	—
Details	Husband killed in conflict.

Date	July 9, 1985[g]
Name/Home	Kharib Ibtisam Harb /—
Age/Status	28 /—
Organization	SSNP/PPS

Place of Attack	SLA post, Lebanon
Casualties	2 to 6 wounded
Details	Left videotape: wearing a red hat and uniform, she asked her parents to forgive her and that she wanted "to kill as many Jews and their assistants as she could."[hi]

Date	September 11, 1985[j]
Name/Home	Miriam Khaierdin /—
Age/Status	18/—
Organization	SSNP/PPS
Place of Attack	SLA checkpoint in Hatzbaya, Lebanon
Casualties	2 wounded
Details	—

Date	November 26, 1985[k]
Name/Home	Al Taher Hamidah /—
Age/Status	17 /—
Organization	SSNP/PPS
Place of Attack	Falous village of Jezzin, in South Lebanon
Casualties	—
Details	Drove car with 100 kg of explosives into SLA checkpoint.

Date	July 17, 1986[l]
Name/Home	Norma Abu Hassan /—
Age/Status	26 / high school teacher
Organization	Hezbollah SSNP/PPS
Place of Attack	Against Lebanese Agents
Casualties	7 wounded
Details	A Christian.[m] Blew herself up when she saw soldiers searching for her.[n]

Date	November 11, 1987[o]
Name/Home	Sahyouni Soraya /—
Age/Status	20 /—
Organization	SSNP/PPS
Place of Attack	Beirut airport, Lebanon
Casualties	6 killed, 73 wounded
Details	Carried suitcase with explosives. Case exploded by remote control.

Date	November 14, 1987[P]
Name/Home	Shagir Karima Mahmud /—
Age/Status	37 /—
Organization	Syrian Socialist National Party (SSNP/PPS)
Place of Attack	AUB Hospital, Beirut, Lebanon
Casualties	7 killed, 20 wounded
Details	Carried explosive charge hidden in bag.

The suicide attack by Khyadali Sana, a.k.a. Sana Youssef Mehaydali or Sana'a Mehaidl, on April 9, 1985, is considered the first suicide attack carried out by a woman in the Israeli-Palestinian Conflict (IPC) area. Sana, about 16 or 17, is also one of the youngest female bombers. The attack occurred in south Lebanon in Bater Al Shuf Jezzin. Sana joined the Syrian Social Nationalist Party (SSNP/PPS) three months before she drove the car that exploded near an Israeli Defense Force (IDF) convoy, killing two Israeli soldiers and wounding two others. She had stated that her motive was to "avenge the oppressive enemy." Known to her admirers as "the Bride of the South," she explained her motive was to liberate the south from the Zionist terrorists' occupation.[22] Heather A. Andrews writes that it was Mehaydali's last wish to be called the bride of the south; "Consequently, the female Islamic suicide terrorist still fulfills the ultimate societal goal of marriage, albeit without its constraints."[23]

In November 1987, two women carried explosives concealed in a bag. Sahyouni Soraya, 20, killed six and wounded 73 when her bomb detonated by remote control at the Beirut airport on November 11. On November 14, Shagir Karima Mahmud, 37, detonated her explosives at the AUB Hospital in Beirut, killing seven and wounding 20.[24]

On July 9, 1985, Kharib Ibtisam Harb, 28, attacked an SLA post, wounding between two and six people. Harb left videotape of herself dressed in a red hat and uniform. She asked her parents to forgive her and stated that she wanted "to kill as many Jews and their assistants as she could."[25]

Twenty-six-year old Norma Abu Hassan, a high school teacher, is one of the few female suicide bombers to be a Christian.[26] Her attack against Lebanese agents occurred in Jezzin. She blew herself up when she saw soldiers searching for her.[27] Seven people were wounded. The Hezbollah and SSNP/PPS claimed responsibility.

The Kurds Conflict in Turkey

Kurdistan is the homeland to over 20 million Kurds. The Treaty of Sevres that divided up the Ottoman Empire following World War I recognized Kurdistan as a nation. But the world has long forgotten Kurdistan as a nation. "The Kurds, inhabiting parts of Turkey, Iraq and Iran are the largest national group without a country."[28] By 1990, a Kurdish separatist movement appeared in southeastern Turkey. The government banned Kurdish political parties and arrested and exiled Kurdish leaders. In 1992, the Kurdistan Workers Party (PKK) announced a war government and mounted an insurgency.[29]

Kurdistan Workers Party (PKK)

The Kurdistan Workers Party, known as the PKK after its Kurdish name, Partiya Karkeren Kurdistan, is another name for the Kongra-Gel (KGK). Its other names include: Kurdistan Freedom and Democracy Congress, KADEK, Kurdistan People's Congress, Freedom and Democracy Congress of Kurdistan. The PKK was founded in 1974 as a Marxist-Leninist separatist organization and was formally named the Kurdistan Workers Party in 1978. It is a secessionist secular Islamic movement. The group primarily consists of Turkish Kurds. Its campaign of armed violence began in 1984. The result has been some 30,000 casualties. The PKK's goal is to establish an independent, democratic Kurdish state in southeast Turkey, northern Iraq, and parts of Iran and Syria, according to the U.S. State Department.[30]

The State Department reports that the PKK's strength numbers about 4,000 to 5,000 people, of which 3,000 to 3,500 are in northern Iraq. The group has thousands of sympathizers in Turkey and Europe. The PKK operates primarily in Turkey, Iraq, Europe, and the Middle East.[31]

Although PKK members shared the same Muslim beliefs, Islam was not the essential characteristic. PKK leader Abdullah Öcalan's orders provided the incentive and justification for suicide attacks. Öcalan reached the status of God in the organization. It was on this leader's orders that suicide bombings started and eventually stopped.[32]

The PKK has used suicide bombings in its attempt to persuade the

Turkish government to accept their demands for Kurdish autonomy.[33] PKK's suicide campaign began on June 30, 1996, and ended on July 5, 1999. The PKK suicide attacks ended as they had begun, with a decree by Öcalan.[34] The purpose of the PKK is not based in religion, but in the cause of and devotion to its leader.[35] The military efforts ended in 1999 for Öcalan and his group because he withdrew from martyrdom. He began advocating an end to the civil war and started a peace process. After he was arrested, he apologized in court to families of soldiers who had died in the war, said the war was a mistake and offered to be a mediator if his life were spared. He received a sentence of life in prison.[36]

As in Sri Lanka, women in Turkey were allowed to fully participate from the early stages of terror organizations. Women carried out 14 of 21 suicide attacks (66 percent) conducted by the PKK in Turkey. This number includes both successful and unsuccessful missions.[37]

On June 30, 1996, the first female PKK bomber killed six Turkish soldiers and wounded 30 others. The attacker strapped a bomb to her stomach as if she were pregnant.[38] On October 29, 1996, in Sivas, Turkey, 29-year-old Otas Gular dressed as a pregnant woman, detonated her bomb and killed a policemen. This attack was the third bombing by PKK females who appeared to be pregnant. Öcalan had urged his troops to imitate Hamas by becoming human bombs.[39] On October 25, 1996, 17-year-old Laila Kaplan disguised as a pregnant woman and attacked police headquarters in Adana, killing 5 and wounding 12 people.[40] (See Table 4.2.)

Table 4.2
Female Suicide Bombers
Kurds–Turkey Conflict, 1996–2005

Date	June 30, 1996[a]
Name/Home	Unknown /—
Age/Status	—/—
Organization	PKK
Place of Attack	Turkey
Casualties	6 killed, 30 wounded
Details	First female PKK bomber. Turkish soldiers killed. Bomb strapped to her stomach as if she were pregnant.

Female Suicide Bombers

Date	October 25, 1996[b]
Name/Home	Laila Kaplan / —
Age/Status	17 / activist
Organization	PKK
Place of Attack	Police headquarters in Adana.
Casualties	5 killed, 12 wounded
Details	Disguised as pregnant woman.

Date	October 29, 1996[c]
Name/Home	Otas Gular / —
Age/Status	29 / —
Organization	PKK
Place of Attack	Sivas.
Casualties	2 killed, 1 wounded
Details	Killed policemen. Dressed as pregnant woman, accompanied by another group member. Third bombing by PKK females appearing to be pregnant. Őcalan had urged his troops to imitate Hamas by becoming human bombs.

Date	November 17, 1998[d]
Name/Home	Ozen Fatima, a.k.a. Fatma / —
Age/Status	29 / —
Organization	PKK
Place of Attack	Outside a police station in Yuksekova, southeast Turkey.
Casualties	6 wounded
Details	Bomb strapped to body, missed target of military convoy.

Date	December 1, 1998[e]
Name/Home	Unknown Kurdish woman / —
Age/Status	— / —
Organization	—
Place of Attack	Outside supermarket, Lice.
Casualties	1 killed, 22 wounded
Details	Supermarket frequented by Turkish soldiers.

Date	December 24, 1998[f]
Name/Home	Unknown / —
Age/Status	— / —
Organization	—
Place of Attack	Outside Army barracks in Batman.

Casualties   1 killed, 22 wounded
Details   Killed passer-by.

Date   March 4, 1999[g]
Name/Home   Unknown /—
Age/Status   —/—
Organization   —
Place of Attack   Main square of Batman.
Casualties   4 wounded
Details   Bomb may have gone off prematurely as suspected target was
                  police station.

Date   March 27, 1999[h]
Name/Home   Esma Yurdakul /—
Age/Status   21 /—
Organization   —
Place of Attack   Istanbul.
Casualties   10 wounded
Details   —

Date   July 5, 1999[i]
Name/Home   Rusen Tabanci /—
Age/Status   19 /—
Organization   —
Place of Attack   Adana.
Casualties   17 wounded
Details   Flashed "V" for victory and detonated bomb on body.

Date   May 21, 2003[j]
Name/Home   Unknown /—
Age/Status   —/—
Organization   —
Place of Attack   Ankara Crocodile coffee shop.
Casualties   —
Details   Unclear whether shop was target or if bomb detonated in the
                  ladies room while she hid, possibly as a result of being
                  scared off by the presence of a policeman.

Date   May 2003[k]
Name/Home   Unknown / —
Age/Status   — / —
Organization   DHKP/C
Place of Attack Istanbul
Casualties   1 wounded
Details   —

Also on October 25, 1996, another woman met her death, but for a different reason. Turkan Adiyaman was shot by her own group (PKK). She had refused to volunteer. She was shot in front of Leyla Kaplan as an example of the fate that befalls shirkers. Kaplan then performed the bombing.[41] In other instances, little is known about missions that are not successful. Such is the case with an unsuccessful PKK mission by a female bomber in August of 1998 that was to take place in Adana.[42]

5

The Conflict in Sri Lanka

"[Suicide bombing is a] self sacrifice.... If we have a target and use conventional operations we normally lose 15 or 16 fighters. With self sacrifice we can achieve the same objective and only one dies."

–Thamilvili, Black Tigress, LTTE[1]

Tamil separatism has been a part of Sri Lanka since it gained independence from India in 1948. The civil war began in 1983 and continues but with a cease-fire in place between the Buddhist Sinhalese majority and the mostly Hindu Tamil minority.[2] The Liberation Tigers of Tamil Elam (LTTE) have been fighting for a homeland for minority ethnic Tamils during this time. They accuse the government of discrimination.[3] The Tamil Tigers have been fighting for a separate homeland in Tamil majority areas in the north and the east of the country. More than 60,000 people were killed in the nearly two decades of fighting in Sri Lanka.[4]

On February 21, 2002, the Sri Lankan government and Tamil Tiger rebels agreed to a permanent cease-fire as part of a Norwegian initiative to end almost two decades of civil war.[5] The cease-fire is still in effect.

Liberation Tigers of Tamil Eelam (LTTE)

The Liberation Tigers of Tamil Eelam (LTTE) were founded in 1976. Velupillai Prabhakaran formed the group with aid from India. Its insurgency against the government of the Sinhalese Buddhist majority of Sri Lanka began in 1983.

Although the LTTE operates throughout the island of Sri Lanka, it controls most of the northern and eastern coastal areas. It is headquartered in northern Sri Lanka, and its leader has an extensive network of checkpoints and informants.[6] The LTTE's organizations support Tamil separatism by lobbying foreign governments and the United Nations and uses international contacts and the large Tamil diaspora in North America, Europe, and Asia to obtain weapons, communications, funding, and supplies.[7]

LTTE's strategy includes guerrilla and terrorist tactics. "The LTTE is the most powerful Tamil group in Sri Lanka," reports the U.S. Department of State.[8] Prabhakaran established the LTTE with women and men. The women's fighting commando unit, Birds of Freedom, formed in 1983.

Estimates of the LTTE's strength range between 8,000 and 10,000 armed combatants in Sri Lanka. It has a core of 3,000 to 6,000 trained fighters and 4,000 women.[9]

Because the Tamil society is traditional, women see membership in the LTTE as an opportunity to perform like males. Some women believe they reach the position of equality only because of the male leader, Prabhakaran. Beyler writes, "The LTTE has justified women's involvement as its way of assisting women's liberation and counteracting the oppressive traditionalism of the present system."[10] Women who were raped by the enemy were no longer considered women or mothers by society. The way to redeem their status was to undertake a man's task and die for a good cause.

"There have been massive human rights abuses in the north and east in Tamil areas," writes Mia Bloom.[11] The abuses include rape, dehumanizing checkpoint searches, murder, widespread torture, and systematic campaigns of disappearances. Thus, women's reasons for joining the LTTE range from personal experiences to experiences of the Tamil community as a whole. Women have been exposed to violence through the years of armed conflict, but they are not represented in the official peace process or in local or national leadership positions.[12]

Lisa Kruger's study revealed that LTTE men and women "are motivated to participate in the group's terrorist activities for similar reasons.

Similarities are rarely recognized since reporting tends to focus on rape and women's emancipation as the main motives."[13] Further, she writes that men and women share motivations of nationalism, revenge for suffering and oppression, poverty, and educational restrictions, but that women may also be motivated by elements pertinent to them, such as oppression of women and the desire to redeem oneself from incidents of sexual violence.[14]

The LTTE, like the Kurdish Workers Party (PKK) in Turkey, does not have religion as the common ground, but rather the goal of establishing a land of their own, based upon a common nationality and the personality of their leaders, Vellupilai Prabhakaran for the Tamils, and Abdullah Öcalan for the Kurds.[15]

Eelam, or freedom, the goal of LTTE, is joined together with the pursuit of like personal, societal freedom for female recruits. As a member of LTTE, a woman can redeem herself (e.g., from having been raped). The sacrifice of the female bomber is equated with an extension of motherhood. To the organization and to her family, suicide bombing becomes an acceptable offering for women who can never be mothers. Women's identity is a core symbol of the nation's identity, and to the LTTE, their nationalism.[16] Female martyrdom is necessary to overcome the individual and collective shame of dishonor that rape causes. These factors, among others, allow the LTTE to exploit "its female cadre, who are used as 'throw-aways' or 'as artillery.'"[17]

Suicide Bombing and LTTE Female Members

The LTTE began suicide bombings in 1987. It followed the Hezbollah, whose suicide terror attacks against Western targets began in Lebanon in April 1983.[18] The LTTE usually targets senior political and military officials in Sri Lanka. It is the only organization that has succeeded in assassinating two heads of state by suicide bombings: former Indian Prime Minister Rajiv Gandhi in May 1991 and President Ranaginghe Premadasa of Sri Lanka in May 1993.[19]

The LTTE suicide squads are motivated by a strong nationalistic spirit and the charismatic leadership of Prabhakaran. It is the most active group in the use of suicide terrorism, but it has not succeeded in achieving an independent Tamil state.[20] Yoram Schweitzer, an International Center for Terrorism researcher, characterizes the group as "unequivocally the most effective and brutal terrorist organization ever to utilize suicide terrorism."[21]

The LTTE has perpetrated the most attacks, over 200, and 30 percent to 40 percent involved women bombers.[22] Women are trained and go on suicide missions like men. Many are recruited when they are children and perform suicide missions as early as ten years old, states Clara Beyler.[23] A cyanide capsule is carried to use in case a bomber is caught. Beyler relates an interview with an ex–LTTE cadre in hiding by the French philosopher Bernard-Henri Levy: "Part of their training includes hiding a hand-grenade in women's vaginas. This exercise was also imposed on all the other non-virgin members in the training camps."[24]

Heather A. Andrews, author of *Veiled Jihad:* writes about two recent female bombing activities by the LTTE. (See Table 5.1.) She states, a "noteworthy incident occurred on January 5, 2000, when a female bomber targeted the office of Prime Minister Siramavo Bandaranaike. Thirteen people were killed, but the Prime Minister was not at her office at the time. This attack was not claimed by anyone, but the LTTE was suspected."[25]

A second incident involving a Black Tigress occurred on July 7, 2004. Andrews writes the attack "resulted in the death of five policemen. The apparent target was Cabinet Minister and Ealam Peoples Democratic Party (EPDP) leader Douglas Devananda. The EPDP is a rival party of the LTTE. This marked the first suicide bombing since the ceasefire agreement was signed in February 2002 between the LTTE and the Sri Lankan Government."[26]

Failed suicide attacks by the Tamil Tigers have been few, in terms of not being able to kill their target. Even when they have failed in killing their target, one or several others have been killed in the attack.[27]

Table 5.1
Female Suicide Bombers
LTTE–Sri Lankan Conflict, 1991–2004

Date	May 21, 1991
Name/Home	Gayatri, a.k.a. Thenmuli Rajaratnam a.k.a. Dhanu. Tanu aliases: Anbu and Kalaivani.

	Dhanu's stand-in, Subha / Jaffna, Sri Lanka[a] /—
Age/Status	late 20s /—
Organization	LTTE
Place of Attack	Gandhi was campaigning in southern state of Tamil Nadu. The explosion occurred in town of Sriperumbudur, approximately 30 miles from Chennai, capital of Tamil Nadu.[b]
Casualties	16 to 18 killed, 33 wounded
Details	Most famous LTTE bomber. Killed India's Prime Minster Rajiv Gandhi by detonating an explosive vest after bowing down at Gandhi's feet during an election rally.[c] Explosive device was highly sophisticated and powerful with a foolproof triggering mechanism, electric detonator and a well-concealed body jacket to house the device. Plastic explosive of the RDX variety was used; 2 mm steel balls were used to create an intense impact; six grenades containing cyclonite explosives, known as C4-RDX, each fitted with 2,800 splinters of 2 mm were held in a denim belt using a silver wire connected to the 9-volt battery with two toggle switches to detonate it. The device was enclosed in a casing of trinitrotoluene (TNT). Dhanu appeared to have intimate knowledge of the function and its sequence.[d]
	First attacker to use a suicide belt. Four brothers killed in conflict; her home looted, she was gang-raped.[e]

Date	October 24, 1994[f]
Name/Home	Unknown /—
Age/Status	—/—
Organization	LTTE
Place of Attack	Thotalaga (Grandpass) Junction in Colombo
Casualties	59 killed
Details	Leader of the opposition and United National Party candidate for the presidential elections, Gamini Dissanayake, was killed.

Date	November 11, 1995[h]
Name/Home	Unknown /—
Age/Status	—/—
Organization	LTTE
Place of Attack	Near the Slave Island Railway Station in Colombo

Casualties	17 (15 children, a police personnel and one soldier) killed
Details	—

Date	November 24, 1995[i]
Name/Home	Two women /—
Age/Status	—/—
Organization	LTTE
Place of Attack	Targeted the headquarters of the Sri Lankan Army
Casualties	16 killed, 52 wounded
Details	Exploded bombs concealed in their vests.

Date	July 4, 1996[j]
Name/Home	Unknown /—
Age/Status	—/—
Organization	LTTE
Place of Attack	Stanley Road, Jaffna town
Casualties	20 killed, 60 wounded
Details	Jaffna military commander Brigadier Ananda Hamangoda was killed. Bomber detonated explosives strapped to her waist as a minister's motorcade stopped. Target was housing and construction minister Nimal Siripala de Silva, who escaped with minor injuries.

Date	February 6, 1998[k]
Name/Home	Female cadre /—
Age/Status	—/—
Organization	LTTE
Place of Attack	SLAF roadblock near the Rio Cinema at Slave Island
Casualties	8 (6 soldiers and 2 civilians) killed
Details	Exploded when cadre failed to penetrate the roadblock.

Date	May 14, 1998[l]
Name/Home	Unknown /—
Age/Status	—/—
Organization	LTTE
Place of Attack	Jaffna
Casualties	1 killed
Details	Bomber wore abdominal belt bomb. Target was killed: Brigadier Larry Wijeyaratne, one of the Sri Lankan Army's top commanders.

Date	March 18, 1999[m]
Name/Home	Unknown /—
Age/Status	—/—
Organization	LTTE
Place of Attack	Near a police station in Colombo
Casualties	3 killed, 8 wounded
Details	Target was Chief Inspector Mohammed Nilabdeen, head of the terrorism investigation unit. He was wounded.

Date	July 25, 1999[n]
Name/Home	Unknown /—
Age/Status	—/—
Organization	LTTE
Place of Attack	Trincomalee Harbor
Casualties	1 killed
Details	Targeted a docked ship, hours before it was to take on passengers.

Date	August 4, 1999[o]
Name/Home	Unknown /—
Age/Status	—/—
Organization	LTTE
Place of Attack	Vavuniya, northern Sri Lanka.
Casualties	10 killed (9 police commandos and one civilian), 18 commandos injured
Details	Bomber threw herself at a police truck.

Date	December 18, 1999[p]
Name/Home	Gunanayagam Leela Lakshmi/Batticaloa
Age/Status	—/—
Organization	LTTE
Place of Attack	Election meeting at the town hall in Colombo
Casualties	21 killed, over 100 injured
Details	Failed attempt; target was President Chandrika Kumaratunga. She was injured in one eye from shrapnel. Among those killed were four police personnel, including Colombo's Deputy Inspector-General T.N. De Silva. Injured included three senior ministers and some foreign journalists, including a Japanese television crew.

Female Suicide Bombers

Date	January 5, 2000[q]
Name/Home	Unknown /—
Age/Status	—/—
Organization	Not claimed, but suspected LTTE
Place of Attack	Prime Minister's Office, Flower Road in Colombo.
Casualties	11 to 13 killed, 27 to 29 wounded
Details	Prime minister not harmed.

Date	March 2, 2000[r]
Name/Home	Unknown /—
Age/Status	—/—
Organization	LTTE
Place of Attack	Inner Harbour Road in Trincomalee
Casualties	1 killed
Details	Target was Col. Piyal Abeysekara, who survived, but his driver was killed.

Date	October 30, 2001[s]
Name/Home	Unknown /—
Age/Status	—/—
Organization	LTTE
Place of Attack	MV *Silk Pride*, off port of Point Pedro on northern Jaffna peninsula
Casualties	3 soldiers: 4 bombers, including 2 women killed
Details	A suicide boat attack on an oil tanker

Date	July 7, 2004[t]
Name/Home	Thiyagaraja Jeyarani /—
Age/Status	—/—
Organization	LTTE
Place of Attack	Kollupitiya Police station next to the prime minister's official residence, Colombo.
Casualties	5 killed
Details	Target was Cabinet Minister and Ealam People's Democratic Party's (EPDP) leader Douglas Devananda. Marked the first suicide bombing since the cease-fire agreement of February 2002 between the LTTE and the government.

The First Female LTTE Suicide Bomber

In 1991, Dhanu became the first LTTE female suicide bomber[28] and is the most famous.[29] On December 18, 1999, Gunanayagam Leela Lakshmi attempted to assassinate the Sri Lanka president, Chandrika Kumaratunga, at an election rally. The president was wounded. Her attack killed approximately 20 people and wounded over 100 others. Lakshmi is from the eastern town of Batticaloa. She had been a member of LTTE for ten years and was a member of the rebel Black Tigers squad.[30] Women like Lakshmi and Dhanu are most likely part of the reason Luca Ricolfi reports that the "LTTE became the world's foremost suicide bombers and proved the tactic to be so unnerving and effective that their

Dhanu, a Sri Lankan Tamil, center, carried the bomb which killed former Indian Prime minister Rajiv Gandhi. The picture was taken minutes before the explosion, May 21, 1991 (AP Photograph).

methods and killing innovations were studied and copied, most notably in the Middle East."[31]

Dhanu

On May 21, 1991, Dhanu, whose real name was Gayatri[32] and Thenmuli Rajaratnam[33] and was also known by the aliases Anbu and Kalaivani, killed India's Prime Minster Rajiv Gandhi by detonating an explosive vest after bowing down at Gandhi's feet during an election rally in the state of Tamil Nadu. Eighteen people were killed.[34] (See Table 5.1.)

Only three people had security clearance to present garlands. Dhanu was seen by witnesses as moving toward Gandhi and bending down, genuflecting to pay respects, by touching his feet. The explosion occurred in the town of Sriperumbudur, near Madras. Dhanu appeared to have intimate knowledge of the bomb's function and its sequence. Parts of her body were flung in different directions and only the torso was not recovered.[35]

Dhanu's father, A. Rajaratnam, was a former government clerical servant. In 1966, he was a member of the Ilankai Thamil Arasu Kadchi, organized as the Puli Padai (Tigers Army), to oppose the Sinhalese government. A. Rajaratnam left government service and lived in Madras, where he died a poor man in 1975.[36]

Robert A. Pape rates Dhanu as one of the three most deadly suicide terrorists in the past 20 years. The other two most deadly suicide terrorists were males: Mohamed Atta, who organized and led the September 11, 2001, attacks, and Saeed Hhotari, a member of Hamas who blew up himself and killed 21 Israelis outside a discotheque in Tel Aviv.[37] According to Pape, these three suicide bombers were basically ordinary people. They were not religious fundamentalists, impoverished, impulsive, delusional, depressed, detached or not able to enjoy life. Rather, the opposite was true in each case. They worked for months planning their missions and attended dress rehearsals. They trained and worked closely with others. Pape writes:

> For them, suicide attack was not an escape — it was a duty. From smiles to statements of satisfaction in their final moments on earth, the world's most deadly suicide terrorists took evident pride in what they saw not as crimes but as sacrifices for their communities.[38]

Dhanu was the first attacker to use a suicide belt. Dhanu was in her late twenties and had a history of experience with violence. Four of her brothers were killed in conflict; her home in Jaffna, Sri Lanka, looted; and she was gang-raped. Pape describes Dhanu as a remarkably beautiful woman whose motivation was most likely revenge for the harm she suffered at the hands of the Indian soldiers.[39]

Dhanu was trained by the Black Tigresses of the LTTE, who prepare members especially for suicide terrorism. Pape states that members perform only one mission. Joining the Black Tigresses involves three steps. First, a woman is carefully selected. The primary requirement is that the candidate be highly motivated to complete the mission. Mental stability is more crucial than tactical military competence. Second, the suicide attackers are trained in camps that are separate from the others. Third, the Tigers and Tigresses conduct dress rehearsals near the location of the proposed attack and study the films of past operations.[40]

Pape writes that Dhanu's behavior weeks before the assassination does not indicate evidence of depression or personal trauma. Rather, "her activities suggest a person enjoying the good things in life."[41] Money and encouragement from the LTTE enabled her to go to the market, the beach and restaurants each day. She purchased dresses, jewelry, cosmetics and her first pair of glasses. Pape writes, "in the last twenty days of her life, she took in six movies at a local cinema."[42]

Pape explains that it is understood that women in Sri Lanka who are thought to be rape victims by Sinhalese or Indian soldiers will never be allowed to marry or procreate. Martyrdom is understood and an accepted option for such women. Pape concludes: "Dhanu clearly had nerves of steel. She clearly understood the consequences of her actions and worked hard to ensure that her mission would surely succeed."[43]

Karla J. Cunningham suggests that Dhanu represents "some contradictory themes that arise when considering women's roles in LTTE."[44] In the organization women are trained on an equal footing with men and share combat experience. Yet women's use as suicide bombers comes from their general exclusion from the established "profile"—young males— used by many policy and security forces which allows women to better avoid scrutiny and reach their targets.[45]

The Challenge of Reintegrating LTTE Women in Society

The conflict in Sri Lanka presents the challenge of reintegrating the women members of the LTTE into society. Dilshika Jayamaha interviewed LTTE women fighters in 2003 and 2004. Jayamaha posed the question: "Perhaps they [LTTE] are emancipating a people, but what of themselves? This question becomes more significant when analyzing the former women combatants, who are re-entering civilian roles."[46]

Violence makes a culture what it is and forces "new constructs of identity, new socio-cultural relationships, new threats and injustices that reconfigure people's life-worlds, new patterns of survival and resistance,"[47] writes Jayamaha. The new sociocultural construct forged by violence allows these women to walk through their worlds with modern and non-traditional confidence. They are empowered and believe they are making a path for all women's emancipation. They believe the LTTE training has made them more confident and assertive. The real question is whether they will be able to transform their society.[48]

Although Tamil women fighters may be pulled back into more normal lives, they will retain a difference that society will have to contend with, according to Jayamaha. One former woman fighter, Girija, said, "Society looks on us with tremendous respect."[49]

Former fighter Nila said,

> After I returned home people treated me with honor and respect. Often they did not quite know how to treat me.... I felt separate. They treated me like I was special. I asked myself why they didn't treat me like an ordinary person.[50]

Special but separate, Jayamaha writes. Possibly respected out of obligation and maybe resented, "Like veterans of many wars, these women combatants will likely find that peacetime society is not quite sure how to handle them."[51] Jayamaha concludes that how well women fighters are reintegrated into peacetime society will be a key indicator of Sri Lanka's shift to the logic of peace.[52]

6

The Chechen-Russian Conflict

"I know what I am doing, paradise has a price, and I hope
this will be the price for Paradise."
— Khava/Hawa' Barayev's last words
First Black Widow[1]

The mountainous region of Chechnya has important oil deposits,
as well as natural gas, limestone, gypsum, sulfur, and other minerals. Its
mineral waters have made it a spa center. Major production includes oil,
petrochemicals, oil-field equipment, foods, wines, and fruits. For centuries, the Chechen people's history and relationship with the regional
power, Russia, has been full of turmoil.[2]

When the Soviet Union collapsed in 1991, 14 regions became independent nations. After Dzhokhar Dudayev was elected president of
Chechnya, he declared Chechnya independent. Russian President Boris
Yeltsin refused to recognize Chechnya's independence and, in 1994, sent
in troops. This was the beginning of the first Chechen-Russian War, and
it lasted until 1997. The Russian force numbered 45,000. In 1995,
Dudayev was killed by a Russian rocket. The Chechens took hostages as
the war continued and became more destructive. Aslan Maskhadov led
the Chechen forces, which pushed the Russian army to retreat from
Grozny in 1995.

In 1996, the Chechens launched a major counteroffensive with 5,000
troops led by Maskhadov and invaded the capital of Grozny. Yeltsin was
unwilling to use maximum force and destroy Grozny to defeat the rebels,

so the Russians agreed to a cease-fire. Maskhadov was at the forefront of peace negotiations in 1995 and 1996, which Moscow undertook to withdraw its forces from the republic. The war produced 70,000 casualties on all sides.[3] After the Russians withdrew, Chechnya continued to refuse to accept Moscow's authority. Chechens elected Maskhadov president in January 1997 because of his war record and because he promised a more peaceful future than younger and more radical rival candidates, including Shamil Basayev. On one point he was always firm, however: Chechnya must be independent.[4] The name of the capital was changed from the Russian Grozny to the Chechen Djohar. In 1999, terrorist bombs exploded in Moscow and other Russian cities. Russian authorities blamed Chechen paramilitary commanders. Chechen insurgents entered the neighboring Russian territory of Dagestan to help Islamic fundamentalists seeking to create separate nation. Russian troops were successful in recapturing the breakaway areas of Dagestan.

The second Chechen-Russian War began in 1999 when Yeltsin sent nearly 100,000 Russian troops into Chechnya. The Russians occupied much of Chechnya, pulverized Grozny, and drove the rebels into hills. The war created 250,000 refugees.

In 2000, despite Russian claims of imminent victory, the war continued. The Russians were unable to defeat the rebels in the mountainous areas. The United Nations called for investigations of alleged human rights abuses by Russian troops and by Chechen rebels. New Russian President Vladimir Putin agreed to the human rights investigation as the war continued.[5]

The Second Chechen War is an ongoing conflict in which the major combat occurred from 1999 to 2002. But flare-ups continue. At issue is the degree of autonomy Chechnya should have and whether Chechnya should remain within the Russian Federation or whether it should become an independent nation.[6]

The conflict of an Islamic democracy versus Islamic militancy within Chechnya is further complicated by Russia's desire to prevent secession. After determining the status of Chechnya, numerous challenges must be overcome, including security, the return of refugees, reconstruction, the rebuilding of the economy, and dealing with corruption. Because of these circumstances, it will be difficult to achieve a prompt resolution of the conflict, especially since there are various nations jostling for influence, Anup Shah concludes.[7]

Chechen rebels

The Chechen rebels emerged in the early 1990s and are led by Aslan Maskakov and Shamil Basayev.

Aslan Maskhadov

Maskhadov is the Chechen rebel leader. Maskhadov was born in 1951 in exile in Kazakhstan and began his career as an officer in the Soviet army. After the collapse of the Soviet Union, he became breakaway Chechnya's chief of staff in 1992. He was the rebel leader during the first Chechen-Russian War and became President of Chechnya in 1997.

When Chechen rebel forces crossed into Dagestan in 1999 and Moscow held Chechens responsible for a wave of bomb attacks across Russia, Russia accused Maskhadov of having lost control. When Maskhadov urged resistance, Moscow branded him a terrorist and withdrew its recognition of his presidency. Russia sent troops back into the republic, described Maskhadov's government as unlawful, and tried to build support for a parliament made up of Chechens in exile. During fierce fighting, Maskhadov's government was removed from power and a pro–Moscow administration was set up.

Maskhadov continued to be the official leader until he was killed on March 8, 2005, by Russian security forces in a village north of Grozny.[8]

Maskhadov's successor is Abdul-Khalim Saydullayev; but it seems likely to many analysts that Saydullayev will be unable to control guerilla leader Shamil Bassayev and that Bassayev is poised to become the new leader of the divided resistance. Even though Russia viewed Maskhadov and Bassayev as close allies, their connection was complicated and their differences many.[9]

Shamil Basayev

The most widely recognized leader is the field commander for the rebels, Shamil Basayev. Basayev was born in Chechnya in 1965. He came to prominence in 1995 during the first Chechen war when as a field commander he led a hostage-taking raid at Budennovsk, Russia. He has long threatened a series of "kamikaze" attacks inside Russia, arguing that Russian civilians were legitimate targets.[10] He claimed to have organized the seizing of a Moscow theater in 2002, during which 129 people died.[11] He has also boasted to have trained Chechen female suicide bombers — the infamous Black Widows brigade. He has come to call himself Abdallah Shamil Abu Idris.

Suicide and Hostage Taking Attacks

Attacks attributed to Chechen rebels include:

1. February 6, 2004: Moscow subway bomb kills 41 people and injures 100.
2. May 9, 2004: A bomb kills Moscow-backed Chechen President Akhmad Kadyrov during Victory Day ceremony in the Chechen capital, Grozny.
3. August 24, 2004: Two passenger planes crash almost simultaneously after leaving Moscow, killing all 90 people onboard.
4. August 31, 2004: A female suicide bomber kills 10 people outside a Moscow subway station.
5. September 1, 2004: At least 326 children and adults killed after rebels seize a school in Beslan.[12]

In 2003, women had been responsible for about half of the suicide bombings, according to Yoram Schweitzer.[13] Viv Groskop contends that the origin of Chechen female bombers is completely different from bombers in Arab countries, where terrorism is closely linked to Islamic fundamentalism. Far from being freedom fighters with an equal right to die for their beliefs, Chechnya's female martyrs are more likely to be forced, blackmailed or brainwashed to their deaths. Even when they have chosen their mission, it is not because of a religious or a political cause, but for personal reasons: to avenge the death of a husband or a brother. More often than not, they are pawns in a man's game.[14]

There are some similarities between the Chechen rebels and Palestinian organizations like the al Aqsa Martyrs Brigade. They are reluctant to give females full membership or gender equality. "Women do not participate in their terrorist activities, yet they were accepted as would be martyrs to carry out suicide bombings in the names of these organizations," Clara Beyler states.[15] In fact, Beyler writes that the Chechens have claimed responsibility for the suicide bombing of Khava/Hawa' Barayev on their official website, but not for another female suicide bomber, Luisa Gazueva.[16] In June 2000, Barayev, a 22-year-old relative of the leader of the Moscow Theater hostage takers, Movsar Barayev, drove a truck packed with explosives into a Russian army base in the family's home village of Alkhan-Khala, six miles south of Grozny.[17] Barayev became the first female suicide bomber for the Chechen rebels.[18]

Table 6.1
Female Suicide Bombers
Chechen–Russian Conflict, 2000–2003

Date	June 9, 2000[a]
Name/Home	Hawa, a.k.a. Hawaa' Barayev, Khava Barayeva, with one male /—
Age/Status	20 or 22 /—
Organization	Chechen rebels
Place of Attack	Building housing Russian Special Forces, Alkhan-Khala, six miles south of Grozny.
Casualties	27 soldiers killed
Details	Drove into forces' housing. Hawa's last words, "I know what I am doing, paradise has a price, and I hope this will be the price for Paradise."[b] First Black Widow.

Date	June 10, 2000[c]
Name/Home	Ajsa Gasujewa /Urus-Martan
Age/Status	22 /widow
Organization	Chechen rebels
Place of Attack	Headquarters, Urus-Martan.
Casualties	9 killed, 12 wounded
Details	Husband, two brothers and a sister killed in conflict. Husband had been wounded and captive; the same day General Gadschijew, the military commander of Urus-Martan, visited him in the hospital and drilled a bayonet into his

chest. Gadschijew would not release the bodies of her husband and brothers.

Date	April, 29 2001[d]
Name/Home	Unknown /—
Age/Status	—/—
Organization	Chechen rebels
Place of Attack	Chechnya
Casualties	—
Details	—

Date	June 2001[e]
Name/Home	Unknown (2) /—
Age/Status	—/—
Organization	Chechen rebels
Place of Attack	Federal forces building Alkhan-Yurt, Chechnya
Casualties	More than 80 killed
Details	—

Date	November 29, 2001[f]
Name/Home	Aizan, a.k.a. Luisa Vakhaevna Gazueva /—
Age/Status	Late 20s /widow
Organization	Chechen rebels did not associate with this attack
Place of Attack	Urus Martan
Casualties	2 killed, 2 wounded
Details	She attempted to kill Commander Gaidar Gadzhiev. Former member of an armed group. Husband and two children killed in conflict.

Date	October 23, 2002[g]
Name/Home	Unknowns 18 women worked with 32 males Known: 2 sisters, Ayshat and Khadizhat Ganiyeva, a.k.a. Fatima and Khadzhad Ganiyeva, and Zareta Bayrakova[h] /—
Age/Status	—/— Ayshat married at 26.[i]
Organization	Chechen rebels
Place of Attack	Moscow Theater Center or Moscow Dubrovka House of Culture
Casualties	170 killed or 165 by special forces and 5 by Chechens.[j] Some

129 hostages and 41 guerrillas were killed when Russian special forces took over the building. A gas used by the forces to incapacitate the hostage-takers caused most of the deaths.

Details	First time in the history of female suicide terrorism that such a team was established, signaling a shift from an individual action to a group structure.[k]

Date	December 27, 2002[l]
Name/Home	Unknown /—
Age/Status	—/—
Organization	Chechen rebels
Place of Attack	Outside a government building, Grozny
Casualties	72 killed
Details	Basayev pushed the button on the remote control of the explosive devices in the vehicles. The operation on blowing up the compounds was carried out by one family, the father, son and daughter, whose mother and older brother were killed by Kadyrov's men. Basayev said, "Shaheeds do not resort to personal revenge. They were taking revenge for our desecrated religion, for our entire nation, for our land, and for the entire Islamic Ummah."[m]

Date	February 6, 2003[n]
Name/Home	Unknown /—
Age/Status	—/—
Organization	Chechen rebels
Place of Attack	Russia
Casualties	—
Details	—

Date	May 1, 2003[o]
Name/Home	Unknown, 1 woman and 2 men /—
Age/Status	—/—
Organization	Chechen rebels
Place of Attack	Government complex in northern Chechnya
Casualties	59 killed
Details	Truck bomb suicide attack

Female Suicide Bombers

Date   May 12, 2003[p]
Name/Home   Unknown: 1 female and 1 or 2 males /—
Age/Status   —/—
Organization   Chechen Shaheeds (attackers)
Place of Attack Government compound in Znamenskoye in northern Chechnya
Casualties   59 to 60 killed, 197 wounded
Details   Drove an explosives-laden truck into compound. Explosion had the force of at least 1.3 tons of TNT and left a crater some 16 feet deep and 33 feet wide.

Date   May 14, 2003[q]
Name/Home   Shakhidat Baimuradova and Zulai Abdurzakova /—
Age/Status   46 and 52 /—
Organization   Chechen rebel leader Shamil Basayeu Basayev
Place of Attack During Muslim festival near the villages of Belorechye and Eleskhan-Yurt east of the capital, Grozny
Casualties   12 to 18 killed, 140 to 145 wounded
Details   Targeted Chechen Administrator Mufti Akhmed Kadyrov. Kadyrov escaped injury. One source said Kadyrov was not present.

Date   June 5, 2003[r]
Name/Home   Lidia Khaldykharoyeva /—
Age/Status   25 /—
Organization   Planned by Shamil Basayev, Chechen warlord
Place of Attack Mozdok air base, in Russia's North Ossetia province, which borders Chechnya
Casualties   17 to 18 killed, 24 wounded
Details   Targeted a Russian Air Force bus. Bomber boarded the bus wearing a nurse's white coat and declared, "God is great." She lived in Saratov Province. Zarema Muzhikhoyeva was supposed to set off the bomb.[s] (See Table 6.2.) Another report says that she threw herself under the bus as it slowed down for a railway pass and blew up.[t]

Date   June 20, 2003[u]
Name/Home   Unknown female and male /—
Age/Status   —/—
Organization   Chechen rebels

Place of Attack	Targeted Russian government buildings
Casualties	8 killed, 25 wounded
Details	Truck bomb

Date	July 5,-2003[v]
Name/Home	Zulikhan Elikhadzhiyeva a.k.a. Alikhadzhiyeva, (male),and unknown (2)—some sources say 2 women /—
Age/Status	19, or 20, or -30, 20 /—
Organization	Chechen rebels
Place of Attack	Tushino, a Moscow suburb with an open-air rock festival
Casualties	14 to 20 killed; 40 to 50 to 60 wounded
Details	Two women came up to the perimeter of the Tushino airfield north of Moscow, where they were stopped from entering the concert.[w] Detonated their bombs 10 minutes apart with second causing most casualties. First bomber killed only herself. Another bomb was found at an entrance and defused by the police. Family claims she was kidnapped by her half-brother Danilbek, a Chechen fighter, and taken to Moscow.[x]

Date	July 12, 2003[y]
Name/Home	Unknown /—
Age/Status	—/—
Organization	Chechen rebels
Place of Attack	Mozdok, North Ossettia
Casualties	15 killed
Details	Blast on bus carrying workers to nearby Prokhladny Air Force base.

Date	July 27, 2003[z]
Name/Home	Unknown /—
Age/Status	27 to -30 /—
Organization	Chechen rebels
Place of Attack	Military base Southeast of Grozny
Casualties	—
Details	Bomber detonated her explosives as the son of Kadyrov was reviewing troops. Security forces were searching for another female bomber suspected to be on a mission to assassinate Kadyrov. Husband killed in conflict.

Date	October 2003[aa]
Name/Home	Unknown /—
Age/Status	—/—
Organization	Chechen rebels
Place of Attack	Chechnya
Casualties	—
Details	—

Date	December 5, 2003[bb]
Name/Home	Unknown plus 2 to 3 others/—
Age/Status	—/—
Organization	Chechen rebels
Place of Attack	Southern Russia
Casualties	42 killed; more than 150 wounded
Details	Bombed commuter train.

Date	December 9, 2003[cc]
Name/Home	Unknown, possibly 2 /—
Age/Status	—/—
Organization	Chechen rebels
Place of Attack	Outside National Hotel, Red Square, heart of Moscow
Casualties	5 to 6 killed, 11 to 14 wounded
Details	She was said to be looking for the State Duma. Belt packed with 2.5 kg of plastic explosives and ball bearings. Similar to, but lower quality than, bomb used at rock concert.

Date	December 2003[dd]
Name/Home	Unknown (2) /—
Age/Status	—/—
Organization	Chechen rebels
Place of Attack	Southern Russia
Casualties	44 killed
Details	Train blast

Date	Dec 2003[ee]
Name/Home	Unknown (2) /—
Age/Status	—/—
Organization	Chechen rebels
Place of Attack	Meters from the Kremlin, Moscow

Casualties	5 killed, 12 wounded
Details	—

Date	August 24, 2004[ff]
Name/Home	Nagayeva and Satsia Dzhebirkhanova / Grozny, Chechnya
Age/Status	—/—
Organization	Black Widows
Place of Attack	Two Russian passenger planes were blown up almost simultaneously.
Casualties	89 killed
Details	Federal Security Service found traces of explosives in wreckage, leading them to believe two women were involved. Earlier, they had been taken into custody when they arrived at Moscow's Domodeveo airport accompanied by two Chechen men. Police officers confiscated their passports and handed them over to a police captain for a further check. The captain let them go without checking them. The women got their tickets for the later flights in the same building. The crashes took place ahead of a regional election in Chechnya.

Date	August 31, 2004[gg]
Name/Home	Unknown /—
Age/Status	—/—
Organization	Black Widows
Place of Attack	Row of shops by Metro Station, outside Rizhskaya subway station in northeastern Moscow
Casualties	8 to 9 killed, 18 to 51 wounded
Details	Bomber was walking toward the entrance when she saw police checking commuters' bags and blew herself up. Her head was found on the subway station's roof. The blast was so powerful that a nearby car erupted in flames. Bomb was stuffed with shrapnel and other small metal objects. Police said the device was planted in a Zhiguli parked near the train station.

Date	September 3, 2004[hh]
Name/Home	32 attackers; 1 female known, 2 spotted /—
Age/Status	—/—
Organization	Autonomous groups with al Qaeda connection
Place of Attack	Beslan School No. 1, Beslan, North Ossetia, a southern Russian Republic

Casualties   350+ killed, 180+ were children

Details   Sophisticated strike. A shredded black belt and bloodied camouflage utility vest found in hall next to cafeteria where a female suicide bomber detonated herself. Female suicide bombers who openly disagreed with the Colonel (the leader) about the children hostages were killed when he detonated their bombs by remote control.

Six of the seven suicide attacks in 2003 were carried out by women, killing 165 people. Since the beginning of the second Chechen War, female bombers have taken part in more than 18 major attacks. Not all women were widows.[19] The Chechen rebels hold the distinction of having killed the largest number, 170, in Moscow in October 2002 when they — with a high percentage of women — held hostages in the theater center. The police killed 129 captives and 41 rebels in a rescue effort.[20] Many of the women in the Moscow Theater Center siege of 700 hostages remain unknown, but estimates are that 18 women were known participants. Among those known female participants were two sisters, Ayshat and Khadizhat Ganiyeva, a.k.a. Fatima and Khadzhad Ganiyeva.[21]

Mia Bloom writes that, in the beginning, the Al Ansar Mujahideen limited women's roles to supplying medical aid, food and water, to carrying weapons and ammunition, and helping maintain the guerrillas' morale during battles. Women's primary role was to raise children to become Mujahideen as adults.[22]

The September 2004 attack on Beslan School No. 1 in Beslan, North Ossetia, a southern Russian Republic, killed over 350 people, including over 180 children. Hundreds were wounded.[23] The strike was sophisticated. Female suicide-bombers who openly disagreed with the colonel (the leader) about using the children as hostages were killed when he detonated their bombs by remote control.[24]

Two Sisters, Ayshat and Khadizhat Ganiyeva, and Moscow Dubrovka House of Culture

The 18 females dressed in black, wearing black explosive belts, worked with 32 males. This attack marked the first time in the history

of female suicide terrorism that such a team was established, signaling a shift from an individual action to a group structure.[25]

According to Viv Groskop, two sisters who were suicide bombers stand out, Fatima and Khadzhad Ganiyeva. Chechen warlord Shamil Basayev paid U.S. $1,500 per sister to Rustam Ganiyev, a brother and Chechen fighter not involved in the siege, to send the sisters to Moscow for the attack.[26]

Their father, Sulumbek Ganiyev, sheds light on what took place with his daughters previous to the takeover:

A woman, one of the armed Chechens who seized a crowded Moscow theater October 23, 2002, poses with a pistol inside the theater on October 25 (AP Photograph/Russian NTV).

In September some woman came to them. About 30, in a jacket, woman's height. Then Ayshat and Khadizhat left. They said they were going to their grandmother's in Khasavyurt. I think they were lying. For 10 days they were gone. But on 25 September Ayshat and Khadizhat departed completely. We did not go to the police because it was a disgrace — the girls had left us. We searched through relatives. They were nowhere to be found; we thought they had been killed. And then rumors crept a round the village that the Sulumubek daughters had died in Moscow. If only I had known, I would have broken their legs so that they would stay home.[27]

The woman who came to see Ayshat and Khadizhat resembled Kurbika Zinabdiyeva, also known as Gekhayeva, a resident of the town of Ulus-Kert in Shatoyskiy Rayon. Thirty-five-year-old Zinabdiyeva and

Movsar Barayev, right, a leader of the armed Chechens who seized a crowded Moscow theater, is shown with another male captor and a woman captor inside the theater on October 25, 2002 (AP Photograph/Russian NTV).

15 year-old Amina Dugayeva were arrested. One week after Zinabdiyeva and Dugayeva were arrested, 50 fighters entered Ulus-Kert. The bandits assaulted the head of the administration and took away her service revolver. According to local residents, the main complaint of the fighters was that the townspeople had let the federals arrest Zinabdiyeva and Dugayeva. Although the arrest of the recruiters was officially announced, the women disappeared without a trace. The republic prosecutor's office opened a criminal case related to their kidnapping.[28]

Mystery surrounds the dead women. Officially, very little is known about the women. In 2003, one newspaper reported, "Authorities in Moscow even refuse to say where they buried the bodies. 'We don't want a shrine being created or anything like that,' one official said. Islamic clerics and the managers of the four Muslim cemeteries in Moscow say they never received any of the bodies."[29]

Insights from Hostages and the Moscow Dubrovka House of Culture

From October 23 to 26, 2002, 41 armed Chechen terrorists took control of Moscow's Dubrovka Theater. The Chechen warlord Mosvar Barayev announced to an audience of about 800 that Russian forces must immediately leave Chechnya. He told the crowd that they did not plan to return home because "theirs was a suicide mission."[30] Anne Speckhard *et al.* report that in the end, Russian Special Forces killed all the terrorists. The terrorists shot five hostages.[31]

According to Radio Free Europe/Radio Liberty (RFE/RL), some 129 hostages and 41 guerrillas were killed when Russian Special Forces took over the building. A gas used by the forces to incapacitate the hostage-takers caused most of the deaths. A female survivor of the siege, speaking to RFE/RL's Tatar-Bashkir Service, said: "Everybody saw the gas and everybody realized what was happening. [The hostage takers] had enough time to blow up everything, but they purposely didn't do it. It is very strange. I do not know why [they didn't do it]."[32]

The fact that "they didn't do it," and that some hostages survived the terrorists' not blowing up the theater, has lent insight into suicide terrorism and into the role of women who participate. It also provides a possible answer to the survivor's question of why. Anne Speckhard *et al.*, a group of Russian scholars, began interviewing hostages to learn their psychological responses to being taken captive by terrorists who were willing to commit suicide to advance their cause. At the same time, the scholars realized that the hostages' observations of and interactions with the suicidal terrorists during the siege presented a rare opportunity to observe a suicidal terrorist in his or her last moments of life.[33]

One hostage explained that the takeover was confusing because it began on stage during the musical about World War II. The terrorists, in camouflage uniforms, shot automatic rifles into the air, shouting, "You are hostages."[34] Initially, almost everyone thought the terrorists were part of the drama's special effects.

The hostage reported that the takeover was very organized. The terrorists instructed people to put their arms behind their heads and pass their mobile phones to the aisles. Technical operator glass and ventilation system covers were broken. Explosives were placed in the balcony and on the stage.[35]

The terrorists were able to create a nonhysterical environment and bond with the hostages because many hostages later expressed positive feelings toward them and regret that they had been killed. The terrorists were very skilled in trauma bonding. Hostages, for example, were granted such freedoms as letting children and pregnant women go, allowing some people to look for medicine, to smoke, or to drink juice. As time went on, the barriers eroded further when the rebels told of their beautiful country.[36]

The terrorists set up and watched television footage of the very events they had put into action. They also took photographs and made movies of their activities.[37] The hostages reported that the command structure was clear and that the hierarchy existed within and beyond the theater. The lead terrorists were in communication with others. The highest in the command structure was outside the theater.[38]

Almost all of the female suicidal terrorists who participated in the takeover of the Russian Dubrovka House of Culture remain faceless and nameless. An exception is 26-year-old Zareta Bayrakova, who was named. (See Table 6.1.) Speckhard et al. give insight into the role of the women. One hostage reported that in the early stages a Chechen woman held her gun ready. When the bombs were in place, she put it away.[39] When recalling that all terrorists were heavily armed, the same hostage provides this insight: "The women wore officer's army belts and put explosives there. They were in black. Every woman had a pistol revolver and a grenade."[40] Later in the takeover another hostage recalled: "[The women] all wore masks and scarves, but (over time) they took them off. The younger women opened their faces — it was too hot. But the women older than 30, who were widows, didn't take them off."[41]

More meaningful is that another hostage reported that the women terrorists couldn't decide anything. This hostage said, "If we asked for the toilet they said 'ask the men.'"[42] Speckhard et al.'s hypothesis is significant: "This lack of authority vested in the women may be the very reason that the hostages lived through the storm."[43] One hostage recalled that although some of them smelled gas and heard shots, "Those inside maybe could not realize it and were waiting for an order perhaps (to detonate the bombs)."[44]

But other exploration of hostage responses revealed the women terrorists were perceived as more severe than the men. One hostage said: "It was possible to speak with the men, but with the women I had no desire to speak. The women had read only the Koran."[45] Speckhard *et al.* reasons this perception of severity may reflect the female terrorists' inability to make decisions or grant allowances.[46]

The hostages also believed the women would be the first to die. Men sometimes went out, but the women sat there as if they were ready for death. When the special forces arrived, the same was true, the men left to deal with them and the women remained to detonate the bombs for which they had no authority to do so on their own. One hostage stated that the men were active and that the women were passive to the end.[47]

A Grozny agent reported a similar view of the female members. The agent had studied the personalities of the female terrorists in the group and concluded that if "anyone there blows themselves up it will have to be the girls. Men do not want to die; if they did want it, they had already had many opportunities."[48]

The Grozny agent reported that it was not difficult to find women who have lost someone and who were not knowledgeable because they grew up amid the ruins of war. For these reasons recruiters have a lot of material to work with. The agent said:

> The recruiters work for money. According to unconfirmed information some relatives of female terrorists who were wiped out at Dubrovka also received several thousands dollars apiece. But the suicide terrorists themselves are not mercenary and go to their deaths voluntarily. I do not know of a single female suicide terrorist who would have committed the terrorist act under threat. Such people are vocationally unsuited and could blow the operation at any moment. Deceived — yes, overwhelmed and scarred — yes. But all the same, in the end they all go to their deaths voluntarily and want this death.[49]

Profiles, Other Black Widows

Ajsa Gasujewas

In 2000, Ajsa Gasujewa, 22 and from Urus-Martan in Chechnya, became the first Chechen suicide attacker that year. (See Table 6.1.) Mainat Abdulajewa gives insight into Gasujewa's method of attack:

> On the 10th June, 2000, a young woman surged through the crowd and took the Russian General Rassul Gadschijew by his arm. "Do you still know me?" she asked. In the next moment there was an immense detonation. The General and eight of his bodyguards were killed instantly. In addition a dozen injured people with splinter wounds. Also the woman herself was killed.[50]

Abdulajewa believes that the Russian military's killing of 16 of Gasujewa's closest relatives within a year from the beginning of the war led her to commit the death act. Among the relatives Gasujewa lost were her husband, two brothers, one sister, several cousins and nephews.[51]

The day that Gasujewa's husband, a Chechen rebel, was wounded and taken captive, General Gadschijew, the military commander of Urus-Martan, visited him in the regional hospital. "He had no questions to the patient, he stepped forward to him and drilled the bayonet into his chest," reports Abdulajewa.[52]

Gasujewa spoke to the general twice for the release of her husband's and brother's bodies, but Gadschijew refused. Abdulajewa writes, "During her last visit he promised, in front of witnesses, to bury her alive if she dared again to appear in front of him."[53] Gasujewa left home and wasn't seen for two weeks until she appeared on June 10, 2000, in front of the headquarters gate. Abdulajewa believes Gasujewa was willing to die and take others with her as an act of personal revenge.[54]

Zarema Muzhikhoyeva

Zarema Muzhikhoyeva did not complete her mission successfully. (See Table 6.2.) The 22-year-old widow lost her husband in the fighting against the Russians. On July 9, 2003,[55] she tried to detonate one pound of military-issued explosives in a bag at a busy café on Moscow's main Tverskaya Street. A policeman was killed while attempting to defuse her bomb.[56] Muzhikhoyeva's intended target was a McDonald's restaurant, but she entered the closest café, where she tried to detonate the defective bomb and was caught.[57] She is in prison in Moscow[58] serving a 20-year sentence.[59] Muzhikhoyeva was supposed to set off the explosion that occurred on June 5, 2003, but she became ill at the last moment and was sent to Nalchik for treatment. Lidia Khaldykharoyeva detonated the bomb in her place.[60] (See Table 6.1.)

Table 6.2
Female Suicide Bombers
Who Did Not Complete Their Mission,
Chechen–Russian Conflict, 2000–2003

Date	December 19, 2000[a]
Name/Home	Mareta Duduyeva /Grebenskaya, Shali district, Chechnya
Age/Status	17 / single
Organization	Shamil Basayev
Mission	Attempted to run a truck stuffed with explosives into the military commandant's office in Leninsky district of Grozny.
Outcome	Captured when her bomb-laden truck failed to detonate.
Details	Two of her accomplices ran out of the truck after federal troops fired. Duduyeva was injured and lost control of the vehicle, and ran into a concrete block. When she was being dragged out of the cabin she tried to explode a grenade, then freed herself and ran away from the truck, shouting, "It will blow up now!"
	Act might have been ordered by field commander Shamil Basayev, who tried to avenge the death of his younger brother, Shirvani. The act also might have been prepared by field commander Ruslan Tsagorayev.
	No other relatives had died in the war; not a religious attack.

Date	Between December 27 and 31, 2002[b]
Name/Home	2 /—
Age/Status	—/—
Organization	Chechen rebels
Place of Attack	Religious ceremony in Chechnya
Casualties	Unknown

Details	Targeted Chechnya's pro–Moscow leader (now Chechen president) Akhmad Kadyrov.

Date	July 10, 2003[c]
Name/Home	Zarima, a.k.a. Zarema Muzhikhoyeva /Achkoi-Martan, Chechnya
Age/Status	22 / Her husband died fighting for Chechen independence before she gave birth.
Organization	Black Fatima, Chechen rebels
Mission	Attack near the Imbir restaurant in 1st Tverskaya-Yamskaya Street in the heart of Moscow. One pound of military-issue explosives in bag. Explosives similar to those at rock concert. An FSB bomb disposal expert, Sergei Trofimov, was killed.
Outcome	Captured and sentenced to 20 years in Moscow prison.
Details	First bomber to be captured alive. She responded, "'Now I know why everyone hates the Russians!'— adding that she would return and 'blow you all up.'"[d]
	Muzhikhoyeva received her final instructions from a woman called Lyuba, who drugged her before sending her on her failed mission.

Viv Groskop writes that Muzhikhoyeva lived in poverty and desperation that is characteristic of a people that has known only war for a decade.[61] She was born in Bamut, Achkhoy-Martanovskiy Rayon, Chechnya. Her mother abandoned her when she was one year old. Her father, Musa Muzhikhoyev, died when she was eight, after a Chechen stabbed him in a fight over money in Achinsk. She was 14 when the first Chechen campaign began. Bamut was shelled and bombed.[62]

Muzhikhoyeva was raised by her grandparents in Achkoi-Martan, which was destroyed in the first war.[63] Her grandfather, Khamzat Magomedovich, remembers that they hid in the basement from December 1994 to April 1995 and said of Muzhikhoyeva, "She was very afraid. She couldn't even cry. She sat there as if she were dead."[64] They left for Troitskoye in Ingushetia, where she attended school. The grandfather describes her life during that time,

> Zarema went to school and was an average student. Six of us lived
> in a room that was three meters by four. We slept on the floor,

then in the morning we would gather up all the rags and throw them in a corner in order to have a place to walk.

Zarema would get up in the morning, eat, and spend the whole day sitting by the window. She did not have any duties around the house. And anyway, where would they come from? We had no chickens, no cow. She finished eight grades in school, more or less. There was no work, and she sat like that at the window until she was 17 and got married.[65]

Muzhikhoyeva attended school from age seven to 15 and then, pregnant, she left school to marry.[66] According to Groskop, during the second invasion her husband was killed in Chechnya's war for independence. The grandfather recalled that the husband died in an auto accident.[67] Lawrence Uzzell reports that her husband was killed in a business dispute unrelated to the war and that his family took custody of only her child, a daughter, Rashana.[68] Groskop reports Chechen tradition dictates that Muzhikhoyeva and her baby belonged to her husband's family, who "treated her as a household slave."[69] Muzhikhoyeva escaped in an effort to have custody of her child. To survive she did whatever necessary, including stealing and borrowing money.

Uzzell writes that Muzhikhoyeva missed her daughter. She sold her grandmother's jewelry for U.S. $600, then got Rashana on the pretext that she wished to have time with her. In reality she planned to take her daughter to Moscow to begin a new life. Relatives stopped them at the airport, "beat her up, and left her disgraced, ostracized and forlorn."[70]

People knew Muzhikhoyeva as a person easily persuaded.[71] A group of Chechen independence fighters gave Muzhikhoyeva a loan, with their repayment plan for her to pay them back with her life by performing a suicide mission. Her family would also receive money. When her training was complete she was "sent to a safe house in Moscow where a woman with the code name 'Black Fatima' looked after her."[72] Although Muzhikhoyeva confessed that she wanted to avenge her husband's death, she said "she was drugged regularly in her orange juice, which gave her headaches."[73] Groskop writes that her confession indicates Muzhikhoyeva's "motives lie somewhere between choice and coercion."[74] Uzzell reports that Muzhikhoyeva's motive was the money. She had heard that a suicide bomber's family would receive U.S. $1,000. This amount was more than enough to pay back her grandparents for the jewelry she had stolen.[75]

In the spring of 2003, Muzhikhoyeva spent two weeks in a guerrilla training camp. Uzzell describes that time:

> A one-legged guerrilla leader — perhaps Shamil Basayev himself, she said — told her that it was wrong to sacrifice one's life simply for money, that one should do this only for the sake of one's religious faith. But she was not interested in his suggestion that she get the money she needed by staying in the camp and marrying one of his guerrillas. "I wanted to die — not to sit in the woods like a rat."[76]

Muzhikhoyeva offers contradictory statements as to why she did not complete her mission. On July 7, two handlers, Igor and Andrei, took her on a reconnaissance drive around Moscow. The next day the two men had her make a videotape for her relatives. Muzhakhoyeva said that it was important that her relatives see that video, so that they would know "that I had died and had cleansed myself of my shame, that I was a good woman and would not trouble them further." Uzzell writes that this contradiction to her previous statement that she could not kill herself is understandable, given that she was such a desperate and downtrodden person. The next day she was given her explosive belt and feared the men might know her real thoughts. She said, "but I was much helped by our traditions which forbid looking directly into a man's eyes."[77]

Igor, alias Ruslan, her handler, did not tell Muzhikhoyeva she would be performing a suicide mission, but she suspected that she would be. She lived outside of Moscow in Tolstopaltsevo for a few days before the bombing with Igor and Andrei, an explosives expert, and two other women, Marem and Zulikhan Elikhadzhieva, who performed the July 5, 2003, rock festival explosion. When Muzhikhoyeva saw the results of the rock festival explosion, she said, "I saw how it would look. If I tell you that I felt sorry for all of them you won't believe me. To be honest, I felt sorrier for Zulikhan than for the others, she was the only one of the dead whom I had seen alive that very morning. To be completely honest, I felt sorriest of all for myself."[78]

Most sad are Muzhikhoyeva's words uttered after she changed into casual but stylish clothes for the bombing: "I had never worn a baseball cap. I gazed into a mirror and really liked the way I looked; I had never dressed that way. For a few seconds I was simply happy."[79]

During Muzhikhoyeva's trial, she expressed several times that she feared her organizers would kill her. First, she told investigators that she had tried unsuccessfully to detonate the bomb. Later she admitted she had confessed because she was afraid that the organizers of her bombing mission would have her killed. She was also afraid of the police thinking the terrorists might have paid them to kill her. She feared her attorney because he wore black clothing like traditional martyrs. Muzhikhoyeva would only sip water from the bottled water belonging to her attorneys because she was afraid of being poisoned.[80]

This underlying fear of her organizers explains her behavior the day she failed to detonate her bomb. She said they were following her and she believed they could detonate the bomb by remote control.[81] According to her attorneys, Muzhikhoyeva had tried to get herself arrested by behaving suspiciously. Rather than turning herself in and arousing the suspicion of the organizers, she behaved in ways to call attention to herself. First, seated at a table outside Mon Café, she stared and made faces at a group of men sitting inside because the men would not be terrorists sitting inside a café they planned to blow up. When these actions failed to get the men's attention, she showed them bomb switches and stuck out her tongue. When the owner attempted to approach Muzhikhoyeva, she told him to stop because she had a bomb. He then called the police. Muzhikhoyeva then left the café and was soon arrested.[82]

Muzhikhoyeva is credited for identifying other terrorists for the police. Significantly, she identified a "photofit of Black Fatima as 'Lyuba,' a middle-aged Chechen who directed her attack."[83] Lyuba met Muzhikhoyeva when she flew in from Ingushetia, a region bordering Chechnya. There she had been prepared for her mission by converts to Wahabism. The Wahabis are a conservative strain of Islam brought to the region by Arab fighters. Lyuba took Muzhikhoyeva to a safe house. She then gave Muzhikhoyeva orange juice that made her dizzy and confused. The security officials believe the juice was mixed with a mind-altering drug intended to break down inhibitions as she prepared to die.[84]

Lyuba had given Muzhikhoyeva a bomb in a rucksack and instructed her to blow herself up in the McDonald's restaurant in Pushkin Square. Muzhikhoyeva did not know Moscow well and entered a small café instead. Her attack was thwarted when the TNT failed to detonate. Muzhikhoyeva said to her interrogators, "I pressed the button about 20 times but the bomb didn't go off."[85]

Conclusion

The Chechen outrage was caused by the crimes Russian forces committed against Chechen civilians during war, according to Mia Bloom. Russian forces were known to kill children and civilians and demand payment for the return of their corpses. The war is horrible and stories abound "about Russian soldiers laughing as they charge Chechen fathers 300 rubles (nearly $25) not to rape their daughters."[86] Thus, the society from which these female suicide bombers emerged was one steeped in violence.

7

The Palestinian-Israeli Conflict

"I was hoping to be the first woman, where parts of my body can fly everywhere."

–Reem al-Raiyshi
Palestinian Female Bomber[1]

A Palestinian State

At the center of the Israeli-Palestinian conflict have been the West Bank and Gaza Strip. Israel occupied these lands during the 1967 war. The conflict is a part of the greater Arab-Israeli conflict and is an ongoing conflict between Israel and Palestinians.[2] The Oslo Accord marked the main political outcome or achievement of the first intifada, or uprising, from 1987 to 1993.[3]

Since the Oslo Accord, the government of Israel and the Palestinian Authority (PA) have been officially dedicated to a two-state solution. Unresolved issues remain. The status and future of the West Bank, Gaza Strip and East Jerusalem are of primary concern. These areas are the proposed state of Palestine. The nature of a Palestinian state and the fate of the refugees are to be settled. Security issues for Israel and Palestine have to be resolved.[4]

The aim of the 1993 interim agreement between Israel and Palestine "is, among other things, to establish a Palestinian Interim Self-Government Authority, the elected Council, (the 'Council') for the Palestinian people in the West Bank and the Gaza Strip, for a transitional period not exceeding five years, leading to a permanent settlement based on Security Council Resolutions 242 and 338."[5] This agreement was no longer acceptable in the second intifada.[6]

The Camp David efforts from July 11 to 25, 2000, moved directly to final status talks without Israel having withdrawn.[7] After Ariel Sharon, accompanied by hundreds of Israeli police, on September 28, 2000, went to what the Jews call the Temple Mount and the Arabs call Haram esh Sharif, the second intifada began. After prayers the next day, the Palestinians rioted, tossing stones at police outside the compound and at Jewish worshipers in the Western Wall plaza far below. Police used gas, then rubber-coated steel slugs. Suddenly, though, people were dying. Later the police admitted using snipers with live ammunition. The Arabs called it murder, and even many Israeli commentators were flabbergasted. One newspaper columnist wrote that, in Israel now, Jewish lives were sacrosanct, whereas Arabs were just numbers, easy to kill in the powerful pretext of security.[8]

The intifada was marked by Palestinian and Israeli violence and by Israel's "unprecedented use of tanks, missiles, and attack helicopters."[9] The Camp David agreements were never approved. Supporters of Palestine perceive the conflict as an illegitimate military occupation of Palestine, supported with military and diplomatic assistance from the United States. Supporters of Israel see the conflict as a campaign of terrorism committed by Palestinian groups such as Hamas, Islamic Jihad, and Fatah, and supported by other states in the region and most of the Palestinians. Each group cites the Geneva conventions and the United Nations Charter to support its view.[10]

Al-Aqsa Martyrs Brigade, Palestinian Nationalists

The al-Aqsa Martyrs Brigade appeared at the beginning of the 2000 Palestinian intifada to attack Israeli targets with the aim of driving the Israeli military and settlers from the West Bank, Gaza Strip, and Jerusalem, and to establish a Palestinian state. The U.S. State Department reports, "numerous public accusations suggest Iran and Hezbollah are providing support to al-Aqsa elements."[11] The al-Aqsa Martyrs Brigade is a group of West Bank militias affiliated with Palestinian leader

Yasser Arafat's al-Fatah. It is one of the driving forces behind the current Palestinian intifada.[12]

Initially, the al-Aqsa Martyrs targeted only Israeli soldiers and settlers in the West Bank and Gaza Strip. In early 2002, it began terrorist attacks against civilians in Israeli cities. The group's ideology is based in Palestinian nationalism, not in political Islam.[13]

Palestinian Islamic Jihad (PIJ)

The Palestinian Islamic Jihad (PIJ) is also known by the following names: Islamic Jihad of Palestine, PIJ-Shaqaqi Faction, PIJ-Shalla Faction and Al-Quds Brigades. The PIJ is located and operates primarily in Israel, the West Bank, and the Gaza Strip. Primary leadership resides in Syria, though other leadership elements reside in Lebanon as well as other parts of the Middle East. Militant Palestinians formed the PIJ in the Gaza Strip during the 1970s. The group is committed to the creation of an Islamic Palestinian state. Their attacks are against Israeli military and civilian targets inside Israel and the Palestinian territories. According to the U.S. State Department, the PIJ is also committed to the destruction of Israel.[14]

The Israel Security Agency (ISA) reported that the Islamic Jihad perpetrated 106 terror attacks in 2004 compared to 71 in 2003. There was one unsuccessful suicide attack in 2004, compared to six in 2003. High-trajectory weapon fire increased from two terrorist attacks in 2003 to 17 in 2004, an increase of 750 percent.[15]

Hamas

The Hamas and Palestine Islamic Jihad used suicide attacks to derail the 1995 Oslo Interim Agreement. The agreement was designed to serve as the foundation of a peace process between Palestinians and Israelis.[16] The Israel Security Agency (ISA) reports that in 2004, Hamas is responsible for 555 terrorist attacks, compared to 218 in 2003. The number of suicide attacks decreased by 77 percent while the number of Kassam rockets and mortar shells launched increased by 40 percent and 500 percent, respectively.[17]

In late 1987 Hamas formed as an outgrowth of the Palestinian branch of the Muslim Brotherhood. Its goal is to establish an Islamic Palestinian state in Israel. It is loosely structured; some elements work clandestinely and others operate openly through mosques and social service institutions. Senior leaders are spread throughout the Gaza Strip, Syria, Lebanon, Iran, and the Gulf States. Hamas's strength is concentrated in the Gaza Strip and the West Bank and the group has confined its attacks within Israel against the country's military and citizens.[18]

Hamas (Harkat el-Mukawma el Islamiya, or "The Islamic Resistance Movement") was inspired and aided by the Hezbollah. According to Yoram Schweitzer, an International Center for Terrorism researcher, Hamas and PIJ had a close liaison with Hezbollah and the Iranian Revolutionary Guards, and it "gained momentum after Israel deported a few hundred operatives to Lebanon in 1992."[19] In the beginning Hamas attacked military targets but it quickly began attacks on civilians in central cities and crowded areas.

The withdrawal of IDF forces from the Gaza Strip began on the night of September 11, 2005, and was completed in the morning of September 12.[20] At this time, the Hamas-associated Al-Mustaqbal research center presented another study on the future of the Palestinian-Israeli conflict. The study's main conclusions were, "Hamas (and the other terrorist organizations) will not disarm; they will continue the armed struggle while moving its focal point to the West Bank, and will not consent to submit to pressure exerted by the Palestinian Authority and the international community."[21] After the disengagement, escalation of Palestinian terrorism was followed by an IDF killing and air strikes in the Gaza Strip, arrests of wanted terrorists, and a closure of the West Bank.[22]

"Will history repeat itself?"[23] asks Raphael Israeli of the Truman Institute for the Advancement of Peace at Hebrew University in Jerusalem, Israel. Do the Palestinian women who have become "Islamikaze" (his term for suicide bombers) martyrs free themselves? Israeli refers to the prediction of Frantz Fanon in *A Dying Colonialism* that women in the Algerian struggle for independence from 1954 to 1962 would liberate themselves by taking part in the violence.

Suicide bombers were imported from the Hezbollah, who were very effective in using them against Americans and Israelis, Israeli writes. Initially the Hamas fundamentalists who opposed the Palestinian Authority used them, but now they are used by secular groups such as al-Aqsa Brigade and Fatah and Force 17, which are elements of Fatah, the principal component of the PA. Thus, once the exclusive tool of Muslim radicals, the "Islamikaze" are expanding.[24]

Palestinian Terrorism Linked to Islamic Fundamentalism

During the first intifada, because many men were put into prison, women took over their roles.[25] Karla J. Cunningham writes that women collaborated with more experienced males, learned how to plant bombs but not detonate them, and then progressed to actually detonating them. Ahlam Al-Tamimi on two occasions and Ayman Razawi in a separate incident performed in cooperation with males or in tandem with males or an organization. These roles changed when Wafa Idris detonated a bomb January 22, 2002, in Jerusalem. She was eventually confirmed by the Israelis as the first official female bomber and claimed by the al-Aqsa Martyrs Brigade.[26] (See Table 7.1.) In spite of these confirmations, significant uncertainty surrounds the authenticity of her attack as an al-Aqsa Martyrs Brigade planned suicide, according to Cunningham. Idris more likely meant to plant the bomb, but al-Aqsa learned the importance of using female bombers because three incidents followed Idris, with Darin Abu Aysheh, Ayat Akhras and Andalib Takafka, all in 2002.[27] (See Table 7.1.)

Table 7.1
Female Suicide Bombers
Palestinian-Israeli Conflict, 2000–2004

Date	August 29, 1969, and September 6, 1970[a]
Name/Home	Leila Khaled (or Khalid) /—
Age/Status	25 /—
Organization	Popular Front for the Liberation of Palestine
Place of Attack	Rome-Athens flight TWA #840
	Amsterdam-New York flight El Al #219
Casualties	0
Details	Many sources consider Khaled a forerunner of suicide bombing.

Date	January 27, 2000[b]
Name/Home	Unknown/—

Age/Status	—/—
Organization	—
Place of Attack	Busy shopping area of central Jerusalem
Casualties	2 killed
Details	—

Date	August 1, 2001[c]
Name/Home	Ahlam al-Tamimi, accomplice /—
Age/Status	20 / student and journalist
Organization	Hamas
Place of Attack	Sbarro pizzeria, West Jerusalem
Casualties	15 killed
Details	Al-Tamimi was arrested in 2001 for giving logistical support to Hamas, which attacked Sbarro pizzeria. In July 2001, she carried a bomb disguised as a beer can into a West Jerusalem supermarket. She placed the bomb on a shelf after shopping and walked away. Bomb exploded, but did not hurt anyone. In August, she worked with an accomplice posing as a girlfriend of the man who carried a bomb in guitar case into Sbarro pizzeria. The man, a Hamas bomber, walked in and she walked away. Now jailed in Hadarim, a particularly violent, maximum security Israeli detention center in the south.

Date	January 27, 2002[d]
Name/Home	Wafa Idris, a.k.a. Wafa Idrees, Shahanaz Amouri a.k.a. Idriss /Al-Amari Refugee Camp near Ramallah
Age/Status	26 or 28 / divorced, no children/paramedic for the Red Crescent
Organization	al-Aqsa Martyrs Brigade
Place of Attack	Shopping district, Jaffa Road, Jerusalem
Casualties	1 or 2 killed, 30–150+ wounded
Details	She had three brothers in the Fatah. Family originally from Ramla, Israel. Originally recruited in connection with brother's planned suicide attack. Her intended role was to carry a knapsack with explosives across a checkpoint. Her brother would then later use them. Armed with more than 10 kilos of explosives, Idris detonated the explosives. Some reports indicate it is not certain whether the explosion was intended, or if the bomb exploded too soon. As her body

lay in the middle of Jaffa Road, it was covered haphazardly with a rubber sheet. Her right arm was torn off, lying several inches from her body. Idris's attack made the al-Aqsa the first Palestinian terrorist group to use a female suicide bomber.

Date	January 28, 2002[e]
Name/Home	Shihaz Amudi / —
Age/Status	20 /from Al-Najah University in Nablus, West Bank
Organization	—
Place of Attack	—
Casualties	—
Details	Identity remains a mystery. The university's director said no such person was on the student roll, and Palestinian security sources said no one of that name was known to be living in the Nablus area.

Date	February 27, 2002[f]
Name/Home	Darin Abu Aysheh, a.k.a. Dareen Abu Ashai, dareen Abu Eishi, Dareen Abu Aisheh, Daaren Abu Aeshah, Dareen Abu Aisha / the village of Beit Wazan, Samaria, in the West Bank
Age/Status	21 / single and student, Al-Najah University, Nablus
Organization	al-Aqsa Martyrs Brigade
Place of Attack	Checkpoint Israeli Maccabim roadblock in West Ramallah (West Bank) on a road between Tel Aviv and Jerusalem
Casualties	4 wounded
Details	She went to Hamas to volunteer but was turned down. Her parents said she was religious. The bombing came after Israeli troops killed four armed Arabs in gun battles and a Palestinian employee shot dead an Israeli factory manager in an attack that was apparently politically motivated. In photo, headband reads, "Izzedine Al Qasam Brigade," the military wing of Hamas, as she holds a knife in one hand and holds up her index finger making the "one" symbol, meaning one God, Allah. (See Chapter 2.)

Date	March 29, 2002[g]
Name/Home	Ayat al-Akhras a.k.a. Eiat al Achras / Dehaishe refugee camp near Bethlehem

Age/Status	18 /engaged to Shali Abu Laban
Organization	al-Aqsa Martyrs Brigade
Place of Attack	Jerusalem supermarket Kyriat Hayovel
Casualties	2 killed, 22 or 28 IDF wounded
Details	The attack was part of a wave of Passover attacks that came after Israeli attacks against Arafat's headquarters. Carried explosives in black purse. First cousin killed in conflict. Her taped martyr statement said, "I am going to fight instead of the sleeping Arab armies who are watching Palestinian girls fighting alone."[h]

Date	April 12, 2002[i]
Name/Home	Andalib Suleiman Takatka, a.k.a. Andaleeb Taqataqah / Bethlehem
Age/Status	20 or 21 /—
Organization	al-Aqsa Martyrs Brigade
Place of Attack	Mahane Yehuda market bus stop in Jerusalem
Casualties	6 killed, 60 to 90 wounded
Details	Detonated a belt full of explosives. Israeli security said, "The bomb was manufactured from three tubes of plastic explosives and a battery, which were placed in a black purse to camouflage it.... A number of days prior to the attack Taqataqah was videotaped dressed in black and holding a Koran."[j] Her attack undermined U.S. Secretary Colin Powell's efforts to move ahead on peace talks. Her name means nightingale in Arabic.

Date	May 19, 2003[k]
Name/Home	Hiba Daraghmeh, a.k.a. Hiba Da'arma, Heiba Daragmeh /Tubas village in the Jenin district
Age/Status	19 / Palestinian student at Quds Open University, English literature major
Organization	Islamic Jihad (PIJ) and al-Aqsa Martyrs Brigade
Place of Attack	Entrance of mall in Afula
Casualties	3 killed, 52 to 83 wounded
Details	Family members said she dreamed of teaching English. First Islamic Jihad bomber, fifth female bomber.

Date	May 20, 2002[l]
Name/Home	Irena Polichik (accomplice to Issa Badir, 16-year-old male) / Dehaishe refugee camp
Age/Status	26 / married
Organization	Fatah
Place of Attack	Crowded park in Rishon Le Zion, Israel
Casualties	2 killed, 51 wounded
Details	Arrested. First misidentified as Marina Pinsky. She drove the car for the bombers. Claimed she did not know the youths were suicide bombers, but her husband knew. Immigrated from Ukraine, Russia, 1991. Married to Ibrahim Sarachane, 33. Badir and Polichik carried out the attack that was supposed to be done by Arin Ahmed, who backed out. Christian. Previously worked as a prostitute in Tel Aviv. She stole Pinsky's ID card and brought it to Bethlehem, where a forged copy was made.

Date	August 2003[m]
Name/Home	Unknown (3) /—
Age/Status	—/—
Organization	al-Aqsa Martyrs Brigade
Place of Attack	Ha'ayin, Israel
Casualties	2 killed, 10 wounded
Details	—

Date	October 4, 2003[o]
Name/Home	Hanadi Tayseer Jaradat /Jenin
Age/Status	27 or 29 /single, trainee lawyer in Jenin
Organization	Palestinian Islamic Jihad
Place of Attack	Maxim Restaurant in Haifa, Israel
Casualties	21 killed, 60 wounded
Details	Fiancé and brother killed in conflict. Hanadi was the sister of Fadi Jaradat, an Islamic Jihad militant who was killed, along with a cousin, Salah Jaradat, in June 2003 during an IDF operation to arrest them. In 1999, graduated from Jarash law school in Jordan. She was said to be religious; she prayed daily and read the Qur'an. A childhood friend described Jaradat as a very determined woman, self-confident, and stubborn in her pursuit of success and personal achievements.

Date	January 14, 2004[p]
Name/Home	Reem al-Reyashi, a.k.a. Reem Raiyshi, Rheim Saley al-Riyashi / Gaza City
Age/Status	21 or 22 / Wife and mother of son, 3, and daughter, 18 months
Organization	Hamas and al-Aqsa Martyrs Brigade
Place of Attack	Erez Crossing point between Israel and the Gaza Strip
Casualties	4 killed, 7 to 10 wounded
Details	First Hamas female suicide bomber; first mother in Israel. Requested medical help, blew up at inspection checkpoint at the entrance to the Erez industrial zone. Made video (anti–Zionist). Ten pound bomb with ball bearings and screws. Came from middle-class family. Husband had no knowledge of her plans. She tricked soldiers by saying she had a metal implant in her leg that would trigger metal detectors. While soldiers were getting a female soldier to search her, Reem entered the building and blew herself up. Her last statement: "My wish was fulfilled in the manner I wanted."[q]

Date	September 22, 2004[r]
Name/Home	Zeybab Ali Issa Abu-Salam, a.k.a Zeinab Ali Issa Abu Salem, a.k.a. Zainab Abu Salem / Askar Refugee Camp, on eastern outskirts of West Bank city of Nablus
Age/Status	18 / high school graduate
Organization	Fatah al-Aqsa Martyrs Brigade
Place of Attack	French Hill junction hitchhiking post in northern Jerusalem
Casualties	2 killed, 16 to 17 wounded
Details	Eighth female bomber since the renewal of conflict in September 2000. The week previous to her death, Israeli troops had killed five men from an al-Aqsa cell and an 11-year-old girl. Border policeman demanded she undergo a body search. When second officer arrived, she detonated a bomb that weighed between six and 11 pounds and was wrapped with shrapnel.

The first suicide attack within the borders of Israel occurred on April 16, 1993. Tamam Nabulsi, a male member of the Hamas, blew his car up alongside an Israeli bus parked near Mechola in the Jordan Valley. Two were killed and five were wounded.[28]

From 2002 on, the Palestinians saw the United States increasing its support for Israel's treatment of the territories it had occupied since the 1967 war. The United States did nothing when Yasser Arafat, President of the Palestinian Authority, was placed under virtual house arrest in Ramallah by the Israeli army. At the same time, Western nations were pressuring Arafat to condemn Palestinian terrorist activities. V.G. Julie Rajan writes that these factors heightened despair and forced the rebel groups to search for ways to gain global support, publicity and action. By 2002, Palestinian females entered as bombers against Israel and became a force to be reckoned with. Women were first officially allowed to engage in suicide bombing in January 2002.[29]

The suicide bombings "signaled the unleashing of a new terror weapon" becoming the "'smart bomb' of the poor,"[30] Barbara Victor writes. When these bombers became superstars in the West Bank and Gaza, Yasser Arafat and his factioned secular group recognized the bombers' effects on the morale of the Israeli society. More importantly, they observed a shift in public opinion from his secular organization to the radical Islamic movements.

Shaul Kimhi and Shemuel Even obtained their statistics from IDF sources and divide suicide attacks in Israel into two sub-periods: preceding and following the Temple Mount Intifada. In the period preceding the Intifada, from April 1993 to September 29, 2000, 61 suicide terrorist attacks occurred with 43 people, or 70 percent, blowing themselves up. The remainder were captured. Two organizations were involved during this time: Hamas, 41 attacks, Islamic Jihad, 20.[31]

In the period following the beginning of the intifada, from September 29, 2000, to the beginning of May 2004, 274 terrorist acts occurred, with 142 people, or 52 percent, blowing themselves up in 132 attacks. The remainder were captured. More than four organizations were involved during this time: Hamas, 99 attacks; Fata, 70; Islamic Jihad, 67; National Front, 10; and other organizations, 28.[32]

Arafat's presidency of the Palestinian Authority was at risk in the summer of 2000, writes Victor. Arafat, seen as having consented too much to the Americans and Israelis, found his control weakened. To avoid a militant Islamic regime, control his streets and to elevate his power, he approved the use of suicide bombing. The present intifada thus began in September 2000 with the use of the al-Aqsa Martyrs Brigade in the name of Allah. While Arafat was then seen as having been responsive to his people's criticism, he had difficulty in getting the masses involved in military operations. This difficulty gave birth to the use of female suicide bombers.[33]

Victor expands upon the significance of Arafat's role. Specifically on January 27, 2002, Arafat spoke to over 1,000 Palestinian women at his compound in Ramallah. Arafat told the crowd, "Women and men are equal. You are my army of roses that will crush Israeli tanks."[34] But Arafat's use of the phrase, "*Shahida* all the way to Jerusalem" was more important.[35] Previous to his speech, there was no feminized version of the masculine form of the Arab word for martyr, *shahide*. Victor describes this avid speech:

> [Arafat] repeated it [*shahida*] over and over again until the crowd, with raised fists, took the cue and chanted along with him: "*Shahida, Shahida* ... until Jerusalem. We will give our blood and soul to you, Abu Amar [Arafat's nom de guerre], and to Palestine."
>
> "You," he continued, his arm sweeping across the group of women and young girls, "are the hope of Palestine. You will liberate your husbands, fathers, and sons from oppression. You will sacrifice the way you women have always sacrificed for your family."[36]

Arafat's speech was in the morning. In the afternoon of January 27, 2002, Wafa Idris "blew herself to pieces" in a downtown Jerusalem shopping mall. (See Table 7.1.) She is the only suicide bomber not to leave a videotaped confession.[37]

Women join politically violent organizations for reasons similar to men's, such as political change, Cunningham concludes. The argument that women join for personal reasons suggests women do not choose their participation. Women who join for public reasons are suspect because their motivations for freedom are looked upon collectively as well and individualistically or their ideology is not fully developed. This perception makes women helpers to men rather than an advocate in their own right.[38]

Warrior women want expanded roles within the organization and tend to stay in the group. Cunningham writes, "what is equally clear is that for most observers ... this choice seems so foreign and unnatural to women that there must be an explanation beyond simply that women want to fight for their respective causes."[39]

Cunningham suggests four guidelines for evaluating roles of women in terrorist and politically violent organizations: be aware of limited data, the possibility of denial and deception, that invisibility does not mean passivity or powerlessness and organizational versus societal imperatives. The secretive nature of groups makes it difficult to obtain reliable information. All in all, terrorist organizations are very aware of societal biases but will work to make those biases work for the benefit of the organization's goals. Societies in extreme conflict will in turn loosen their constraints on women to facilitate the convergence of individual and terrorist organizational interests.[40]

Scope of Female Suicide Bombers

Some of the Palestinian women did not complete their missions. These women were either arrested or refused to carry out the bombings. Clara Beyler reports, "Out of the 20 suicide bombings since the beginning of the year 2002, 4 have been committed by women. In the first six months of 2002, women have participated more and more in the Israeli-Palestinian conflict and represented one fifth of the suicide killers. The rapidity and willingness of other women to imitate female suicide bombers, and the present inability to profile them point to a changing situation to which society needs to understand and adapt."[41]

Only since 2002 have women been allowed to be on an equal footing with men and perform suicide missions. According to Beyler, the Fatah employed women on the battlefield to gather information. Leila Khalid is an early example in the 1970s. (See Tables 4.1 and 7.1.) Women have volunteered to be martyrs, but Hamas, for example, has not embraced their participation. On the other hand, the al-Aqsa Martyrs Brigade has assisted women to become martyrs. Beyler describes the al-Aqsa: "This terrorist organization, born with the Intifada, ... in October 2000, is more secular than other more fundamentalist organizations such as Hamas."[42]

In Palestinian society, women have more rights than women in other fundamentalist countries and are permitted to choose political action, such as suicide bombing, writes Beyler. Women can vote, hold office, drive cars, own property and have equal access to universities. They are not confined to their homes and are not required to wear a veil. When a woman martyrs herself she is honored. Her picture is displayed and Palestinians attend her funeral. In spite of all of her rights and the honor given her, her participation in suicide bombing surprised the Palestinian society. Beyler writes that honor was not always the reason women performed suicide attacks. To transcend mortality and to receive economic gain for their families were underlying reasons.[43]

Aspects of the Lives of Some Female Suicide Bombers

In other parts of the book, I have chosen to present the female suicide bomber in the context of the power of the society in which she lives and of society being a part of the larger global community. An ethics of form is needed in the examination of the female suicide bomber. In this section I seek to present the women empathetically and in more than strictly historical terms.[44]

A pitfall in attempting an ethics of form that it is necessary to be aware of the relationship between political violence and media environments. Hilla Dayan writes that, in some cases, the images and stories of female political violence help destabilize fundamental dispositions of gender. But she warns, the enigmatic and ambivalent personal stories are enfolding, almost overshadowing the violent act itself. Examples are: Ayat al-Akhras's unwanted planned marriage; Wafa Idris's social marginality as a divorcee; Reem Salah Al-Raiyshi being forced to commit the death act as punishment for her infidelity and having suicidal tendencies; and Latifa Abu Dara'a's reported mental illness. Dayan writes,

> Latifa Abu Dara'a's case is particularly interesting, because it almost entirely ignores the man who was actually designated to carry out

the would-be suicide operation, and exclusively focuses on her personal life, when her 'mere' function was to carry the explosive belt across the military checkpoint.... Their private stories always loom over these personae.[45]

Just as a pitfall exists, so does the responsibility to humanize women who bomb, concludes Dayan.

Barbara Victor includes an ethics of form in her book, *Army of Roses: Inside the World of Palestinian Women Suicide Bombers*. She provides the political context and the bombers' personal dimension. This is particularly so in her background information on Wafa Idris. Raphael Israeli credits Idris as having "established the precedent of the first Palestinian woman who went to her death willingly and by choice."[46]

Wafa Idris, al-Aqsa Martyrs Brigade

On January 27, 2002, Wafa Idris, a divorced paramedic for the Red Crescent, who was 26 or 28, exploded at a shopping district on Jerusalem's Jaffa Road. Reports were not able to determine whether the explosion was intended or if the bomb exploded too soon. Idris had lived at the Amari Refugee Camp near Ramallah. One person was killed and 90 were wounded.[47] (See Table 7.1.) According to Heather A. Andrews, author of *Veiled Jihad: The Threat of Female Islamic Suicide Terrorists*, "Shiraz Amudi was actually the mistaken identity of Wafa Idris who of course blew herself up on January 27, 2002. According to quite a few sources, there was an identity mistake for a few days before properly being identified as Wafa Idris. Idris's mother has previously been uncertain because of the name mix-up, but knew it was her daughter a short time later."[48]

Wafa Idris's actions have religious significance, writes Raphael Israeli. At first personal motives were attributed to Idris as the reasons for committing suicide. When Palestinians justified her act and predicted more women might follow her example, "the religious aspect broke into the open."[49] Some, like Jamila Shanti, the head of the Women's Activities of the Palestinian Islamic Movement, believed, because martyrdom was a high calling, women were to be excused from normal restrictions. The head of Hamas, Sheikh Yassin, believed women had a role, but they must be accompanied by a chaperone. Necessity led him to later amend his

Top left: Wafa Idris killed herself and an Israeli man in a bombing attack in downtown Jerusalem on January 27, 2002 (AP Photograph/Nasser Nasser). *Bottom:* Israeli police inspect the body of suicide bomber Wafa Idris at the site of her attack in downtown Jerusalem (AP Photograph/Jacqueline Larma).

position to say that in the case of martyrdom, where a woman is not expected to return, she could go alone, but he also stated that women were not needed at the moment in the movement.[50]

Idris's motivation was a sense of hopelessness under occupation and

Israeli forensics team investigates the scene around the remains of Wafa Idris on January 27, 2002 (AP Photograph/Jerome Delay).

rage, writes Cunningham. Her motivation was nationalist rather than religious zeal. Skepticism about Idris is due to three things. Idris was not a known figure in a terror organization, thus less likely to be identified as a potential suicide bomber. She did not carry out the attack in a normal fashion; she carried the bomb in a backpack instead of having it strapped to her waist. It appeared that she did not intend to detonate explosives. No note or martyr's video was left behind.[51]

Posthumously, Wafa Idris received earthly glory. The Arab world stage praised the woman who heroically defended her country. Newspaper accounts labeled her a modern Jeanne d'Arc and elevated her to a great heroine. Israeli writes that no one gave higher praise than the Egyptian psychologist, Dr. 'Adel Sadeq, head of Psychiatry at Cairo's Ein Shams University. He compared her to Jesus Christ. Saddam Hussein erected a memorial in her honor. Raphael Israeli speculates that Idris was seen as a ray of hope designed to absorb the attacks of the ongoing struggle with

Israel even though Egypt and Jordan had signed a peace agreement with Israel.[52]

The response to her attack inside and outside of Palestine was a turning point for the al-Aqsa Martyrs Brigade, according to Cunningham. They were now willing to use women attackers and to use attackers against civilian targets within Israel. By the end of February 2002, they had created a women's unit named after Idris.[53]

What was Wafa Idris really like? In Barbara Victor's interview with Idris's mother, Mabrook Idris said that Wafa was only 12 at the beginning of the first intifada in 1987. The loss of her friend's eye during the conflict affected Wafa deeply. Some friends and relatives alluded to other reasons why Wafa became a martyr: Wafa's desire for pretty clothes; her bouts with melancholy and depression; and that she had become a "constant target for mocking after her husband divorced her."[54]

Wafa and Ahmed married in 1991 when Wafa was 16 and Ahmed 26. In 1998, she delivered a premature stillborn infant. According to Ahmed, Wafa then lost all interest in life, stopped eating and talking, did not leave her bed to clean or cook. Ahmed believed that while Wafa had not disgraced him, she had disobeyed him. Mabrook said Wafa's husband divorced her because she could not have more children. As a divorced woman, Wafa could not marry again. It was as though she had nothing to live for. Was martyrdom Wafa's way out?[55]

At 26 years of age, Wafa, divorced and allegedly sterile, was returned to her childhood home by her husband where she became a financial burden. Wafa's childhood home was filled with other children without a father present. Mira Tzoreff, professor of women's history in the Middle East at Ben Gurion University, says that Wafa's intent is not important:

> Wafa Idris was not chosen by mistake. She was from the lowest social economic strata of Palestinian society and she didn't have a father. All her problems with her failed marriage and sterility made her an abnormal person. She could never remarry, and her chance to be self-sufficient was zero. There is no doubt that the people who chose her, if they did, did so because they knew she had no future. And I'm quite certain that the recruiters asked themselves how the family would react if they found out that she had been chosen as the first woman suicide bomber.[56]

It is credible for families who live far below the poverty line to sacrifice a child for martyrdom so others could have a better life. Palestinian families of suicide bombers received monetary rewards and the martyrs don't die, they go to Paradise where they have a better life.[57]

Victor interviewed other friends and relatives who had different conclusions about Wafa's reasons for becoming a martyr. Wafa's aunt claimed Wafa got divorced not because she couldn't have children but because she did not want them. She said:

> She was too independent. She preferred to study. There is no truth about her being sterile. Wafa was a fighter with a strong sense of patriotism. She was destined to become a martyr.[58]

There was agreement among people who knew Wafa that she had a sensual smile, soft brown eyes, and curly dark hair and found her work at the Palestinian Red Crescent satisfying, Victor writes. Wafa's mother said that Wafa had told her that volunteer nursing was the only thing that gave her purpose. Wafa's brother thought she should earn money but says: "Wafa always said that she could never take money for saving lives. It was her contribution to the struggle."[59] The director of the Red Crescent office in Ramallah said that Wafa was willing to brave bullets to evacuate the wounded.

Israeli law states that when a suicide bomber dies while committing an act of terrorism with Israel, the body is never returned to the family, explains Victor. It is buried in an unmarked grave in a large cemetery in northern Israel. If the martyr dies within the Occupied Territories or Gaza, the body is returned for a proper Muslim burial. But in Wafa's case, her mother Mabrook "honored her daughter's memory with an empty pine box."[60]

The Fatah eulogized Wafa this way: "Wafa's martyrdom restored honor to the national role of the Palestinian woman, sketched the most wonderful pictures of heroism in the long battle for national liberation."[61]

Missions Not Completed

The Israel Defense Force (IDF) reports, "Since September 2000, more than 50 women have been arrested by security forces who were to carry out suicide terrorist attacks or aid in their execution. In October 2004 only, 14 women have been arrested ready to perpetuate a suicide terrorist attack."[62] The IDF web site offers photos of some female bombers who did and did not complete their missions.

Wafa Samir Ibrahim Bas

On June 20, 2005, Wafa Samir Ibrahim Bas was arrested at Erez crossing at the Gaza border. She was wearing about 20 pounds of explosives stitched to her underwear. She had agreed with the Abu Rish Brigade, a militant faction with links to Fatah's al-Aqsa Brigade, to detonate in a crowded area of the Soroka Hospital in Beersheva, Israel. She said that she did not intend to blow up the hospital because many Arabs were treated there and considered Tel Hashomer near Tel-Aviv instead.[63] (See Table 7.2.)

Wafa Samir Ibrahim Bas was a 21-year-old Palestinian and a student at Al-Quds Open University.[64] She is described as having "big, brown eyes and her black hair was tied in a ponytail." Because her gait appeared strange, security officials stopped her to ask her to remove her (continued on page 146)

Table 7.2
Female Suicide Bombers
Who Did Not Complete Their Mission
Palestinian–Israeli Conflict, 1969–2005

Date	1969[a]
Name/Home	Randa Nabulsi /Nablus
Age/Status	—/—
Organization	—
Mission	Jerusalem supermarket
Outcome	Captured
Details	Sentenced to 10 years

Date	1987[b]
Name/Home	Etaf Aliyan, a.k.a. Atef Eleyan, a.k.a. Elian /—
Age/Status	—/—
Organization	Palestinian Islamic Jihad
Mission	Jerusalem police station
Outcome	Captured

Details	Apprehended before she could drive a car loaded with explosives into the police station. Jailed in Israel for ten years and released in 1997. She was a senior Palestinian Islamic Jihad activist.

Date	August 3, 2001[c]
Name/Home	Ayman Razawi, a.k.a. Imman Ghazawi, Iman Ghazawi, Immam Gazawi, a.k.a. Iman Asha / Nabulus
Age/Status	23 /married mother of two
Organization	Fatah
Mission	Tel Aviv bus station
Outcome	Captured before she could plant an 11-pound bomb.
Details	Hid bomb packed with nails and screws in laundry detergent box. Husband requested her to do the attack to clear the family name and improve the family's status. Brother was also involved in the attack.

Date	August 31, 2001[d]
Name/Home	Abir Hamdan / Nablus
Age/Status	26 /engaged to Fatah militiaman and had romantic ties to other operatives
Organization	Fatah
Mission	Attacked a restaurant in Hadera
Outcome	Killed while she was transporting a bomb in a taxi from Tulkarm to Nablus. Explosion occurred prematurely during preparations for the attack.
Details	She wanted to improve her status in Palestinian society.

Date	March 21, 2002[e]
Name/Home	Kahira Saadi and Sana'a Shahada, accomplices to male bomber, Hashaika /— Al-Ram and Kalandia refugee camp
Age/Status	26 /married, mother of four, ages 6, 8, 11, 12; 27 /girlfriend and facilitator of Nasser Shawish, a senior PIJ operative from Jenin, who had recently been arrested;
Organization	Fatah, of al-Aqsa
Mission	King George Street, Jerusalem; 3 killed, 80 injured.
Outcome	Captured

Details   They purchased a bouquet of flowers which male bomber
                   Hashaika held to blend in with the crowd on Mother's Day.
                   Shahada walked fifty meters behind Sa'adi Hashaika
                   because she was wearing traditional Arab clothing and did
                   not want to arouse suspicion.
                   They were arrested. Saadi is serving three life sentences
                   plus 80 years in an Israeli jail for her role in helping the
                   male get into Jerusalem.

Date   April 11, 2002[f]
Name/Home   Shefa'a Alkudsi, a.k.a. Shfaa al-Koudsi / Tulkarm
Age/Status   26 /divorced with 6-year-old daughter
Organization   —
Mission   Maale Adumin near Jerusalem
Outcome   Arrested by Israel Defense Forces (IDF)
Details   Admitted she planned an attack disguised as a pregnant
                   woman. Admitted shooting and killing Israeli motorists at
                   random. Friends said she tortured animals, skinned a cat
                   alive and had a series of disastrous love affairs. When a
                   lover rebuffed her, she stabbed him with scissors.
                   She had prepared a will bidding her daughter and family
                   goodbye. She was arrested when she was preparing to leave
                   to commit an attack with a young male. She intended to
                   carry an explosive charge under a maternity dress. The
                   young man was to wear an additional explosive charge and
                   place a third charge at the attack site before they deto-
                   nated the charges they carried on their bodies. She was to
                   detonate her explosive belt first, and then her partner
                   would detonate his, and then the third charge would det-
                   onate.

Date   May 22, 2002[g]
Name/Home   Arin Ahmed / Bethlehem
Age/Status   20 /student, business administration
Organization   —
Mission   Supposed to commit bombing in Rishon Le Zion during
                   last week of April with 16-year-old Issa Badir (who went
                   through with the mission)
Outcome   Arrested in June 2002 by the IDF

Details	Volunteered to carry out an attack to avenge the death of her fiancé.

Date	May 30, 2002[h]
Name/Home	Tauriya, a.k.a. Tawriya Hamamra / village near Jenin in the West Bank
Age/Status	25 / dressmaker, florist
Organization	Fatah al-Aqsa Martyrs Brigade
Mission	Israeli capital
Outcome	IDF arrested her in Tulkarm.
Details	Conflicting information from sources. From northern Samaria; confessed that she backed out of a planned suicide bombing on the Israeli capital, Jerusalem, due to discontent with handlers.[i] She also said that her reasons were personal, not political. She said: "I didn't feel fear. I am not afraid of dying. I went for personal reasons. I was afraid of how God would look on me if I came for impure reasons."[j] She volunteered for the al-Aqsa Martyrs Brigade. Reports vary on amount of training she received: from one hour to two days.

Date	June 13, 2002[k]
Name/Home	Shireen Rabiya /—
Age/Status	15 /Youngest of 16 children
Organization	—
Mission	Bethlehem
Outcome	Captured before fitted for explosive belt. Because of age and lack of weapons, Israeli security forces released her.
Details	Recruited by uncle with complicity of school principal. Had difficulty in school. Uncle convinced her that her afterlife would be more rewarding.

Date	June 14, 2002[l]
Name/Home	Unknown (2) /—
Age/Status	—/—
Organization	—
Mission	Israel
Outcome	Arrested by Israel Security Forces
Details	—

Female Suicide Bombers

Date	July 27, 2002[m]
Name/Home	Umaya Mohammed Danaj / —
Age/Status	28 / —
Organization	—
Mission	Israel
Outcome	Arrested on her way to commit bombing
Details	—

Date	August 3, 2002[n]
Name/Home	Amna'a Mouna, a.k.a. Amana Mona / Ramallah
Age/Status	— / journalist and Fatah activist
Organization	Fatah
Mission	On the way to Ofra, an Israeli settlement
Outcome	Border police stopped her. She was armed with two pistols and three hand grenades. Was put in prison near Tel Aviv where authorities use her as a leader of inmates because of her ability to instill fear.
Details	Used pseudonym, Sally. One of two known females to commit murder before becoming a bomber. On January 17, 2001, she met an Israeli male teen, Ofir Rahum, on Internet chat room. On a promise for sex, he agreed to meet her at a central bus station in Jerusalem; instead she drove him to a deserted area between Jerusalem and Ramallah where two male members of Fatah killed Ofir with 18 rounds from two Kalashnikovs. Two weeks after the murder, she was stopped by border police.

Date	October 20, 2004[o]
Name/Home	Echlem Jawarish / —
Age/Status	29 / widow
Organization	Al-Aqsa Brigade
Mission	Bethlehem area
Outcome	Captured
Details	She tried several times to detonate herself at the crossing but did not succeed. IDF troops arrested her on the way to carry out a suicide attack. She wore stockings that contained approximately 20 pounds of explosives. Lost her husband and brother who were senior members of the al-Aqsa Martyrs Brigade during clashes with IDF troops 18 months previous to attempted attack.

Date	June 20, 2005[p]
Name/Home	Wafa Samir Ibrahim Bas, a.k.a. Wafa al-Bass / resident of the Jabaliya refugee camp in northern Gaza.
Age/Status	21 / Palestinian student at al-Quds Open University
Organization	Abu Rish Brigade militant faction links to Fatah, al-Aqsa Brigade
Mission	Erez crossing, Gaza border
Outcome	She was caught wearing about 10 to 20 kilograms of explosives in her stockings. She had agreed with the brigade to detonate in a crowded area of the Soroka Hospital, Beersheva, Israel. Said that she did not intend to blow up the hospital because many Arabs were treated there and considered Tel Hashomer instead.
Details	She stated her reason as: "My dream was to be a suicide bomber. I wanted to kill 20, 50 Jews. Yes, even babies."[q] Because she was a burn victim, she had permission to travel to southern Israeli city Beersheba for medical treatment, a day before a planned summit in Jerusalem between Israeli Prime Minister Ariel Sharon and Palestinian Authority President Mahmoud Abbas.

Female Suicide Bombers for Whom the Date of Mission or Capture Was Not Found or Incomplete

Date	NA[r]
Name/Home	Patan Dragma / Loben A-Sharkia
Age/Status	—/ mother of 7
Organization	—
Mission	City of Ariel
Outcome	Captured
Details	Captured while carrying a 15 to 20 kilogram bomb on her way to explode.

Date	NA[s]
Name/Home	Haula Hashash / Ballata
Age/Status	19 /—
Organization	Hamas, Palestinian Islamic Jihad (PIJ)
Mission	—
Outcome	Imprisoned

Details	She considers herself a daughter of her people. She believes that as long as her people are killed, Palestinians will fight back.

Date	NA[t]
Name/Home	Raida Jadana / Nablus
Age/Status	22 /—
Organization	—
Mission	—
Outcome	Imprisoned
Details	She doesn't believe she did anything wrong but would not repeat her actions.

Date	NA[u]
Name/Home	Ayat Allah Kamil /Kabatya
Age/Status	20 /—
Organization	Hamas, Jihad
Mission	—
Outcome	Arrested and imprisoned
Details	Became a martyr "because of my religion. I am very religious. For the holy war [Jihad], there is no difference between men and women."[v]

Date	NA[w]
Name/Home	Baid Yaam / Ballata refugee camp
Age/Status	26 /—
Organization	Hamas, Palestine Islamic Jihad
Mission	—
Outcome	Imprisoned
Details	She believes every Palestinian is a soldier because there is no organized army; this is war. Outside the prison is a battlefield and the answer is to convert to Islam.

long dark cloak. As she calmly took off her clothing down to a T-shirt and jeans, she tried to set off the explosives still hidden beneath her jeans. She was desperate and "clawed at her face, screaming."[65]

The Israeli Intelligence publicized Bas's case to demonstrate that terrorist threats continued despite a letup in the intifada as a result of the Palestinian-Israeli cease-fire agreed to at the Sharm el-Sheikh summit in

February 2005. Scars were apparent on Bas's neck and hands. The scars were the result of a kitchen gas explosion that occurred six months earlier.[66]

After a press conference, Bas said that she did not regret her decision to perform her mission. She said: "My dream was to be a martyr. I believe in death." When asked whether her actions might prevent other Palestinians from getting health care, she responded, "So what?... They pay you the cost of the treatment, don't they?" Then asked whether she would have killed babies and children, she replied, "Yes, even babies and children. You, too, kill our babies."[67]

In the final analysis, Bas showed remorse and concern for her personal welfare when she said, "I don't want my mother to see me like this. After all, I haven't killed anyone.... Will they have pity on me?"[68] Bas broke down and cried and said that she did not tell her mother of her plans and asked her for forgiveness. "I am sorry, mother, forgive me, I should have listened to you."[69]

Incarcerated Suicide Women

Visiting incarcerated women who failed to detonate their explosives is one way to obtain information. In 2005, Manuela Dviri, a journalist, playwright and writer, visited an Israeli jail that holds the "suicide women near the finest Israeli villas, in the heart of the most fertile area of the country, the Plain of Sharon."[70] Dviri's son Jonathan was killed in 1998 by a Hezbollah rocket. In 2005, she received the Peres Reward for Peace and Reconciliation for her work with Saving Children, an Israeli-Palestinian project which refers Palestinian children to Israeli hospitals for free treatment.

Dviri describes the women's conditions in the Israeli jail. To get to the women one must climb and descend many flights of stairs. The 30 women between 17 and 30 years of age are kept behind seven or eight iron doors and gates that are at the end of long corridors. Their female guard is young and unarmed.[71]

From January 2002 to January 2003, 38 women who intended to perform suicide attacks were arrested either on the way to their targets or before they put on their explosive belts, reports Victor. Two of the 38 women admitted to having committed murder before making their final decision to become a suicide bomber.[72] (See Table 7.2.) Given these figures and the research done by Dviri, Table 7.2 underrepresents the number of unsuccessful female bombers.

Dviri reports on her visits with unsuccessful female suicide bombers including Ayat Allah Kamil, 20, from Kabatya; Baid Yaam, 26, from the Ballata refugee camp; and Kahira Saadi, 27, from Jenin. (See Tables 7.1 and 7.2.) Ayat Allah Kamil said that she became a martyr because of her religion and that in the holy war there's no difference between male and female martyrs. She spoke of male martyrs being welcomed in to paradise by 72 beautiful virgins. She said that a woman martyr "will be the chief of the 72 virgins, the fairest of the fair."[73]

Dviri asked Kamil how and when did she have the idea to martyr herself. Kamil replied: "I asked merciful God to help me, and he sent me the idea of making an official request to the right person — who, in my case, was a girl like me — my request was granted and I joined up."[74] Although Kamil says that she would rather take the lives of soldiers and not civilians, she also adds that destiny does not "take any notice of what you are or what you do."[75]

Baid Yaam and also of the Hamas Jihad said: "The Israeli army doesn't distinguish between men and women or the old and the young; we haven't got an organized army, I haven't anything against you [as a civilian who might die as a result of martyrdom] personally, but that's war, and every Palestinian, whether a man or a woman, is a soldier."[76]

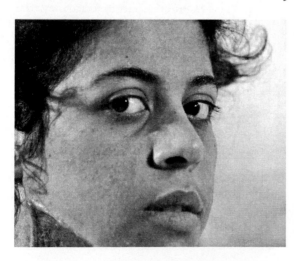

Palestinian Wafa al-Bass, in Hashikma prison in Ashkelon, Israel, was suspected of trying to carry out a suicide bombing June 20, 2005 (AP Photograph/Ronen Zvulun, Pool).

Dviri asks what are their dreams for the future. Kamil responded: "Of the world becoming Islamic, a world in which we will all live in peace, joy and harmony, all of us.... And you'll be able to remain Jewish, whatever you want; it doesn't matter, but in an Islamic world."[77]

The female prisoners who were members of the Hamas Jihad are in agreement that they are part of a war, that outside is a battlefield and that they must fight back as long as their people are being "slaughtered."[78]

Dviri describes Kahira Saadi as "one of the jail celebrities."[79] She is the mother of four and is serving three life sentences plus 80 years. Her husband is also in jail. The children are with her mother-in-law. For the first two years, Saadi had no visitors, but at the time of the interview she said that her children were beginning to come to see her. In February 2002, she and a male accomplice executed an attack that claimed the lives of three people and injured 80. Saadi claimed that she, herself, did not kill anyone, but that her role was to help the male get into Jerusalem. She gave him some flowers to hold.

Dviri asked Kahira Saadi whether she felt remorse for ruining her life and the lives of her family. Saadi said, "I did it to defend them. I'm not sorry, we're at war. But perhaps I wouldn't do it again. It was an impulse."[80] Saadi agreed that her real reason was different from her official one, but said she would not tell the real reason.

8

United States Policies and New Strategies

> It's a matter of time before we have a woman detonate herself at a school, a shopping mall, a grocery store, a movie theater, a museum, a bus/subway terminal or elsewhere because the attention, or profile, remains on a 20 to 30–something, Arabic-looking male, which excludes a tremendous recruiting pool for terrorists wanting to catch us off-guard and inflict as much terror, shock, and destruction as possible. A woman suicide bomber would absolutely fit that bill.
>
> — Jennifer Hardwick, senior director,
> Terrorism Research Center, Inc.[1]

Effects of Terror

In 2000, Yoram Schweitzer wrote, "The greatest potential risk suicide terrorism may pose in the future is if terrorists carry out operations combined with other spectacular tactics such as blowing up airplanes or the use of Weapons of Mass Destruction."[2] He believed that if these tactics occurred, they would be viewed as a strategic threat. In 2001, on September 11, the future risk became a reality.

Acts of terror upon civilian populations cause fear and insecurity among the people.

Since 2000, suicide attacks by Hamas, Palestinian Islamic Jihad (PIJ) and al-Aqsa Martyrs Brigade have resulted in a high number of casualties among the Israeli civilian population and threatened the Israeli public's sense of personal security. Schweitzer explains, "This effect was intensified by the fact that the terror campaign accompanied a peace process, which was supposed to bring tranquility to the relationships between Israelis and Palestinians.... The suicide factor in the Palestinian terror campaign thus had strategic ramifications on the Israel-Palestinian peace-process."[3]

Not all of the specific goals of the terrorist organizations that have used suicide attacks have been met, but their methods have had useful and definite effects for them. The policy created within the United States and elsewhere is, in large part, a response to terrorism.

The United States's first response to terrorism was to go to war in Afghanistan. The United States and its allies used their armed forces to find and destroy the terrorist group and their allies. They succeeded in toppling the Taliban government. In its report, the 9/11 Commission concluded this strategy of war should be balanced with other elements of national power such as diplomacy, intelligence and economic policy.[4] The United States and governments around the world continue the struggle to find that balance.

The fact that policies and strategies are developed is one powerful effect of terrorism. Efforts to prevent and control attacks are ongoing around the globe. Efforts are strong, but emphases sometimes shift.

Combatants, such as the Palestinians, who do not have military forces capable of competing against the opposing force have used suicide bombers as a tactical act of warfare. But by virtue of President George W. Bush's statement in 2005 that the United States is involved in "a global struggle against violent extremism"[5] represents a shift in policy away from war and more toward diplomacy. "The continuing patriotism and tolerant nature of American Muslims need to be spotlighted more by Bush and given a leading voice in the U.S. effort to overcoming Islamic extremism abroad. That one step would help immediately to transform the 'war' into a more sustainable struggle for common human values," concluded the *Seattle Post*.[6] Not long after using the new terminology, President Bush said he was not in favor of the new term, "global struggle against violent extremism." He said, "no one checked with me."[7] Perhaps it is more a battle over language within the National Security Council, writes Larry Johnson.

Evident also is a shift in the approach of Muslim leaders in the

United States. After the 9/11 terrorist attacks, the leaders insisted that the terrorism had nothing to do with Islam. After the London attacks of 2005, policy shifted to constructive intervention "to persuade American Muslims — especially the young — to beware of preachers peddling extremism and terrorism."[8]

United States Domestic Security and Foreign Policy

In 2001, the U.S. Congress passed the Patriot Act, which gives the government new powers to catch terrorists.[9] Another initiative of Congress after 9/11 was the creation in 2002 of the Department of Homeland Security to defend the country from attacks on U.S. soil.[10] In July 2004, in its *Report*, the 9/11 Commission detailed the circumstances surrounding the September 11, 2001, attacks. On the face of it, the United States counterterrorism policy is straightforward:

First, make no concessions to terrorists and strike no deals;
Second, bring terrorists to justice for their crimes;
Third, isolate and apply pressure on states that sponsor terrorism to force them to change their behavior; and
Fourth, bolster the counterterrorism capabilities of those countries that work with the U.S. and require assistance.[11]

The policy also has measures concerning international terrorism, specifically, American hostages and weapons of mass destruction. These regulations state, "The U.S. Government will make no concessions to individuals or groups holding official or private U.S. citizens hostage.... Preventing terrorist access to or use of weapons of mass destruction ... is one of our government's highest priorities."[12] The government has other programs and initiatives under way in relation to these regulations.

In November 2002, when the Department of Homeland Security was created, it began greater Internet surveillance and computer security efforts.[13] The department also sought to have national preparedness that resonates down to the community levels.[14] Some communities and organizations interested in safety have developed literature to help citizens be better prepared. For example, Aurora Protection Specialists, located in Boca Raton, Florida, has developed an educational book to help citizens be prepared for a possible attack, *C/B/R/N: Chemical/Biological/Radiological/Nuclear Disaster Familiarization and Overview Manual.*[15]

The law that created the Department of Homeland Security contains provisions that have raised privacy concerns. Mariano-Florentino Cuellar wrote that one of the government's disturbing policies is focusing on a person's national origin or race, "commonly referred to as 'profiling.'"[16] She maintains that the use of profiling or any anti-terrorism enforcement strategy depends on the context. "Scientific precision is not possible in this area, and may not be desirable," Cuellar writes.[17] Benefits may outweigh the costs in a particular context. She concludes the justification for profiling is plausible. The demand for new enforcement strategies to reduce a terrorist threat that can never be completely removed helps to shape the justification.[18]

Governments must learn how to deal with the risk of possible attack. Edmund Andrews asks, "Should the federal government continue to be the main provider of terrorism risk insurance?"[19] If Congress doesn't set aside funds, then the cost of a repeat of September 11 "would all be borne in the form of future budget deficits."[20]

The Citizens for Legitimate Government says that a global myriad of activity to prevent terrorism is taking place. New laws appear and old laws are revisited. In July 2005, for example, the Italian parliament passed anti-terrorism laws allowing police to take DNA samples from suspects without formally charging them; precise plans will be revealed on how Britain's police will run the Internet in the event of an attack; and, in the United States, the Senate has made permanent most of the expiring and controversial provisions of the anti-terrorist USA Patriot Act, that allows "federal agents to use roving wiretaps and to search library and medical records."[21]

The Senate voted on December 22, 2005, to extend the USA Patriot Act for one month.[22] The extension gave Congress time in 2006 to revise the antiterrorism law that would have expired at the end of the year. Before the USA Patriot Act was to sunset on December 31, 2005, Senator Charles E. Grassley (R–Iowa) explains a few important provisions of the Senate version of the proposed new Patriot Act legislation: a limit of seven days after execution of a search warrant; and enhanced oversight of the Foreign Intelligence Surveillance Act that allows authorized review of business records in investigating persons alleged to have ties with terrorism.[23]

The U.S. Attorney General would report to Congress the number of applications made for orders approving requests for business records and the total number of granted in any of the following: items from a library; tangible items from a person or entity primarily engaged in the sale, rental, or delivery of books, journals, magazines, or other similar forms of print or digital communication; records related to the purchase of a firearm, health records; and tax returns.[24]

Some of the other issues of concern over government regulation are: expansion of the FOIA exemption framework and restriction of the public's ability to access sensitive government information[25]; a new set of investigative guidelines that Attorney General John Ashcroft issued in May 2002[26] that "permit federal law enforcement agents to attend any religious meeting or event that the public can attend. It is well settled that agents may carry concealed recording equipment"[27]; and "how do we protect our constitutional democracy without contravening constitutional and democratic commitments"[28] in issues such as prisoner abuse at the hands of American troops at Abu Ghraib and at Guantanamo Bay, Cuba; and red-flagging civil liberties and due process rights of airline passengers.[29]

I asked Rear Admiral D.M. Williams, Jr., USN (Ret.), "What is the relationship between domestic security and foreign policy?" He answered:

> The problem with terrorism in the United States is that it threatens the existence of our way of life. You increasingly see that in all manner of things. I was talking to a friend and he was complaining about the Patriot Act and the authority that government organizations were being given and I made the observation to him that when I used to attend federal law enforcement luncheons, there were present the heads of all the federal law enforcement agencies. There were 25 to 30 people in the room that were all head of some federal law enforcement organization. The structure was very fragmented. Why? It was so nobody would have enough authority. I think the United States consciously went about establishing a structure where nobody

would have authority to be abusing people's civil rights and intruding in their private lives. Well, then comes along the World Trade Center and people began talking about how law enforcement agencies were not cooperating with each other and you start sweeping all these agencies under the same umbrella and you begin to develop a structure where certain officials have a lot of authority and are going to start doing things that the average citizen would not have been subjected to in the past and would consider it very Orwellian. Some people would shrug and not think anything of it, but others would say, "We are really getting into civil liberties and intruding on our way of life and why?" It gets back to where we started this conversation. The more difficult it is to discern who the evildoers are, the more your rights and mine are going to be infringed upon, so that the people who are responsible for the protection of society at large will infer that they have no other means available to them than to infringe on people's rights.[30]

Look at the antagonism that is associated with the infringing on rights. From bitter personal experience, I have to say I am very fearful of giving people in positions of power authority and I think Lord Acton was precisely correct when he said, "Power corrupts and absolute power corrupts absolutely" because people who have that kind of authority, the more they exercise it, the more you become at risk for it being abused. So the response to the very circumstance that the terrorists are creating could be very destructive of our society and the way we live. To some extent, it already has. When I was a lieutenant commander working in the office of legislative affairs, Senator Hartke refused to be searched before he got an airplane. He said, "I'm a U. S. Senator. You don't need to do this to me." The people at the airlines said, "If you are not subjected to the search, you do not get on the airplane." He was very indignant about it. The upshot of that was he lost his next re-election bid because everyone out there was saying, "If I have to go through this, so does he." That was 1974. Look how far we have come.[31]

To the concern of how terrorists are to be treated by the United States, Williams replied:

The debate is going on now in the United States about the treatment of terrorists. Are they entitled to prisoner of war status? They

155

are not under any kind of organized command structure. They are not accountable to some government as in the case of a state actor. The military people are in uniform, they have a chain of command, they abide by the rules of warfare that have evolved over the centuries in terms of what constitutes legitimate targets and what does not. I defy anyone to show me a target of a bomber in Iraq in recent days that somebody would describe as a legitimate objective of combat.[32]

As Americans who have flown often since 9/11 know, thorough searches in airports are now routine. In the interview, Williams gives insight into practices all citizens now experience as a result of terrorism in the following discussion:

MW: I have not seen any full body cavity searches at the airport, but I have read some articles in the newspaper about women being required to disrobe.[33]

RS: I have been traveling some and at one airport a woman was required to remove her prosthetic leg. I thought that was a bit much. My hometown airport has the most thorough searches of all airports that I have frequented.

MW: I have to say that the best airport I have been in was O'Hare in Chicago. I brought my wife, Libby, through there in a wheelchair. I could understand that was going to create some concern for them. They handled the situation very well and we got through there in expedited fashion. I gave them high marks. I have queued up in Dulles International Airport for 15 to 20 minutes waiting to go through security because they had so many problems and when I got to the security checkpoint, I had to take off my shoes and socks. I had a fingernail file in my briefcase which I guess gave the same signature on an X-ray machine as a pocket knife. I was subjected to some real scrutiny. The third time they ran the briefcase through the X-ray, I realized that and said, "I think I left a fingernail file in there." So when they came back, I told the guy, "Open it and see if there is a fingernail file in the bottom of that pouch."[34]

On the issue of recordkeeping on U.S. citizens, Williams affirmed that the country has "people wanting to keep records on financing. People wanting to keep all sorts of records about your life." I told him "That bothers me." He agreed, "It should. I have seen what people can do with that kind of information and it is not good."[35]

Continued Human Rights Watch

One of the concerns about human rights involves Chechen women. Peter Baker reports that, for many years, Russian soldiers have stormed into homes in Chechnya in the middle of the night to seize young men claiming they are separatist fighters. Often the men were tortured or killed or they disappeared. With the increase in female suicide bombers, Russian forces are abducting Chechen women from their homes. The Russian military denies seizing women. They say the incidents are invented. Human rights investigators are concerned.[36]

Human rights advocates report "many innocent Muslim-appearing women are suffering from a generalized apprehension about 'black widows.'"[37] Human rights activists believe that the authorities' reaction to attacks by increasingly scrutinizing Chechen women leads to wrongful imprisonment, discrimination and abuse.[38]

Does the strategy of a continued human rights watch have any effect on terrorism? I asked Williams whether he believed that it did. He said:

> To a certain extent, it may have some impact. You have to abide by laws in order to be seen doing that, but I am not sure that it has much of an impact on preventing terrorism. Although people would say, "If you mistreat prisoners and they are subsequently released, you have created an enemy in the prisoner and everybody that is close to the prisoner — family, relatives, and friends." So, to that extent you might have some effect, but I don't see that strong of a correlation there.[39]

New Approaches by the United States

One word in Barbara Ehrenreich's new counterterrorism strategy is feminism. "Or, if that's too incendiary, try the phrase 'human rights for women.'"[40] After reading Carmen Bin Ladin's book, *Inside the Kingdom: My Life in Saudi Arabia*, a sustained and serious effort to gain human rights for women, Ehrenreich proposes a new worldwide approach to fighting terrorism. If this country were to embrace a feminist strategy against the insurgency, we'd have to begin by addressing our own dismal record on women's rights.

Some argue that the role of women in suicide bombing is too small in proportion to that of men to justify attention. I do not agree with this premise, but the conclusion could follow that we need to focus on the larger issues of the entire groups that perpetrate these acts. In so doing, we may find some solutions.

In a 2005 interview with Reuters about his new book, *Dying to Win: The Strategic Logic of Suicide Terrorism*, Robert A. Pape said that a broad misunderstanding of the terrorism issue is taking the U.S.-led war in the wrong direction. The war could, in fact, be fueling an increase in suicide terrorism. Before the U.S.-led invasion of Iraq in March 2003, he said there was "never in Iraq's history a suicide terrorist attack" but since then they have doubled every year. Pape has compiled a comprehensive database on every suicide terrorist attack in the world since 1980, using Arabic, Hebrew, Tamil and Russian-language sources. By contrast, the U.S. government did not begin collecting data until 2000, which provides it with only "a partial understanding" of what has been driving suicide terrorism, Pape believes.[41]

After the terrorist attacks in London on July 7, 2005, Pape said, "Since 2002, Al Qaeda has been involved in at least 17 bombings that killed more than 700 people — more attacks and victims than in all the years before 9/11 combined."[42]

Pape's study shows that most attackers are citizens of Saudi Arabia and other Persian Gulf countries where United States troops have been stationed since 1990. The remaining attackers come from America's allies in the Muslim world — Turkey, Egypt, Pakistan, Indonesia and Morocco.[43] Since 2002, 18 of the countries in which citizens have been killed are those that, Osama bin Laden has said, support American invasions of Afghanistan and Iraq.

Retired General Wesley K. Clark, former Supreme Allied commander of NATO, agrees that the United States must shift a large part of its focus from the elimination of state sponsors to an emphasis on the home front where "national intelligence efforts, special police activities and local community policing efforts" can be more effective.[44]

Specifically, Clark suggests, "To win this war, we must defeat the ideology of terrorism, depriving angry young people of their ability to justify their hateful actions in the name of Allah."[45] Creating meaningful dialogue with Islamists would help us defeat the ideology. Second, he suggests that, in addition to the airways, we must protect U.S. mass transit, rail and other infrastructure. Third, form a volunteer civil defense effort. Fourth, efforts to stop the proliferation of weapons have not progressed as well as they should. For example, the failure of the administration at the recent review conference to strengthen the Nuclear Non-Proliferation Treaty. Fifth, the United States should also intensify efforts to end the Iranian and North Korean nuclear programs, and bring increased resourcing to the control of Russian fissile materials. Sixth, the United States should be working to develop and implement a verifiable biological weapons treaty and strengthen the Chemical Weapons Convention.[46]

Al-Qaeda's post 9/11 strategy was outlined in a lengthy al-Qaeda planning document discovered by Norwegian intelligence. The document said that spectacular attacks on the United States, like those of 9/11, would be ineffective in forcing the United States and its allies to leave Iraq. It proposed that a more effective strategy would be to attack U.S. European allies, in particular, Britain, Poland and Spain. The attack in Spain has happened.[47] On March 11, 2004, Madrid suffered a series of coordinated terrorist bombings on a commuter train system. The attacks killed 191 people and wounded 1,460.[48] In July 2005, Britain was attacked. Only Poland has yet to feel the force of an al-Qaeda attack.

Pape believes terrorists have not been weakened, but have simply successfully changed course enough to make al-Qaeda leaders confident they will succeed in their goal of causing America and its allies to withdraw.[49] Scott Atran says that, if the U.S. is to be successful in preempting and preventing terrorism, it has to identify "the sacred values in different cultures and how they compete for people's affections is surely a first step in learning how to prevent those values from spiraling into mortal conflict between societies."[50]

Preston Taran contends that the United States' lack of "understanding of any belief system outside of their corrupt one causes them to see no distinction between honorable death and suicide."[51] Most important is to recognize the humiliation of a people. The charge that Palestinian parents do not care for their children is not true; they do not wish to see them die in battle. Whose acts are more gruesome or evil is a judgment that the United States and its media outlets make. But Taran replies, "Let no person say martyrdom operations are more brutal than gunning down schoolchildren with their books in hand. Or a father trying to protect his son, and having to witness the bullet killing his son in his arms. Or the cripples which dot the landscape due to Zionist disregard for Palestinian lives."[52]

All religions and many quasireligious ideologies are based on sacred values that in turn are associated with emotions that support feelings of cultural identity and trust. Beliefs "are amplified into moral obligations to strike out against perceived opponents no matter the cost when conditions of relative deprivation get to a point where suicide terrorists actively seek alternatives because of lack of political and economic opportunity," Scott Atran writes.[53]

"In times of crisis, every society routinely calls on some of its own people to sacrifice their lives for the general good of the body politic," Atran reminds. But for militant jihadists, crisis never lets up "and extreme sacrifice is necessary as long as there are nonbelievers (kuffar) in the world."[54]

If political and economic opportunity is provided, the downward spiral can be prevented. It is much more difficult to prevent terrorism once the spiral begins. Rather than focusing on hard lines of defense, a more sensible approach is to persuade Muslim communities to stop supporting religious schools and charities that feed terrorist networks, Atran contends.[55]

What Atran says has been borne out over the past three decades. Initially and officially, Islamist terrorists were concerned with putting into office religious dictatorships in Muslim nations. After two decades they met with defeat, and so they turned to non–Muslim or "infidel" nations.[56] Muslim nations had a peaceful coexistence with the Islamist terrorists by allowing certain activities as long as the terrorists did not attack the governments such as Syria. With the U.S. overthrow of an Islamic government in Afghanistan and the invasion of Iraq, Syria and Saudi Arabia have to deal with the local radicals. Syria is reconsidering its policy. In Saudi Arabia, the radicals not only began terrorizing attacks at home, they also rushed to Iraq to fight. But as American forces are seen in North Africa, those countries as well as others, are witnessing a decline in terrorist activities.[57]

The United States needs to work with the international community as it works to combat terrorism. The mission of the United States should be modified by: not insisting on planetary rights of interference because the government believes the United States' "vision of civilization is humanity's last great hope or that U.S. national security depends on the world accepting a model" of success of one size fits all.[58]

Continued Global Intervention

Research indicates that the use of female and male suicide bombers will continue, and that use of female suicide bombers will increase.[59] "The war in Iraq has energized so many disparate groups that the jihadist network is better prepared than ever to carry on without bin Laden."[60] President George W. Bush has responded by conducting a broad internal review of its anti-terrorism policies. The administration may shift the focus from capturing al-Qaeda leaders to a broader push to defeat "violent extremism."[61]

The Role of the United States

The U.S. should provide leadership, diplomatically, economically, informationally and militarily to combat suicide terrorism, concludes Debra D. Zedalis.[62] The ability to cope with terrorism depends, Yoram Schweitzer believes, on three elements: "the political handling of the basic problems that give rise to the attacks, proactive military and intelligence action against the perpetrators, and the public's ability to endure."[63]

Military action alone is not successful. Scott Atran contends,

> For example, from 1993 through 2003, 311 Palestinian suicide attackers launched themselves against Israeli targets. In the first seven years of suicide bombing, 70 percent (43 of 61 attempts) were successful in killing other people. From the start of the second Intifada in September 2000 through 2003, however, although the success rate declined to 52 percent, the number of attacks increased from 61 to 250, with 129 of those being successful (up from 43).[64]

The abundance of attacks happened even though the State Department funding for strategies to counter and combat terrorism overseas increased 133 percent from September 11, 2001, through fiscal year 2003, according to the final U.S. federal interagency report. These figures include the Iraq conflict that was originally announced as a war necessary to deny weapons of mass destruction to al-Qaeda, the U.S. Department of Defense budget increases and emergency supplemental measures. The bill for foreign operations in the war on terrorism into 2004 exceeded $200 billion.[65] Spending on terrorism is not wasted, but the United States cannot rely exclusively on the military.

Atran proposes a three-layered approach to combat suicide terrorism: protecting targeted populations, use of military and intelligence and work for an understanding of the root causes of terrorism to make it less attractive for recruits. "There is no evidence that most people who support suicide actions hate Americans' internal cultural freedoms, but rather every indication that they oppose U.S. foreign policies, particularly regarding the Middle East." There is an apparent direct correlation between U.S. military aid to states that are politically unstable or ethnically divided and that had human rights abuses by those governments with the rise in terrorism.

Following the Money

Part of the United States' counterterrorism policy pertains to money laundering. "Significant parts of our nation's strategy is to cut off financial support to terrorists. Starving terrorists of their access to money, resources, and support is second only to bringing them to justice in our national strategy."[66] Rear Admiral D.M. Williams speaks to the benefits of following the money:

> One of the policies that I like the most about what the United States has done of late is there has been a much greater emphasis on trying to follow the money that supports the terrorists, because the chances of cutting off the funding are probably higher than other efforts like turning people over for trial, because a country could work to cut off the funding not in the public eye. It is easier to encourage countries to cut off funding because it is not subjected to all of the public scrutiny that would evoke response from

people in their country who support "the cause" that has prompted the terrorist act. These people would object to turning people over for trial but they might never be aware of the efforts to cut off funding.[67]

[Following the money] is a big deal. There is a lot of money flowing to terrorist groups from a lot of different places. Some of it has state sponsorship. Where there is state sponsorship, for example, Iran, you have to get diplomatic pressure from other countries and sometimes that is difficult. The French tend to take a laissez-faire attitude about all these terrorist events and people who were living in France who were alleged terrorists until some of the terrorist activity began to occur in France. Then they became more serious about cooperating in other initiatives associated with it. All that dynamic is coursing through this. Again, with respect to our international response, I do not make any distinction between men and women. I can appreciate the dynamic about target identification and it makes the problem much more difficult, but, in terms of what we should do as a country and the policy that we should be following, I do not make any gender distinction.[68]

Commenting on current day military conflicts, Ray Youngblut, a World War II army veteran, said it well: "The United States does not know who it is mad at."[69] Which, indeed, makes fighting difficult in modern warfare.

Global Intervention

Is continued global intervention a possible strategy for the future? President Bush's policy of going where the terrorists are and rooting them out, as Williams said, is one strategy. He responded:

That is directly related to terrorists. There are other initiatives in proliferation and security that are not specifically directed at terrorists as much as they are directed at countries that are not responsible if they get their hands on some of these nuclear materials and weapons of mass destruction. The president's proliferation and security initiative is directed at that kind of smuggling, but it will have an impact on terrorist activity because some of that material will be caught in these sweeps, as surely as we are talking, whether or not it is intended for terrorists. A couple of years ago, armaments destined for the Palestinians were intercepted by the Israelis. This operation resulted from attempts to prevent materials from going into Iraq, but it ended up catching materials that were destined for Palestine. The president and his administration have a very active agenda on that score about trying to stop illegal arms trade and proliferation of weapons. Other people treat it as an arms control problem but, notwithstanding that is my business, those sometimes tend to have less effect principally because the people you are talking about are not going to comply with those kinds of agreements anyway. So in a terrorist circumstance, I don't think the arms control approach is a particularly useful tool.[70]

In my book *The Women of Afghanistan Under the Taliban*, I found that arms and munitions were being sold to al-Qaeda, before 9/11, by Pakistan, United Arab Emirates and Saudi Arabia. That has to be a factor. Williams responded:

Some people would describe that as state sponsorship of terrorism. Some would say that it was coincidental to state sponsorship of terrorism. I think those kinds of actions will get rooted out by following the money.[71]

Preparedness and Training

Jennifer Hardwick, senior director of the Terrorism Research Center, Inc., near Washington, D.C., stresses that more training is needed on how to identify suicide bombers and what to do in case an attacker strikes. She sees a trend in her audiences. She says:

My most pressing concern is that the U.S. is completely unprepared for suicide bombings, especially by a woman. Homeland Security officials (from DHS and beyond) are not trained on how to identify or what to do in case of a suicide bomber. Airport officials might have nominal training, but school officials, mall security, office guard services, public transit — let alone the civilian population — [are without adequate knowledge and training], and we would see absolute pandemonium if it happened (or when it happens).[72]

In December 2005 the former September 11 Commission reported that the United States is not prepared for the next terror attack.[73]

Debra D. Zedalis writes,

> The official profile of a typical terrorist—developed by the [Department of Homeland Security] DHS to scrutinize visa applicants and resident aliens—applies only to men. Under a program put in place after September 11, 2001, males aged between 16–45 are subject to special scrutiny; women are not.[74]

Zedalis points out that despite the need for a more adequate profile of female suicide bombers there is a level of awareness by some. The DHS Alert 03–025 provided warnings of male and female suicide bombers, and in December 2002, New York City was on heightened alert over a possible attack by a female suicide bomber. But Zedalis, too, concludes, "Terrorists seek out vulnerabilities in the enemy government's countermeasures, so lack of scrutiny of women entering the United States could encourage al-Qaeda to use them."[75]

Lisa Kruger's thesis for the Joint Military Intelligence College, *Gender and Terrorism: Motivations of Female Terrorists*, challenges and

> [I]dentifies unintentional gender bias that severely inhibits the Intelligence Community (IC) from making accurate assessments about the motivations of female terrorists.... The IC predominantly focuses on profiling male terrorists. Gender bias leads analysts to discount the threat when women conduct terrorist attacks for the same reasons as men. This has left the U.S. vulnerable to terrorist acts conducted by women.[76]

The United States has responded to the attacks of 9/11 with much effort to prevent a recurrence. Part of the continued effort must be increased awareness of the female suicide bomber. By so doing, as a nation, the United States can release itself from a false consciousness to a collective consciousness. All over the world, women are now part of the tactic of war.

9

Analysis

Women could very well be the perpetrators of the next 9/11.
— Heather A. Andrews,
*Veiled Jihad: The Threat of Female
Islamic Suicide Terrorists*[1]

Although it may not be possible to draw one profile that represents all female martyrs, the emergence of a continuum is possible. Some women, such as Dhanu, have raw courage and appear to have been resolute in their missions. Others, such as Zarema Muzhikhoyeva, have more difficulty following through but have an acute awareness of the consequences of not completing their mission. In the October 23, 2002, hostage-taking of the Moscow Dubrovka House of Culture, Chechen women worked with the men but lacked decision-making power. On September 1, 2004, over 30 attackers took over the Beslan School No. 1 in North Ossetia, a southern Russian Republic. Nur-Pashi Kulayev survived the attack and his court testimony provides insight into the female bombers who participated. Some hostage takers, he said, objected to taking children hostage, wanting instead to seize the nearby police station. During the trial at the North Ossetian Supreme Court, Kulayev testified, "Two of the militants were female suicide-bombers who openly disagreed with the Colonel [the leader] about the children hostages and were killed when he detonated their bombs by remote control."[2] These particular female bombers displayed courage and had a personal limit on whom and when they were willing to kill when they ask that the children not be taken hostage. Women combatants who do not speak up or appear to have no authority as in the case of the Moscow Dubrovka House of Culture also may have displayed a type of courage.

Information about the lives of suicide attackers is seriously needed to identify risk factors that led them to this type of mission. Listening to their stories does not dishonor the innocent victims but failing to listen will bring more bombings and more victims, states Basel Saleh.[3] The Rev. Dr. Naim Ateek reminds us of our humanity when he says, "When healthy, beautiful, and intelligent young men and women set out to kill and be killed, something is basically wrong in a world that has not heard their anguished cry for justice. These young people deserve to live along with all those whom they have caused to die."[4] As more research on female bombers becomes available, we will have more complete profiles about their lives and their courage with the hope of saving their lives and the lives of those who would be killed.

Emile Durkheim believed it is more important to understand that suicide results from social causes than to know the type of suicide committed. The hypotheses that state that the various incidents of private life are preeminently the causes of suicide do not focus on the real causes. The women combatants who engage in suicide attacks are responding to a force common in their environment, such as desire for freedom, that inclines them to give their lives willingly. The inclination to commit suicide has its source in the moral constitution of groups within a society.[5]

Lisa Kruger, graduate of the Joint Military Intelligence College, in her *Gender and Terrorism: Motivations of Female Terrorists*, demonstrates that, in many cases, the personal reasons women commit martyrdom may not be that different from men, and cites as an example, nationalism.[6] Having been raped in war is not limited to women. Men are raped in war, even though the literature does not much document male rape.[7] "The crime of rape is a human crime, not a gender crime. It's a crime of power, and certainly can be as devastating to either gender."[8]

Mia Bloom concludes, "The reasons for women's participation vary greatly from country to country. Past experience shows that there is generally no single overriding motivation, but rather a number of overlapping motivations working in concert."[9]

My friend's philosophy that "a bomber is a bomber" is true. The devastating results for bombers of either gender are the same. When suicide bombing as a tactic of warfare is reckoned with, the thought in V.G. Julie Rajan's reflection will dissipate: "Recent interest in female suicide bombers is rooted in the seemingly unlimited and unknown power they possess."[10] A civilian woman said to me: "So what. She doesn't live to enjoy her accomplishment." If we believe in Durkheim's concept of altruistic suicide, then living to see an accomplishment is not the goal, dying to realize that goal is. This belief system is a mystery to many. Combatants in the conventional military also are keenly aware they may die so that their nation might stand. When some female bombers have ulterior motives as well, such as avenging honor for their families or themselves, their bombing, too, will be a source of their power and thus command our attention. Rajan writes that their incalculable power lies "as women continue to participate in suicide bombing they symbolically assume the power to disrupt traditional patriarchal female gender notions and thereby destabilize current social political, economic and ethic and religious identities worldwide."[11]

The aim of Raphael Israeli's study of women in the Palestinian-Israeli conflict was to describe the "fascinating process" that Palestinian women use in becoming "Islamikaze" [suicide bomber] martyrs to achieve higher status. He states:

> The paradox is that—while self-immolating young women are glorified posthumously, there seems to be no change in the fortunes of the living women, just as the glorification of the dead Islamikaze males does not raise the status of the deprived youth.[12]

Beyler also points out that the equity females acquire in war has not carried over to gaining equality in societies in times to peace.[13] Yet, some LTTE women are reintegrating into society with a strength that is respected.

In spite of women's participation in suicide bombing, Yoran Schweitzer writes, "women are not likely to take on a dominant role in the terror campaign."[14] Yet, organizations, like Hamas, are sometimes very practical and less ideological. Even those groups based in ideology have evolved from a support role for women to a direct role, as the Islamic Jihad has.

We have but to look at Raphael Israeli's timeline of the development of the "Islamikaze" to be reminded that the use of women in suicide bombing is a tactic of war. Israeli's description of the Palestinian-Israeli conflict leaves no doubt that when we discuss this conflict we should do so in those terms:

The struggle, with its multi-dimensional participants and targets, has acquired some characteristics of a total war, with an awesome impact with respect to casualties, damage, destruction and political reverberations.[15]

Many civilian men, women and children die as a result of war. Jefferson D. Reynolds states it well:

Although the incidence of collateral damage in U.S. combat operations has declined since World War II due to improved technology and strategy, the number of civilians killed in conflict has generally increased. The relationship between concealment warfare strategies and high numbers of civilian casualties generated is evident from conflicts in virtually every corner of the world from Cambodia and Uganda to Kosovo and Colombia.[16]

Reynolds reports that an estimated 62.2 million civilian men, women and children compared to 43.9 million military personnel have been killed in conflict since 1900. The incidence of civilian deaths has increased since the 1949 Geneva Conventions. Reynolds writes that concealment is one cause of the rising numbers. "Concealment warfare is the method of choice with higher frequency among adversaries."[17] This applies also to the Israeli-Palestinian conflict, where civilians in both countries have lost their lives from the fire of the other country.[18]

As in all wars, casualties are not inflicted on one side only. And, although women in conflicts everywhere may cause the death of other women and children (as do men), Israeli presents one view of what the deaths of these Palestinian women may mean:

Ironically, the attempt of young women to make their voice heard could be counter-productive. Their struggle could attract outside sympathy and help, but the indiscriminate killings of other women (and children) might estrange potential Western sympathizers. The Muslims who encourage the women are also those who would deny them equal status sought.[19]

Clara Beyler offers a most sobering insight, "For the generations of post-suicide bombers, one problem caused by these women is that children have a new kind of heroes to look up to: suicide bombers. They take them as role models, and want to grow up to die."[20] While Beyler's insight is particularly alarming when observing the conflict in Sri Lanka where children are half of the population, it causes alarm in the Palestinian and Chechen societies as well.

Observing the fate of female suicide bombers, the deaths of bombers, and societal inequities toward women, commits me to the view that their participation is a tactic of war. Israeli's conclusion contains some sad realities. Indiscriminate killing is not a by-product of female combatants alone. I concluded my book *Women at War: Gender Issues of Americans in Combat* with the thought that in all wars, "women have always been part of for whom the bell tolls in war."[21] Linda Grant DePauw's book, *Battle Cries and Lullabies: A Brief History of Women in War*, covers the period 650 B.C. to the twentieth century. DePauw demonstrates two elements about women and war. One factor is "women have always and everywhere been involved in war."[22] A second is, warfare in the twentieth and twenty-first centuries has seen the "killing of a larger number of noncombatants, most of them women and children ... called collateral damage and ... considered an unavoidable byproduct of combat."[23] Female suicide bombers, as a tactic of war, produces collateral damage as well.

In *Women at War*, I conclude that women have fought in wars as combatants whether or not they were recognized as such.[24] Many return to societies that did not grant equity. In the early 1990s,[25] the United States made progress on including women in combat roles, but the United States needs to do more. In spite of women serving in ground armed conflict in Iraq, Congress in 2004 debated whether to allow women to serve in combat even when they already are.[26] Not many of these women are assigned to career paths that enable them to reach the highest ranks and so they do not receive the same pay as the males who served alongside them in combat.

Lisa Kruger finds support for the hypothesis that women are motivated to participate in terrorist activities for the same reasons as men. She writes, "These findings are vital for intelligence analysts to make accurate assessments about the motivations of female terrorists.... The notion that women are differently motivated than men is largely the result of gender biased reporting."[27] Women and men have the same basic psychological needs and motivations. Reporting characterizes women as passive and motivated only by coercion, manipulation, or desperation and when they commit violent acts they are seen as more ruthless than their males. Kruger says:

> The notion that women are motivated to participate in terrorist activities for different reasons than men is largely the result of gender biased expectations of women's role in violent organizations. Like men, women are motivated by nationalism, ideology, political agendas, revenge for personal suffering, and sense of duty. If we assume women are motivated by gender-specific reasons, we will fail to recognize women as legitimate rational actors in violent organizations.[28]

An interviewee on the Discovery Channel's presentation "Suicide Bombers: Cult of Death," asked, "Who calls it suicide? The occupiers. We call it martyrdom. Martyrs are fighters. We don't have weapons. We do have people who use themselves as a weapon. This is war, not suicide."[29]

The program ended on a note worth remembering: Martyr attacks are no longer confined to a conflict. They are now global, from the battlefields of Iraq to London, the latest evolution of the weaponry of chaos.

Kruger discusses a concept called Groupthink. She writes that it "occurs when individuals do not question the perceived consensus of a group even if some individuals do not agree. Groupthink frequently occurs when analyzing female terrorists because there is limited data and a general concurrence on expected gender roles. As a result, biased assumptions and generalizations are unintentionally perpetuated."[30] Women martyrs are part of the evolution of the weaponry confusion. Heather A. Andrews writes that the government's precautions since 9/11 have a narrow focus. This focus is on certain characteristics that arouse suspicions similar to the perpetrators of the 9/11 attacks, allowing other persons to avoid suspicion. Andrews states, "That being said, the issue becomes one of intelligence interest because these practices are leading to a serious security gap."[31] It will be crucial to examine the tactics of these women in war if we are to avoid other 9/11s.

Abbreviations and Glossary

al-Aqsa martyrs brigade: Palestinian nationalists militant group.

al-Qaeda network: Islamist militant group founded by Osama bin Laden.

Allah: God.

altruistic suicide: suicide that results from strong social bonds. An act of duty and the demands of society oblige suicide.

Anomie: suicide that results from the breakdown of the influence of social norms on society members. The weakening of the social bond.

Armed Islamic Group: Algerian Islamist militant group.

Chechen rebels: militant group committed to establishing an independent Chechnya.

collective consciousness: ideas, norms and social expectations held important by all societal members.

Eelam: freedom.

false consciousness: the ideology that dominates the consciousness of exploited groups and classes and justifies and perpetuates their exploitation.

Fatah: Palestinian political group.

fatwah/fatwa: edict or a formal legal opinion or decree issued by a Muslim authority.

FSB (Federalnaya Sluthba Betopasnosti): Russian Federal Security Service.

Hadith: a traditional story about the Prophet Muhammad.

Hamas: Islamist militant group.

Hezbollah: "Party of God," an Islamist militant group mainly in Lebanon.

intifada: Arabic language term for uprising.

ISA: Israel Security Agency.

IDF: Israeli Defense Forces.

IPC area: Location of the Israeli-Palestinian Conflict, including the four territories of Israel, West Bank, Gaza Strip and Lebanon.

Ismalis-Nizari: Muslim fighters in the eleventh century.

Jamaat al-Islamiyya: Islamist militant group, Egyptian Islamic Jihad, Egypt.

Jihad: holy war.

Kashmir Militant Extremists: Islamist militant group in Kashmir.

***Koran* or *Qur'an*:** Muslim holy book.

LTTE: Liberation Tigers of Tamil Eelam, insurgent group.

Mujahedeen-e-Khalq: Iranian rebel group.

PIJ: Palestinian Islamic Jihad.

PLO: Palestine Liberation Organization, the umbrella group of political and militant groups headed by Yasser Arafat, whose Fatah faction is the biggest single component.

PKK: known as the PKK after its Kurdish name, Partiya Karkeren Kurdistan, usually called the Kurdistan Workers Party, militant group that sought a separate Kurdish state.

***shaheed* or *shahid*:** the Arab word for martyr. Someone who dies in the way of Allah.

***shahida*:** feminized version of *shaheed* or *shahid*.

social facts: often referred to as social forces that are influences put on members by their society or a social institution.

SLA: South Lebanese Army.

SSNP/PPS: Syrian Socialist Nationalist Party. PPS is the Syrian name, Parti Populaire Syrien. A Syrian militant group involved in the Lebanon Civil War.

Chapter Notes

Preface

1. Emile Durkheim, *Suicide: A Study in Sociology,* translated by John A. Spaulding and George Simpson, edited by George Simpson (New York: Free Press, 1897/1996), 48.

2. Debra D. Zedalis, *Female Suicide Bombers* (Carlisle, PA: Strategic Studies Institute, U.S. Army War College), June 2004, 1. April 2, 2005, http://www.carlisle.army.mil/ssi/pdffiles/00373.pdf.

3. Durkheim, 22.

4. Durkheim, 16.

5. Durkheim, 22–23, 25–26, 37; Lisa Ling, "Female Suicide Bombers: Dying to Kill," National Geographic Channel, December 13, 2004.

6. Robert A. Pape, *Dying to Win: The Strategic Logic of Suicide Terrorism* (New York: Random House), 2005, 211.

7. Ling.

8. Durkheim, 125.

9. Durkheim, 225.

10. George Ritzer and Douglas J. Goodman, *Sociological Theory, 6th ed.* (Boston: McGraw-Hill, 2004), 91.

11. Durkheim, 288.

12. Durkheim, 14.

13. Pape, 186–187.

14. Pape, 200–201.

15. Pape, 197–198.

16. Jacqueline Rose, "Deadly Embrace: Book Reviews: *My Life Is a Weapon: A Modern History of Suicide Bombing* by Christoph Reuter, trans. Helena Ragg-Kirkby, and *Army of Roses: Inside the World of Palestinian Women Suicide Bombers* by Barbara Victor," *London Review of Books,* 26 no. 21, November 4, 2004. April 9, 2005, http://www.lrb.co.uk/v26/n21/rose01_.html.

17. Durkheim, 52.

18. Ritzer and Goodman, 93, 107.

19. Ritzer and Goodman, 92.

20. Mariya Rasner, "'Black Widow' Fears Surround a Russian Verdict," *Women's eNews,* February 6, 2005. April 9, 2005, http://www.womensenews.org/article.cfm/dyn/aid/2175/context/cover/; Peter Baker, Foreign Service, "'New Stage' of Fear for Chechen Women: Russian Forces Suspected in Abductions," *Washington Post,* October 19, 2004, A12. April 9, 2005, http://www.washingtonpost.com/wp-dyn/articles/A43296-2004Oct18.html?sub=AR.

21. Zedalis, 1.

22. Zedalis, 12–13.

Chapter 1

1. Plato, The *Republic,* with an English translation by Paul Shorey (New York: G.P. Putnam's Sons), 1930–1935, 452a, 473d.

2. National Commission on Terrorist Attacks upon the United States, *The 9/11 Commission Report: Final Report of the National Commission on Terrorist Attacks Upon the United States* (New York: W.W. Norton), 2004, 1.

3. Paul Thompson, "Abridged 9/11 Timeline," n.d. September 26, 2005, http://billstclair.com/911timeline/main/timelineshort.html.

4. Michael Howard and Ewen MacAskill, "Female Suicide Bomber Kills Six in Iraqi City Declared Free of Terrorists: New Tactics on Two Fronts: First Woman to Detonate Bomb Since 2003 Invasion; 30 Wounded as They Queue to Join Army," *The Guardian* (London), September 29, 2005, S. International, 13.

5. Heather A. Andrews, *Veiled Jihad: The Threat of Female Islamic Suicide Terrorists,* master of science, strategic intelligence thesis, Joint Military Intelligence College, July 2005, 1.

6. Jennifer Hardwick, email, September 9, 2005.

7. Lisa Kruger, *Gender and Terrorism: Motivations of Female Terrorists,* master of science,

strategic intelligence thesis, Joint Military Intelligence College, July 2005, 1.

8. Yoram Schweitzer, "Suicide Bombings: The Ultimate Weapon?" August 7, 2001. April 15, 2005, http://www.ict.org.il/articles/article det.cfm?articleid=373; Debra D. Zedalis, *Female Suicide Bombers* (Carlisle PA: Strategic Studies Institute, U.S. Army War College), June 2004, 2. April 2, 2005, http://www.carlisle. army.mil/ssi/pdffiles/00373.pdf.

9. Yoram Schweitzer, "Suicide Terrorism: Development & Characteristics," April 21, 2000. April 15, 2005, http://www.ict.org.il/ articles/articledet.cfm?articleid=112.

10. Robert A. Pape, *Dying to Win: The Strategic Logic of Suicide Terrorism* (New York: Random House), 2005, 11.

11. Christoph Reuter, *My Life Is a Weapon: A Modern History of Suicide Bombing*, translated by Helena Ragg-Kirkby, (Princeton, N.J.: Princeton University Press), 2004, 4.

12. Clara Beyler, "Messengers of Death: Female Suicide Bombers," February 12, 2003. April 10, 2005, http://www.ict.org.il/articles/ articledet.cfm?articleid=470.

13. Lt Gen Jan C. Huly, "Terrorist Bombing of the Marine Barracks, Beirut, Lebanon," *Henderson Hall News*, October 23, 2003. May 24, 2005, http://www.arlingtoncemetery.net/terror.htm.

14. Sgt. Melvin Lopez Jr., "Terrorist Bombing of the Marine Barracks, Beirut, Lebanon," *Henderson Hall News*, October 23, 2003. May 24, 2005, http://www.arlingtoncemetery.net/ terror.htm.

15. Shaul Kimhi and Shemuel Even, "Who Are the Palestinian Suicide Bombers," *Terrorism and Political Violence*, 16, no. 4 (Winter 2004), 816.

16. Stephen Mulvey, "Russia's Suicide Bomb Nightmare." BBC News Online, February 6, 2004. September 26, 2005, http://news.bbc. co.uk/1/hi/world/europe/3020231.stm.

17. Council on Foreign Relations, "Terrorism: Q&A: Is Suicide Terrorism Becoming More Common?" 2005. May 25, 2005, http:// www.cfr.org/reg_issues.php?id=13|||1.

18. Kimhi and Even, 816.

19. Beyler, "Messengers of Death."

20. Boaz Ganor, "Defining Terrorism: Is One Man's Terrorist Another Man's Freedom Fighter?" International Policy Institute for Counter-Terrorism, June 25, 2001. April 29, 2005, http://www.ict.org.il/.

21. Beyler, "Messengers of Death."

22. Beyler, "Messengers of Death."

23. Preston Taran, "Martyrdom," Arabic Media Internet Network, June 1, 2005. June 22, 2005, http://www.amin.org/eng/uncat/2005/ june/june1.html.

24. Raphael Israeli, "The Promise of an Afterlife Motivates Suicide Bombers," in Lauri S. Friedman (ed.), *What Motivates Suicide Bombers?* (San Diego: Greenhaven, 2005), 36.

25. Zedalis, 1.

26. Robert A. Pape, "Nationalism," in Friedman (ed.), 45.

27. Scott Atran, "Mishandling Suicide Terrorism," *The Washington Quarterly*, Summer 2004, 68–69. May 26, 2005, http://www.twq. com/04summer/docs/04summer_atran.pdf.

28. Pape, *Dying to Win*, 3, 6.

29. Julian Borger, "Rice Changed Terrorism Report," *The Guardian*, April 23, 2005. April 23, 2005, http://www.guardian.co.uk/usa/story/ 0,12271,1468541,00.html.

30. Lauri S. Friedman (ed.), *What Motivates Suicide Bombers?*, 5.

31. Atran, 68–69.

32. Itamar Marcus, "Palestinian Authority TV Portrays Palestinian Martyrdom as a Christian Ideal," May 30, 2002. August 3, 2005, http://www.israel-wat.com/p4_eng.htm.

33. Palestinian Media Watch, translator, "The Beat of the Words," Palestinian Authority Television, May 30, 2002, screening of clip on May 5, 2002. August 3, 2005, http://www. israel-wat.com/p4_eng.htm.

34. Emile Durkheim, *Suicide: A Study in Sociology*, translated by John A. Spaulding and George Simpson, edited by George Simpson (New York: Free Press), 1897/1996, 52.

35. George Ritzer and Douglas J. Goodman, *Sociological Theory, 6th ed.* (Boston: McGraw-Hill, 2004), 93, 107.

36. Peter David, "Islam Advocates Suicide Terrorism," in Friedman (ed.), 10.

37. Rosemarie Skaine, "Neither Afghan Nor Islam," "Symposium on September 11 2001: Terrorism, Islam and the West," *Ethnicities* 2, Issue 2 (June 2002): 143.

38. David, 15.

39. Pape, "Nationalism Motivates," 44.

40. Robert A. Pape in Patricia Wilson, "Religion, Suicide Terrorism Link Disputed in Book," *Reuters*, June 3, 2005. June 4, 2005, http://news.yahoo.com/news?tmpl=story&cid= 578&e=6&u=/nm/20050603/ts_nm/security_ terrorism_dc.

41. Pape, "Nationalism Motivates," 46.

42. Israeli, "The Promise of an Afterlife," 34.

43. Raphael Israeli, "Palestinian Women: The Quest for a Voice in the Public Square through

'Islamikaze Martyrdom,'" *Terrorism and Political Violence*, 16, no. 1 (Spring 2004), 89–90.

44. Israeli, "The Promise of an Afterlife," 37.
45. Israeli, "The Promise of an Afterlife," 38.
46. Osama bin Laden, "American Imperialism Motivates Suicide Bombers," in abstract, Friedman (ed.), 40.
47. Hanley J. Harding, Jr., "Thoughts on Muslim Extremists and Terrorism" (Boca Raton, FL: Aurora Protection Specialists A.L.E.T.A. [Advanced Law Enforcement Training Academy], Special Response Team Anti-Terrorism Training Curriculum), 2005.
48. Harding, "Thoughts."
49. Harding, "Thoughts."
50. Harding, "Thoughts."
51. Fiamma Nirenstein, "Anti-Semitism Motivates Suicide Bombers," in Friedman (ed.), 50.
52. Nirenstein, 54.
53. Nirenstein, 57.
54. George W. Bush, address, Islamic Center of Washington, D.C. September 17, 2001, Friedman (ed.), 17.
55. Dr. Maher Hathout, "What Happens After We Die?," CNN: *Larry King Live*, April 14, 2005.
56. Preston Taran, "Martyrdom," Arabic Media Internet Network, June 1, 2005. June 22, 2005, http://www.amin.org/eng/uncat/2005/june/june1.html.
57. Daniel Pipes, "Despair and Hopelessness Do Not Motivate Suicide Bombers," in Friedman (ed.), 32.
58. Pipes, in Friedman (ed.), 32–33.
59. "Terror 2005: Learning How to Be a Killer on the Net," *Irish Independent*, July 23, 2005.
60. "How Terrorists Train in Cyberspace," *Washington Post* in *The Courier* (Waterloo-Cedar Falls, Iowa), August 7, 2005, A8.
61. "How Terrorists Train in Cyberspace."
62. "Terror 2005."
63. Pape, *Dying to Win*, 237–238.
64. Atran.
65. Ritzer and Goodman, 125, 225.
66. Atran.
67. Atran.
68. Atran.
69. Atran.
70. Pape, *Dying to Win*, 144.
71. Reuter, 6.
72. Schweitzer, "Suicide Bombings: The Ultimate Weapon?"
73. Atran.
74. U.S. Department of State, Counterterrorism Office. *Country Reports on Terrorism, 2004.*

April 2005, "Terrorist Group Profiles," "Al-Qaida," U.S. Navy, May 11, 2005. Available: http://library.nps.navy.mil/home/tgp/qaida.htm. Accessed June 24, 2005.
75. U.S. Department of State, *Country Reports*, "Al-Qaida."
76. U.S. Department of State, *Country Reports*, "Al-Qaida."
77. U.S. Department of State, *Country Reports*, "Al-Qaida."
78. U.S. Department of State, Counterterrorism Office. *Country Reports on Terrorism, 2004.* April 2005, "Terrorist Group Profiles," "Tanzim Qa'idat al-Jihad fi Bilad al-Rafidayn (QJBR)," U.S. Navy, May 11, 2005. Available: http://library.nps.navy.mil/home/tgp/qjbr.htm. Accessed June 24, 2005.
79. Jabin T. Jacob, "Suicide Bombers: A New Front Opens in Iraq," Article no. 1165, Institute of Peace and Conflict Studies, New Delhi, India, September 29, 2003. July 11, 2005, http://www.ipcs.org/ipcs/kashmirLevel2.jsp?action=showView&kValue=1174&subCatID=1022&mod=g.
80. Plato, 452a, 473d.

Chapter 2

1. Lisa Kruger, email interview, September 16, 2005.
2. Council on Foreign Relations, Terrorism Q & A: "Do Women Ever Become Suicide Terrorists," 2005. April 15, 2005, http://cfrterrorism.org/terrorism/suicide2.html.
3. Kim Murphy, "Chechen Women Are Increasingly Recruited to Become Suicide Bombers," in Lauri S. Friedman (ed.), *What Motivates Suicide Bombers?* (San Diego: Greenhaven), 2005, 77.
4. Raphael Israeli, "Palestinian Women: The Quest for a Voice in the Public Square through 'Islamikaze Martyrdom,'" *Terrorism and Political Violence*, 16, no. 1 (Spring 2004), 84.
5. Robert A. Pape, *Dying to Win: The Strategic Logic of Suicide Terrorism* (New York: Random House), 2005, 209.
6. Pape, *Dying to Win*, 208.
7. Clara Beyler, "Messengers of Death Female Suicide Bombers," February 12, 2003. April 10, 2005, http://www.ict.org.il/articles/articledet.cfm?articleid=470.
8. Robert A. Pape, "Nationalism Motivates Suicide Terrorists," in Friedman (ed.), 46.
9. Jacqueline Rose, "Deadly Embrace: Book Reviews: *My Life Is a Weapon: A Modern History of Suicide Bombing* by Christoph Reuter, trans. Helena Ragg-Kirkby, and *Army of Roses:*

Inside the World of Palestinian Women Suicide Bombers by Barbara Victor," *London Review of Books*, 26 no. 21, November 4, 2004. April 9, 2005, http://www.lrb.co.uk/v26/n21/rose01_.html.

10. David Lester, Bijou Yang and Mark Lindsay, "Suicide Bombers: Are Psychological Profiles Possible?" *Studies in Conflict and Terrorism* 27, no. 4 (July-August 2004): 283.

11. Ami Pedahzur, Arie Perliger and Leonard Weinbergy, "Altruism and Fatalism: the Characteristics of Palestinian Suicide Terrorists," *Deviant Behavior* 24, no. 4 (July-August 2003): 405.

12. Israel Security Agency, "Summary of Terrorist Activity 2004," January 5, 2005. April 15, 2005, http://www.mfa.gov.il/MFA/MFAArchive/2000_2009/2005/Summary%20of%20Terrorist%20Activity%202004.

13. Yoni Fighel, "Palestinian Islamic Jihad and Female Suicide Bombers," International Policy Institute for Counter-Terrorism, October 6, 2003. July 7, 2005, http://www.ict.org.il/.

14. Fighel.

15. Fighel.

16. Shaul Kimhi and Shemuel Even, "Who Are the Palestinian Suicide Bombers," *Terrorism and Political Violence*, 16, no. 4 (Winter 2004), 817–818.

17. Kimhi and Even, 818.

18. Debra D. Zedalis, *Female Suicide Bombers* (Carlisle, PA: Strategic Studies Institute, U.S. Army War College), June 2004, 1. April 2, 2005, http://www.carlisle.army.mil/ssi/pdffiles/00373.pdf.

19. Kimhi and Even, 815, 831.

20. Kimhi and Even, 834–835.

21. Birgit Langenberger, "Women's Political Violence — A Case of Emancipation?" *To Kill, to Die: Feminist Contestations on Gender and Political Violence*, March 2004, 4.

22. Langenberger, *To Kill, to Die*, 5.

23. Nida Alahmad, "Response to Birgit Langenberger," *To Kill, to Die*, 5.

24. Belinda Morrissey, *When Women Kill: Questions of Agency and Subjectivity* (London: Routledge), 2003, 24.

25. Morrissey, 24.

26. Morrissey, 25.

27. Morrissey, 25.

28. Morrissey, 27.

29. Tracy L. Conn, "Book Review: When Women Kill: Questions of Agency and Subjectivity by Belinda Morrissey, [London: Routledge, 2003, pp. 213]," 27 *Harvard Women's Law Journal* 285 (Spring, 2004).

30. Rose.

31. Rose.

32. Rose.

33. Morrissey, 24.

34. Lisa Kruger, *Gender and Terrorism: Motivations of Female Terrorists*, thesis, Joint Military Intelligence College, July 2005, abstract.

35. Nicole Speulda and Mary McIntosh, "Global Gender Gaps," Pew Research Center for the People and the Press Commentary, May 13, 2004. August 22, 2005, http://pewglobal.org/commentary/print.php?AnalysisID=90.

36. Speulda and McIntosh.

37. Stephanie Shemin, "Wrongheadedness of Female Suicide Bombers," *Chicago Tribune*, Op-Ed, June 18, 2002. July 2, 2005, http://www.cfr.org/pub4621/stephanie_shemin/wrongheadedness_of_female_suicide_bombers.php.

38. Shemin.

39. Clara Beyler, "Messengers."

40. Barbara Victor, *Army of Roses: Inside the World of Palestinian Women Suicide Bombers* (Emmaus, PA: Rodale), 2003, 2.

41. Victor, 2.

42. Heather A. Andrews, email interview, August 29, 2005.

43. Andrews, email interview, August 29, 2005.

44. Andrews, email interview, August 29, 2005.

45. Kruger, email interview, September 16, 2005.

46. Kruger, email interview, September 16, 2005.

47. Kruger, email interview, September 16, 2005.

48. Kruger, email interview, September 16, 2005.

49. George Ritzer and Douglas J. Goodman, *Sociological Theory*, 6th ed. (Boston: McGraw-Hill), 2004, 92.

50. Saud Abu Ramadan, "Muslim Women Can Be Martyrs Too." United Press International, January 15, 2004, pNA. April 7, 2005, http://www.comtexnews.com.

51. Israeli, "Palestinian Women," 68.

52. Israeli, "Palestinian Women," 67.

53. Rosemarie Skaine, *The Women of Afghanistan Under the Taliban* (Jefferson, N.C.: McFarland), 2002, 53–54.

54. Israeli, "Palestinian Women," 80.

55. Israeli, "Palestinian Women," 81.

56. "Hamas Win...," Reuters.com, Jan. 26, 2006.

57. *Charter of Allah: the Platform of the Islamic Resistance Movement (Hamas)*, translated and annotated by Raphael Israeli, Harry Truman Research Institute, The Hebrew University, Jerusalem, Israel, "The Role of Muslim Women,"

Article 17, n.d. July 2, 2005, http://www.fas. org/irp/world/para/docs/880818.htm.

58. *Charter of Allah.*
59. *Charter of Allah.*
60. Israeli, "Palestinian Women," 83.
61. Israeli, "Palestinian Women," 84.
62. Israel Security Agency, "Summary ... 2004."
63. Hilla Dayan, "Theories of Gender and Nationalism," work in progress. May 13, 2005, http://www.fhk.eur.nl/personal/zuidhof/Hilla_files/Nationalism%20Engendered.doc.
64. V.G. Julie Rajan, "Essay: Subversive Visibility and Political Agency: The Case of Palestinian Female Suicide Bombers," *To Kill, to Die*, 12.
65. Ilene R. Prusher, "Despair and Hopelessness Motivate Suicide Bombers," in Friedman (ed.), 20.
66. Kenneth R. Timmerman, "Children Are Indoctrinated to Become Suicide Bombers," in Friedman (ed.), 76.
67. Rajan, "Essay," *To Kill, to Die*, 13.
68. Rajan, "Essay," *To Kill, to Die*, 13.
69. Rajan, "Essay," *To Kill, to Die*, 13.
70. Rajan, "Essay," *To Kill, to Die*, 13.
71. Clara Beyler, "Female Suicide Bombers: An Update," International Policy Institute for Counter-Terrorism, March 7, 2004. April 15, 2005, http://www.ict.org.il/.
72. Concord Learning Systems, "Russian History (Summary) the Russian Revolution and the Soviet Union, 200 B.C.–2000 A.D.," Concord, N.C.: 1998–2003. May 20, 2005, http://www.laughtergenealogy.com/bin/histprof/misc/russia.html.
73. Murphy, "Chechen Women," Friedman (ed.), 78.
74. Brian Handwerk, "Female Suicide Bombers: Dying to Kill," National Geographic Channel, December 13, 2004. April 3, 2005, http://news.nationalgeographic.com/news/2004/12/1213_041213_tv_suicide_bombers.html.
75. Murphy, "Chechen Women," Friedman (ed.), 77.
76. Murphy, "Chechen Women," Friedman (ed.), 79.
77. Pape, *Dying to Win*, 31–32.
78. Viv Groskop, "Chechnya's Deadly 'Black Widows'..." *New Statesman*, Vol. 133 Issue 4704 (September 6, 2004): 32(2).
79. Mariya Rasner, "'Black Widow' Fears Surround a Russian Verdict," *Women's eNews*, February 6, 2005. April 9, 2005, http://www.womensenews.org/article.cfm/dyn/aid/2175/context/cover/; Peter Baker, "'New Stage' of Fear for Chechen Women: Russian Forces Sus-

pected in Abductions," *Washington Post*, October 19, 2004, A12. April 9, 2005, http://www.washingtonpost.com/wp-dyn/articles/A43296-2004Oct18.html?sub=AR.
80. Beyler, "Update."
81. Beyler, "Update."
82. Pape, "Nationalism," Friedman (ed.), 46.
83. Mohammed Daraghmeh, "In Search of Stealthier Suicide Attackers: Islamic Jihad Encourages Women," Associated Press, May 31, 2003. June 22, 2005, http://sfgate.com/cgi-bin/article.cgi?file=/news/archive/2003/05/31/international1634EDT0609.DTL.
84. Hassan Hathout, *Reading the Muslim Mind* (Plainfield, IN: American Trust, 1995), Chapter 4. Available: April 25, 2000, http://www.islamforum.org/readmind/chp4.html.
85. Fighel.
86. Daraghmeh.
87. Karla J. Cunningham, "Cross-Regional Trends in Female Terrorism," *Studies in Conflict and Terrorism* 26, I. 3 (May-June 2003): 171.
88. Cunningham, 175.
89. Raphael Israeli, "The Promise of an Afterlife Motivates Suicide Bombers," in Friedman (ed.), 35.
90. Yoram Schweitzer, "Female Suicide Bombers for God," No. 88, October 9, 2003. June 6, 2005, www.tau.ac.il/jcss/tanotes/TAUnotes88.doc.
91. Christopher Dickey, "Forward," Victor, xi.
92. Dickey, "Forward," Victor, xi.
93. Hanley J. Harding, Jr., email, "Personal Theory on the Psycho-sociology of Muslim Women Suicide Bombers," May 14, 2005.
94. Harding, email, May 14, 2005.
95. Harding, email, May 14, 2005.
96. Harding, email, May 14, 2005.
97. Harding, email, May 14, 2005.
98. TruthNews, "Female Bomber Disgusted By Fatah Handlers," International Christian Embassy, Jerusalem, May 31, 2002. June 22, 2005, http://truthnews.com/world/2002060103.htm.
99. TruthNews.
100. TruthNews.
101. TruthNews.
102. Murphy, "Chechen Women," in Friedman (ed.), 81.
103. Tom Parfitt, "Meet Black Fatima — She Programmes Women to Kill," (*London Sunday Telegraph*), July 20, 2003, 28.
104. Parfitt.
105. Murphy, "Chechen Women," Friedman (ed.), 81.
106. Zedalis, 7.

107. Pape, "Nationalism," Friedman (ed.), 46–47.

108. Rajan, "Essay," *To Kill, to Die*, 12.

109. Andrews, email interview, August 29, 2005.

110. Andrews, email interview, August 29, 2005.

111. Schweitzer, "Female Suicide Bombers for God."

112. Schweitzer, "Female Suicide Bombers for God."

113. Zedalis, 2.

114. BBC News, "Iraq Says Women Killed Troops," April 5, 2003. June 5, 2005, http://news.bbc.co.uk/2/hi/middle_east/2917107.stm.

115. Pape, *Dying to Win*, 204.

116. Schweitzer, "Female Suicide Bombers for God."

117. Schweitzer, "Female Suicide Bombers for God."

118. Beyler, "Messengers."

119. U.S. Department of State, Counterterrorism Office, "Country Reports on Terrorism, 2004," Chapter 6 Terrorist Groups, April 27, 2005. June 7, 2005, http://www.state.gov/s/ct/rls/45394.htm; Pape, *Dying to Win*, 228.

120. Yoram Schweitzer, "Suicide Bombings: The Ultimate Weapon?" August 7, 2001. April 15, 2005, http://www.ict.org.il/articles/article det.cfm?articleid=373.

121. Yoram Schweitzer, "Suicide Terrorism: Development & Characteristics," April 21, 2000. April 15, 2005, http://www.ict.org.il/articles/articledet.cfm?articleid=112.

122. Cunningham, 173.

123. Christoph Reuter, *My Life Is a Weapon: A Modern History of Suicide Bombing*, translated by Helena Ragg-Kirkby (Princeton, N.J.: Princeton University Press), 2004, 160.

124. Reuter, 161.

125. Reuter, 161.

126. Robert A. Pape in Patricia Wilson, "Religion, Suicide Terrorism Link Disputed in Book" (Reuters), June 3, 2005. June 4, 2005, http://news.yahoo.com/news?tmpl=story&cid=578&e=6&u=/nm/20050603/ts_nm/security_terrorism_dc.

127. Reuter, 161.

128. Pape in Wilson.

129. Pape, *Dying to Win*, 226–227; Isaac Kfir, "Commentary — A Blow to the Peace Process," International Policy Institute for Counter-Terrorism, August 14, 2005. August 16, 2005, http://www.ict.org.il/spotlight/comment.cfm?id=1108.

130. Pape, *Dying to Win*, 226–227.

131. Reuter, 164.

132. Reuter, 165.

133. Zedalis, 2.

134. Schweitzer, "Female Suicide Bombers for God."

135. Diplomat News Service, "The Beslan Attack & Qaeda Link," Vol. 61, Issue 11, September 13, 2004.

136. Baker.

137. Rasner.

138. Council on Foreign Relations, "Terrorism: Q & A: Al-Aqsa Martyrs Brigades," 2004. April 14, 2005, http://cfrterrorism.org/groups/alaqsa.html.

139. U.S. Department of State, *Country Reports on Terrorism, 2004*, April 2005, "Terrorist Group Profiles," "Al-Aqsa Martyrs Brigade," U.S. Navy, May 10, 2005. Available: June 23, 2005, http://library.nps.navy.mil/home/tgp/aqsa.htm.

140. Zedalis, 2.

141. Zedalis, 2.

142. Zedalis, 2.

143. BBC News, "Hamas Woman Bomber Kills Israelis," January 14, 2004. June 4, 2005, http://news.bbc.co.uk/2/hi/middle_east/3395973.stm.

144. Zedalis, 2.

145. Diplomat News Service, "The Beslan Attack & Qaeda Link"; Rasner.

146. Zahid Hussain and Jay Solomon, "Al Qaeda's Changing Face," *Far Eastern Economic Review*, 167, I. 34 (August 26, 2004): 20.

147. Mia Bloom, *Dying to Kill: The Allure of Suicide Terror* (New York: Columbia University Press), 2005, 152–153.

148. Clara Beyler, "Update."

149. Bloom, 153.

150. BBC News, "Iraq Says Women Killed Troops."

151. Bob Roberts, "Gulf War 2: Forces Mystery: Women Suicide Bombers," *The Mirror*, April 5, 2003, 2.

152. Michael Howard and Ewen MacAskill, "Female Suicide Bomber Kills Six in Iraqi City Declared Free of Terrorists: New Tactics on Two Fronts: First Woman to Detonate Bomb since 2003 Invasion; 30 Wounded as They Queue to Join Army," *The Guardian* (London), September 29, 2005, S. International, 13.

153. *Reuters*, "Iraq Woman Bomber Kills Army Recruits in Tal Afar," *New York Times*, September 28, 2005.

154. Sabrina Tavernise, "Suicide Blast by Woman in Iraq Kills 8 Others; 57 Are Hurt," *New York Times*, September 29, 2005.

155. Howard and MacAskill.

156. CNN.com, "Belgian Paper IDs 'Suicide

Bomber,'" December 1, 2005, International Ed. December 17, 2005, http://www.cnn.com/2005/WORLD/europe/12/01/belgium.iraq/index.html; Craig S. Smith, "Raised as Catholic in Belgium, She Died as a Muslim Bomber," *New York Times*, December 6, 2005. December 17, 2005, http://www.nytimes.com/2005/12/06/international/europe/06brussels.html?ex=1134968400&en=bcc647f73eedbcdb&ei=5070.

157. Jackie Spinner, "Female Suicide Bomber Attacks U.S. Military Post," *The Washington Post,* September 29, 2005, A16. December 23, 2005, washingtonpost.com; Christopher Dickey, "Women of Al Qaeda," *Newsweek*, U.S. Ed., December 12, 2005, 26.

158. Dickey.

159. Edward Wong, "Rebels Dressed as Women Attack Iraqi Police Station," *New York Times*, November 5, 2005. November 5, 2005, http://www.nytimes.com/2005/11/05/international/middleeast/05iraq.html?ex=113185800.

160. Associated Press, "Female Bombers Kill 27 in Iraq," *Courier* (Iowa), December 6, 2005, B1; Edward Wong, "Bombers Kill at Least 36 at Baghdad Police Academy," NYTimes.com, News, December 6, 2005. December 18, 2005, http://www.nytimes.com/2005/12/06/international/middleeast/06cnd-iraq.html?ex=1135054800&en=6e369be2d930de44&ei=5070; CNN.com, "Group Pleads for Release of Hostages; Suicide Bombers Kill Dozens in Iraq," December 6, 2005. December 18, 2005, http://www.cnn.com/2005/WORLD/meast/12/06/iraq.main/?section=cnn_topstories.

161. Paul Garwood, "U.S. Military Released Iraqi of Same Name as One of Amman Hotel Bombers," *NC Times*, November 14, 2005. December 18, 2005, http://www.nctimes.com/articles/2005/11/15/military/111405195034.txt; Associated Press, "Iraqi Woman Admits on TV to Jordan Attack," *Courier (*Iowa), A1.

162. Catherine Philp and Rana Sabbagh-Gargour, "Husband and Wife Suicide Team 'Behind Jordan Bomb,'" TimesOnline, November 12, 2005. December 19, 2005, http://www.timesonline.co.uk/article/0,,251-1869041,00.html.

163. Tom Perry and Edmund Blair, "Three Killed, Seven Injured in Two Cairo Attacks," April 30, 2005. May 1, 2005, http://www.reuters.com/newsArticle.jhtml?type=topNews&storyID=8351898.

164. Schweitzer, "Suicide Terrorism: Development & Characteristics."

Chapter 3

1. Jessica Berry, "Fury over Hijacker's Visit to Britain," Telegraph Network, May 27, 2002. July 4, 2005, http://www.portal.telegraph.co.uk/news/main.jhtml?xml=%2Fnews%2F2002%2F05%2F27%2Fnpflp27.xml.

2. Berry.

3. Lauri S. Friedman (ed.), *What Motivates Suicide Bombers?* (San Diego: Greenhaven), 2005, 7–8.

4. Mohammed Daraghmeh, "In Search of Stealthier Suicide Attackers, Islamic Jihad Encourages Women," Associated Press, May 31, 2003. June 22, 2005, http://sfgate.com/cgi-bin/article.cgi?file=/news/archive/2003/05/31/international1634EDT0609.DTL; Berry.

5. Berry.

6. AP caption, "Leila Khaled, former Palestinian guerrilla, speaks as guest of honor to the participants of the May Day rally in Zurich, Switzerland, Tuesday May 1, 2001."

7. Katharine Viner, "I Made the Ring from a Bullet and the Pin of a Hand Grenade," *The Guardian*, January 26, 2001. September 10, 2005, http://www.mqm.com/English-News/Jan-2001/leilakhalid.htm.

8. Luca Ricolfi (Paolo Campana), "Suicide Missions in the Palestinian Area: A New Database," 2004. August 2, 2005, http://www.prio.no/cscw/pdf/micro/techniqes/suicide_missions.pdf.

9. Berry.

10. Berry.

11. Berry.

12. Clara Beyler, "Messengers of Death: Female Suicide Bombers," February 12, 2003. April 10, 2005, http://www.ict.org.il/articles/articledet.cfm?articleid=470.

13. Debra D. Zedalis, *Female Suicide Bombers* (Carlisle, PA: Strategic Studies Institute, U.S. Army War College), June 2004, 7. April 2, 2005, http://www.carlisle.army.mil/ssi/pdffiles/00373.pdf. 7.

14. Zedalis, 7.

15. Christoph Reuter, *My Life Is a Weapon: A Modern History of Suicide Bombing*, translated by Helena Ragg-Kirkby (Princeton, N.J.: Princeton University Press), 2004, 2.

16. Rosemarie Skaine, *Women at War: Gender Issues of Americans in Combat* (Jefferson, N.C.: McFarland), 1999, 51.

17. Israel Security Agency, "Summary of Terrorist Activity 2004, January 5, 2005. April 15, 2005, http://www.mfa.gov.il/MFA/MFAArchive/2000_2009/2005/Summary%20of%20Terrorist%20Activity%202004.

18. Zedalis, 7.

19. Zedalis, 8.

20. Karla J. Cunningham, "Cross-Regional Trends in Female Terrorism," *Studies in Conflict and Terrorism* 26, Issue 3 (May-June 2003): 171.

21. Cunningham, 173.

22. Ashley M. Heher, "Female Suicide Bombers an Extension of an Old Tradition," Cox News Service, April 28, 2002.

23. Israel Security Agency, "Summary ... 2004."

24. Israel Security Agency, "Summary ... 2004."

25. Matthew Lippman, "Essay: The New Terrorism and International Law," 10 *Journal of Comparative and International Law* 302 (Spring, 2003).

26. Lippman, 337.

27. Lippman, 366.

28. Richard A. Falk, "Agora: ICJ Advisory Opinion on Construction of a Wall in the Occupied Palestinian Territory: Toward Authoritativeness: the ICJ Ruling on Israel's Security Wall," 99 *American Journal International Law* 50 (January 2005).

29. Falk, 50.

30. George W. Bush, address before a joint session of Congress on the State of the Union, 40 Weekly Comp. Pres. Doc. 94, 97 (January 20, 2004) in Falk, 99, n43.

31. Falk, 50.

32. Falk, 50.

33. Falk, 50.

34. Wayne N. Renke, "Special Issue Globalization and the Law: Book Review: Why Terrorism Works: Understanding the Threat, Responding to the Challenge, Alan M. Dershowitz," 41 *Alberta Law Review* 771 (December 2003).

35. Renke, 786.

36. Renke, 771.

37. United Nations Office on Drugs and Crime, "Implementing International Action Against Terrorism," 2005. July 14, 2005, http://www.unodc.org/unodc/en/terrorism.html.

38. United Nations Office on Drugs and Crime, "Overview — Conventions Against Terrorism," 2005. July 15, 2005, http://www.unodc.org/unodc/en/terrorism_convention_overview.html.

39. United Nations Office on Drugs and Crime, "Conventions Against Terrorism."

40. UNODC, "Conventions Against Terrorism."

41. Lippman, 340–341.

42. Lippman, 340–341.

43. Lippman, 343.

44. Lippman, 343.

45. Nick Wadhams, "U.S. Seeks to Firm Up Terrorist Sanctions," Associated Press in the *Guardian Unlimited*, July 14, 2005. July 14, 2005, http://www.guardian.co.uk/worldlatest/story/0,1280,-5139772,00.html.

46. Wadhams.

47. Jurist, "Terrorism Law and Policy: World Anti-terrorism Laws," 2003. July 14, 2005, http://jurist.law.pitt.edu/terrorism/terrorism3a.htm.

48. Jurist.

49. CNN.com, "EU Moves to Curb Terror Funding," July 12, 2005. July 14, 2005, http://www.cnn.com/2005/WORLD/europe/07/12/terror.funds.reut/index.html.

50. Mark Trevelyan, "Terrorist Bank Deals Seen as Impossible to Spot," *Reuters*, September 29, 2005. September 29, 2005, http://today.reuters.com/news/NewsArticle.aspx?type=topNews&storyID=uri:2005-09-29T133403Z_01_BAU948325_RTRUKOC_0_US-SECURITY-FINANCE.xml.

51. United Nations News Centre, "Annan Announces New Initiative to Bridge Gap Between Islamic, Western Worlds," July 14, 2005. July 15, 2005, http://www.un.org/apps/news/story.asp?NewsID.

52. Rear Admiral D.M. Williams, Jr., USN (Ret.), interview, May 16, 2005.

53. Heher.

54. Williams, interview, May 16, 2005.

55. Philip Bobbitt, "Facing Jihad, Recalling the Blitz," *New York Times*, July 10, 2005. July 10, 2005, http://www.nytimes.com/2005/07/10/opinion/10bobbitt.html?th&emc=th.

56. Corporal Ray Youngblut, USA (Ret.), 45th Division Infantry, Thunderbird, interview, September 12, 2005.

57. Williams, interview, May 16, 2005.

58. Williams, interview, May 16, 2005.

59. Williams, interview, May 16, 2005.

60. Williams, interview, May 16, 2005.

61. CNN Headline News, July 15, 2005.

62. Jim Hoagland, "The True War: Within, and for, Islam," *Washington Post*, July 14, 2005, A25.

63. Intelligencer Editorial Board, "Global Struggle: War No More," *Seattle Post*, July 28, 2005. July 29, 2005, http://seattlepi.nwsource.com/opinion/234205_wared.html.

64. Intelligencer Editorial Board.

Chapter 4

1. Robert A. Pape, *Dying to Win: The Strategic Logic of Suicide Terrorism* (New York: Random House), 2005, 138.

2. David Johnson, "Major Players in the

Lebanese Conflict: The Governments, Militias, and Countries Involved," All Infoplease, 2000–2005. September 10, 2005, .

3. "Lebanese Civil War," *Wikipedia*, January 13, 2005. October 2, 2005, http://www.infoplease.com/spot/lebanon1.html.

4. David B. Doroquez, "The Israeli-Lebanon Conflict: Past and Present," 2003, 1. September 10, 2005, http://www.doroquez.com/arts/documents/rsoc03.pdf.

5. Council on Foreign Relations, "Terrorism: Q & A: Hezbollah (Lebanon, Islamists)," 2002. July 23, 2005, http://cfrterrorism.org/groups/hezbollah.html.

6. Council on Foreign Relations, "Hezbollah (Lebanon, Islamists)."

7. Council on Foreign Relations, "Hezbollah (Lebanon, Islamists)."

8. Pape, *Dying to Win*, 204.

9. Pape, *Dying to Win*, 205, 206.

10. Council on Foreign Relations, "Hezbollah (Lebanon, Islamists)."

11. Heather A. Andrews, *Veiled Jihad: The Threat of Female Islamic Suicide Terrorists*, MSSI thesis submitted to the Joint Military Intelligence College, July 2005, 37.

12. Yoram Schweitzer, "Suicide Terrorism: Development & Characteristics," April 21, 2000. April 15, 2005, http://www.ict.org.il/articles/articledet.cfm?articleid=112.

13. Andrews, *Veiled Jihad*, 48.

14. Adel Beshara, "Antun Sa'adeh and the Struggle for Syrian National Independence (1904–1949)," Syrian Social Nationalist Party, no date. June 6, 2005, http://www.geocities.com/CapitolHill/Lobby/3577/adel_bechara2.html.

15. Yoram Schweitzer, "Female Suicide Bombers for God," No. 88, October 9, 2003. June 6, 2005, www.tau.ac.il/jcss/tanotes/TAUnotes88.doc.

16. Council on Foreign Relations, "Terrorism: Q & A: Types of Terrorism," 2004. July 23, 2005, http://www.cfrterrorism.org/terrorism/types2.html.

17. Council on Foreign Relations, "Terrorism: Q & A: Syria," 2004. July 23, 2005, http://www.cfrterrorism.org/sponsors/syria.html.

18. Council on Foreign Relations, "Syria."

19. Clara Beyler, "Messengers of Death: Female Suicide Bombers," International Policy Institute for Counter-Terrorism, February 12, 2003. April 10, 2005, http://www.ict.org.il/articles/articledet.cfm?articleid=470.

20. Beyler, "Messengers."

21. Pape, *Dying to Win*, 205.

22. Clara Beyler, "Chronology of Suicide Bombings Carried Out by Women," International Policy Institute for Counter-Terrorism, February 12, 2003. April 15, 2005, http://www.ict.org.il/; Pape, *Dying to Win*, 137; Schweitzer, "Bombers for God"; Debra D. Zedalis, *Female Suicide Bombers*, Carlisle, PA: Strategic Studies Institute, U.S. Army War College, June 2004, 5. April 2, 2005, http://www.carlisle.army.mil/ssi/pdffiles/00373.pdf.

23. Andrews, *Veiled Jihad*, 101.

24. Beyler, "Chronology."

25. Beyler, "Chronology"; Luca Ricolfi (Paolo Campana), "Suicide Missions in the Palestinian Area: A New Database," 2004. August 2, 2005, http://www.prio.no/cscw/pdf/micro/techniqes/suicide_missions.pdf.

26. Pape, *Dying to Win*, 205.

27. Beyler, "Chronology"; Ricolfi; Zedalis, 5.

28. Flash Points: World Conflicts, "Turkey-Kurdistan Conflict Briefing," no date. September 14, 2005, http://www.flashpoints.info/countries-conflicts/Turkey-Kurdistan-web/Turkey-Kurdistan_briefing.html.

29. Flash Points.

30. U.S. Department of State, *Country Reports on Terrorism, 2004*, April 2005, "Terrorist Group Profiles," "Kongra-Gel (KGK)," U.S. Navy, May 11, 2005. June 24, 2005, http://www.ict.org.il/articles/articledet.cfm?articleid=373.

31. U.S. Department of State, "Kongra-Gel (KGK).

32. Beyler, "Messengers."

33. Yoram Schweitzer, "Suicide Bombings: The Ultimate Weapon?" August 7, 2001. April 15, 2005, http://www.ict.org.il/articles/article det.cfm?articleid=373.

34. Schweitzer, "Development & Characteristics."

35. Christoph Reuter, *My Life Is a Weapon: A Modern History of Suicide Bombing*, translated by Helena Ragg-Kirkby (Princeton, N.J.: Princeton University Press), 2004, 165.

36. Reuter, 166.

37. Beyler, "Messengers."

38. Zedalis, 4.

39. Zedalis, 4.

40. Beyler, "Chronology"; Zedalis, 4.

41. Reuter, 165.

42. U.S. Department of State, Bureau of Democracy, "Human Rights, and Labor Turkey Country Report on Human Rights Practices for 1998," February 26, 1998. September 22, 2005, http://www.hri.org/docs/USSD-Rights/1998/Turkey.html.

Chapter 5

1. Dilshika Jayamaha, "Partners in Arms: LTTE Women Fighters and the Changing Face of the Sri Lankan Civil War," 2004, 16. October 3, 2005, http://www.jjay.cuny.edu/terrorism/womencombatants.pdf.

2. "Worlds Apart: The Roots of Regional Conflicts Sri Lanka: The Price of Reconciliation," Britannica.com, 1999. August 2, 2005, http://www.britannica.com/worldsapart/5_timeline_print.html.

3. Simon Gardner and Arjuna Wickramasinghe, "Top Sri Lanka Minister Shot Dead, Tigers Blamed," August 13, 2005. August 13, 2005, http://thestar.com.my/news/story.asp?file=/2005/8/13/worldupdates/2005-08-13T163104Z_01_NOOTR_RTRJONC_0_-212571-2&sec=Worldupdates.

4. U.S. Department of State, Counterterrorism Office, "Country Reports on Terrorism, 2004," Chapter 6 Terrorist Groups, April 27, 2005. June 7, 2005, http://www.state.gov/s/ct/rls/45394.htm; Robert A. Pape, *Dying to Win: The Strategic Logic of Suicide Terrorism*, New York: Random House, 2005, 228.

5. "Peace Deal in Sri Lanka," *BBC News*, February 21, 2002. October 4, 2004, http://news.bbc.co.uk/1/hi/world/south_asia/1833230.stm.

6. U.S. Department of State, "Country Reports on Terrorism, 2004," Chapter 6 Terrorist Groups.

7. U.S. Department of State, Counterterrorism Office, "Country Reports on Terrorism, 2004," Chapter 6 Terrorist Groups.

8. U.S. Department of State, Counterterrorism Office, "Country Reports on Terrorism, 2004," Chapter 6 Terrorist Groups.

9. U.S. Department of State, Counterterrorism Office, "Country Reports on Terrorism, 2004," Chapter 6 Terrorist Groups; Pape, *Dying to Win*, 228.

10. Clara Beyler, "Messengers of Death Female Suicide Bombers," International Policy Institute for Counter-Terrorism, February 12, 2003. April 10, 2005, http://www.ict.org.il/articles/articledet.cfm?articleid=470.

11. Mia Bloom, *Dying to Kill: The Allure of Suicide Terror* (New York: Columbia University Press), 2005, 160.

12. Bloom, 160–161.

13. Lisa Kruger, *Gender and Terrorism: Motivations of Female Terrorists*, master of science, strategic intelligence thesis, Joint Military Intelligence College, July 2005, 67.

14. Kruger, *Gender and Terrorism*, 68.

15. Beyler, "Messengers."

16. Karla J. Cunningham, "Cross-Regional Trends in Female Terrorism," *Studies in Conflict and Terrorism* 26, Issue 3 (May-June 2003): 180.

17. Cunningham, 181.

18. Yoram Schweitzer, "Suicide Terrorism: Development & Characteristics," April 21, 2000. April 15, 2005, http://www.ict.org.il/articles/articledet.cfm?articleid=112.

19. Yoram Schweitzer, "Suicide Bombings: The Ultimate Weapon?" August 7, 2001. April 15, 2005, http://www.ict.org.il/articles/articledet.cfm?articleid=373.

20. Schweitzer, "The Ultimate Weapon?"

21. Schweitzer, "Development & Characteristics."

22. Luca Ricolfi (Paolo Campana), "Suicide Missions in the Palestinian Area: A New Database," 2004. August 2, 2005, http://www.prio.no/cscw/pdf/micro/techniqes/suicide_missions.pdf.

23. Beyler, "Messengers."

24. Beyler, "Messengers."

25. Heather A. Andrews, *Veiled Jihad: The Threat of Female Islamic Suicide Terrorists*, master of science, strategic intelligence thesis, Joint Military Intelligence College, July 2005, 134; *AsiaNow*, "Suspected Suicide Bomber Kills at Least 11 in Sri Lanka," January 5, 2000. May 24, 2005, http://archives.cnn.com/2000/ASIANOW/south/01/05/sri.lanka.explosion/index.html.

26. Andrews, *Veiled Jihad*, 134–135.

27. "Sri Lanka Database — Suicide Attacks by the LTTE," 2001. September 17, 2005, http://www.satp.org/satporgtp/countries/shrilanka/database/data_suicide_killings.htm.

28. Ricolfi.

29. Beyler, "Messengers"; Pape, *Dying to Win*, 226.

30. *AsiaNow*, "Six Dead in Sri Lanka Blast," January 5, 2000. August 20, 2005, http://archives.cnn.com/2000/ASIANOW/south/01/04/sri.lanka.explosion.01/; Yoram Schweitzer, "Suicide Bombings: The Ultimate Weapon?" August 7, 2001. April 15, 2005, http://www.ict.org.il/articles/articledet.cfm?articleid=373.

31. Ricolfi.

32. K.T. Rajasingham, "Sri Lanka: the Untold Story: Rajiv Gandhi's Assassination, *Asia Times*, 1995–2005. July 23, 2005, http://www.lankalibrary.com/pol/rajiv.htm.

33. Isaac Kfir, "Commentary — A Blow to the Peace Process," International Policy Institute for Counter-Terrorism, August 14, 2005. August 16, 2005, http://www.ict.org.il/spotlight/comment.cfm?id=1108.

34. Rajasingham.
35. Beyler, "Messengers"; Kfir; Pape, *Dying to Win*, 226–227; Rajasingham; U.S. Department of State, Bureau of Public Affairs, Office of the Historian, "Significant Terrorist Incidents, 1961–2003: A Brief Chronology," March 2004. April 17, 2005, http://www.state.gov/r/pa/ho/pubs/fs/5902.htm.
36. Rajasingham.
37. Pape, *Dying to Win*, 225.
38. Pape, *Dying to Win*, 220.
39. Pape, *Dying to Win*, 226–227.
40. Pape, *Dying to Win*, 229.
41. Pape, *Dying to Win*, 230.
42. Pape, *Dying to Win*, 230.
43. Pape, *Dying to Win*, 230.
44. Cunningham, 180.
45. Cunningham, 180.
46. Jayamaha, 14.
47. Jayamaha, 14.
48. Jayamaha, 18–19.
49. Jayamaha, 22.
50. Jayamaha, 22.
51. Jayamaha, 22.
52. Jayamaha, 28.

Chapter 6

1. Clara Beyler, "Chronology of Suicide Bombings Carried Out by Women," International Policy Institute for Counter-Terrorism, February 12, 2003. April 15, 2005, http://www.ict.org.il/.
2. Anup Shah, "Crisis in Chechnya," globalissues.org, September 4, 2004. October 5, 2005, http://www.globalissues.org/Geopolitics/Chechnya.asp.
3. David Johnson and Borgna Brunner, "Timeline of Key Events in Chechnya, 1830–2004," 2005. September 30, 2005, http://www.infoplease.com/spot/chechnyatime1.html.
4. "Profiles: Russia's Most Wanted," BBC News, UK Edition, September 8, 2004. October 5, 2005, http://news.bbc.co.uk/1/hi/world/europe/3637126.stm.
5. Johnson and Brunner.
6. "Second Chechen War," *Wikipedia Encyclopedia*, August 1, 2005. August 2, 2005, http://en.wikipedia.org/wiki/Second_Chechen_War.
7. Shah.
8. "Chechen Rebels Acknowledge Maskhadov's Death, Vow to Fight On," *MosNews.com*, March 9, 2005. October 5, 2005, http://www.mosnews.com/news/2005/03/09/chechreaction.shtml.

9. Raven Healing, "Chechnya After Aslan Maskhadov: Assassination of the Rebel President Signals Escalation in North Caucasus," *World War 4 Report*, April 10, 2005. October 5, 2005, http://WW4Report.com.
10. "Profiles: Russia's Most Wanted."
11. "Basayev: Russia's Most Wanted Man," CNN.com, September 8, 2004. October 5, 2005, http://edition.cnn.com/2004/WORLD/europe/09/08/russia.basayev/.
12. David E. Kaplan, "Tangled Roots of an Atrocity (Chechen Terrorism, Russia)," *U.S. News & World Report*, September 20, 2004, Vol. 137, Issue 9, p. 28.
13. Yoram Schweitzer, "Female Suicide Bombers for God," Jaffee Center for Strategic Studies, October 9, 2003, no. 88. June 6, 2005, http://www.tau.ac.il/jcss/tanotes/TAUnotes88.doc.
14. Viv Groskop, "Chechnya's Deadly 'Black Widows'..." *New Statesman*, Vol. 133 Issue 4704, September 6, 2004: 32(2).
15. Clara Beyler, "Messengers of Death: Female Suicide Bombers," International Policy Institute Counter-Terrorism, February 12, 2003. April 10, 2005, http://www.ict.org.il/articles/articledet.cfm? articleid=470.
16. Clara Beyler, "Messengers."
17. Chris Kline and Mark Franchetti, "The Woman Behind the Mask," *Sunday Times* (London), November 3, 2002, Sec. Features; News Review, 1.
18. Debra D. Zedalis, *Female Suicide Bombers* (Carlisle, PA: Strategic Studies Institute, U.S. Army War College), June 2004, 2. April 2, 2005, http://www.carlisle.army.mil/ssi/pdffiles/00373.pdf.
19. Mia Bloom, *Dying to Kill: The Allure of Suicide Terror* (New York: Columbia University Press), 2005, 154, 157.
20. Luca Ricolfi (Paolo Campana), "Suicide Missions in the Palestinian Area: A New Database," 2004. August 2, 2005, http://www.prio.no/cscw/pdf/micro/techniqes/suicide_missions.pdf.
21. Groskop 32(2); Radio Free Europe/Radio Liberty, "Factbox: Major Terrorist Incidents Tied to Russian-Chechen War," September 6, 2004. June 27, 2005, http://rfe.rferl.org/featuresarticle/2004/09/d981dd2d-8b08-41ff-a2e2-ada25338093c.html.
22. Bloom, 154.
23. "Beslan School Hostage Crisis," *Wikipedia*, September 25, 2005. September 30, 2005, http://en.wikipedia.org/wiki/Beslan_school_massacre.
24. Diplomat News Service, "The Beslan

Attack & Qaeda Link," Vol. 61 Issue 11. September 13, 2004; John Kampfner, *New Statesman*, Vol. 133 Issue 4705, September 13, 2004, p. 10(4); "Suspect Retells Beslan's Horror; Leader Blew Up Female Bombers After They Balked at Taking Children Hostage, Court Told," Associated Press, *Toronto Star Newspapers, Ltd., The Record* (Kitchener-Waterloo, Ontario), June 1, 2005, Final Ed., Sec. Front, A7.

25. Clara Beyler, "Female Suicide Bombers: An Update," International Policy Institute for Counter-Terrorism, March 7, 2004. April 15, 2005, http://www.ict.org.il/.

26. Groskop, 32(2).

27. Vadim Rechkalov, "Psychology of Chechen Woman Suicide Bombers Pondered," *Global News Wire*, August 5, 2003.

28. Rechkalov.

29. Mark McDonald, "Chechnya's Eerie Rebels: Black Widows," *Gazette* (Montreal, Quebec), Source: Knight Ridder Newspapers, October 24, 2003, Final Ed., Sec. News; A4.

30. Anne Speckhard, Nadejda Tarabrina, Valery Krasnov and Khapta Akmedova, "Research Note: Observations of Suicidal Terrorists in Action," *Terrorism and Political Violence*, 16, no. 2, (Summer 2004), 305, 306, 308.

31. Speckhard, *et al.*, 305, 309.

32. Radio Free Europe/Radio Liberty, "Factbox."

33. Speckhard, *et al.*, 306.

34. Speckhard, *et al.*, 307.

35. Speckhard, *et al.*, 308.

36. Speckhard, *et al.*, 311, 312, 314, 317, 318.

37. Speckhard, *et al.*, 316.

38. Speckhard, *et al.*, 315, 316.

39. Speckhard, *et al.*, 318.

40. Speckhard, *et al.*, 308.

41. Speckhard, *et al.*, 317.

42. Speckhard, *et al.*, 316.

43. Speckhard, *et al.*, 316.

44. Speckhard, *et al.*, 317.

45. Speckhard, *et al.*, 319.

46. Speckhard, *et al.*, 319–320.

47. Speckhard, *et al.*, 319, 325.

48. Rechkalov.

49. Rechkalov.

50. Mainat Abdulajewa, "Why They Murder: About the Chechen Terrorism," Grosny, September 3, 2004. July 23, 2005, http://www.tamera.org/english/aktuelltext/News/whytheykill.html.

51. Abdulajewa.

52. Abdulajewa.

53. Abdulajewa.

54. Abdulajewa.

55. *RIA Novosti*, "Reference: Terrorist Attacks in Moscow in 1999–2004," September 1, 2004, ACC-NO: 4791672.

56. Zedalis, 6; Richard Beeston, "Black Widow Suicide Bombers Are Extremists' Worst Weapon," *The Times* (London), September 3, 2004, Sec.: Overseas news, 4.

57. Zedalis, 6.

58. Beyler, "Update."

59. Zaur Farniyev (Kommersant), "One Life Sentence for 19 Lives.— Court Hands Down Sentences in Mozdok Bombing Case," Current Digest of the Post-Soviet Press 57, no. 11, Sec.: The Russian Federation — North Caucasus (April 13, 2005).

60. Farniyev.

61. Groskop, 32(2).

62. Rechkalov.

63. Groskop, 32(2).

64. Rechkalov.

65. Rechkalov.

66. Groskop, 32(2).

67. Rechkalov.

68. Lawrence Uzzell, "Profile of a Female Suicide Bomber," *Chechnya Weekly*, 5, Issue 6, (February 11, 2004).

69. Groskop, 32(2).

70. Uzzell.

71. Rechkalov.

72. Groskop, 32(2).

73. Groskop, 32(2).

74. Groskop, 32(2).

75. Uzzell.

76. Uzzell.

77. Uzzell.

78. Uzzell.

79. Uzzell.

80. Anatoly Medetsky, "Counting on FSB's Bombing Testimony," *Moscow Times*, April 5, 2004, Sec: No. 2894.

81. Combined Reports, "24 Years Sought for Would-Be Bomber," *Moscow Times*, April 7, 2004, Sec.: No. 2896.

82. Medetsky.

83. Tom Parfitt, "Meet Black Fatima — She Programmes Women to Kill," *Sunday Telegraph* (London), July 20, 2003, 28.

84. Parfitt, 28.

85. Parfitt, 28.

86. Bloom, 157.

Chapter 7

1. V.G. Julie Rajan, "Essay: Subversive Visibility and Political Agency: The Case of Palestinian Female Suicide Bombers," *To Kill, to Die: Feminist Contestations on Gender and Political Violence*, March 2004, 13.

2. "Israeli-Palestinian Conflict," *Wikipedia Encyclopedia*, August 1, 2005. August 2, 2005, http://en.wikipedia.org/wiki/Israeli-Palestinian_conflict.

3. Rema Hammami and Salim Tamari, "Anatomy of Another Rebellion," *Middle East Report 217*, Winter 2000. August 9, 2005, http://www.merip.org/mer/mer217/217_hammami-tamari.html.

4. "Israeli-Palestinian Conflict."

5. Israel-Palestine Liberation Organization Agreement: 1993, The Avalon Project, Yale Law School, August 9, 2005. August 9, 2005, http://www.yale.edu/lawweb/avalon/mideast/isrplo.htm.

6. Daoud Kuttab, "The Two Intifadas: Differing Shades of Resistance," Palestine Center and the Jerusalem Fund, Information Brief No. 66, February 8, 2001. August 9, 2005, http://www.thejerusalemfund.org/images/informationbrief.php?ID=53.

7. Hammami and Tamari.

8. Neil MacDonald, "Three Days to the Brink," *The Magazine*, October 12, 2000. October 5, 2005, http://www.cbc.ca/news/background/middleeast/threedays.html.

9. Kuttab.

10. "Israeli-Palestinian Conflict."

11. U.S. Department of State, *Country Reports on Terrorism, 2004*, April 2005, "Terrorist Group Profiles," "Al-Aqsa Martyrs Brigade," U.S. Navy, May 10, 2005. June 23, 2005, http://library.nps.navy.mil/home/tgp/aqsa.htm.

12. Council on Foreign Relations, "Terrorism: Q & A: Al-Aqsa Martyrs Brigades," 2004. April 14, 2005, http://cfrterrorism.org/groups/alaqsa.html.

13. Council on Foreign Relations, "Al-Aqsa Martyrs Brigades."

14. U.S. Department of State, *Country Reports on Terrorism, 2004*, April 2005, "Terrorist Group Profiles," "Palestine Islamic Jihad (PIJ)," U.S. Navy, May 11, 2005. Available: http://library.nps.navy.mil/home/tgp/pij.htm. Accessed June 24, 2005.

15. Israel Security Agency (ISA), "Summary of Terrorist Activity 2004," January 5, 2005. April 15, 2005, http://www.mfa.gov.il/MFA/MFAArchive/2000_2009/2005/Summary%20of%20Terrorist%20Activity%202004.

16. Scott Atran, "Mishandling Suicide Terrorism," *The Washington Quarterly*, Summer 2004, 68. May 26, 2005, http://www.twq.com/04summer/docs/04summer_atran.pdf.

17. Israel Security Agency (ISA), "Summary of Terrorist Activity 2004."

18. U.S. Department of State, *Country Reports on Terrorism, 2004*, April 2005, "Terrorist Group Profiles," "Hamas," U.S. Navy, May 11, 2005. Available: http://library.nps.navy.mil/home/tgp/hamas.htm. Accessed June 24, 2005.

19. Yoram Schweitzer, "Suicide Terrorism: Development & Characteristics," April 21, 2000. April 15, 2005, http://www.ict.org.il/articles/articledet.cfm?articleid=112.

20. Center for Special Studies (C.S.S), Intelligence and Terrorism Information Center, "News of the Israeli-Palestinian Conflict: The End of an Era," September 1–15, 2005, 1. October 1, 2005, http://www.intelligence.org.il/eng/eng_n/pdf/t15sep_05.pdf.

21. Center for Special Studies (C.S.S), Intelligence and Terrorism Information Center, "Newsletter: The Hamas-associated Al-Mustaqbal Research Center Presents Another Study," September 28, 2005.

22. Center for Special Studies (C.S.S), Intelligence and Terrorism Information Center, "Newsletter: Escalation of Palestinian Terrorism After the Disengagement," September 28, 2005.

23. Raphael Israeli, "Palestinian Women: The Quest for a Voice in the Public Square through 'Islamikaze Martyrdom,'" *Terrorism and Political Violence*, 16, no. 1 (Spring 2004), 66.

24. Israeli, 66.

25. Graham Usher, "Palestinian Women, the Intifada and the State of Independence: an Interview with Rita Giacaman," *Race and Class* 34, no. 3 (January-March 1993): 31.

26. Karla J. Cunningham, "Cross-Regional Trends in Female Terrorism," *Studies in Conflict and Terrorism* 26, Issue 3 (May-June 2003): 182–183.

27. Cunningham, 184.

28. Shaul Kimhi and Shemuel Even, "Who are the Palestinian Suicide Bombers," *Terrorism and Political Violence*, 16, no. 4 (Winter 2004), 817.

29. V.G. Julie Rajan, "Essay: Subversive Visibility and Political Agency: The Case of Palestinian Female Suicide Bombers," *To Kill, to Die: Feminist Contestations on Gender and Political Violence*, March 2004, 12.

30. Barbara Victor, *Army of Roses: Inside the World of Palestinian Women Suicide Bombers* (Emmaus, PA: Rodale), 2003, 16.

31. Kimhi and Even, 817.

32. Kimhi and Even, 817.

33. Victor, 16–18.

34. Victor, 19.

35. Victor, 20.

36. Victor, 20.

37. Victor, 20.

38. Cunningham, 186.

39. Cunningham, 186.

40. Cunningham, 187.

41. Clara Beyler, "Messengers of Death Female Suicide Bombers," International Policy Institute for Counter-Terrorism, February 12, 2003. April 10, 2005, http://www.ict.org.il/articles/articledet.cfm?articleid=470.

42. Beyler, "Messengers."

43. Beyler, "Messengers."

44. Jacqueline Rose, "Deadly Embrace: Book Reviews: *My Life Is a Weapon: A Modern History of Suicide Bombing* by Christoph Reuter, trans. Helena Ragg-Kirkby and *Army of Roses: Inside the World of Palestinian Women Suicide Bombers* by Barbara Victor," *London Review of Books*, 26 no. 21, November 4, 2004. April 9, 2005, http://www.lrb.co.uk/v26/n21rose01_.html.

45. Hilla Dayan, "Poisoned Cats and Angels of Death: Israeli and Palestinian Combatant Women," *To Kill, to Die: Feminist Contestations on Gender and Political Violence*, March 2004, 11.

46. Israeli, 84–85.

47. Clara Beyler, "Chronology of Suicide Bombings Carried Out by Women," February 12, 2003. April 15, 2005, http://www.ict.org.il/.

48. Heather A. Andrews (Author, Veiled Jihad: *The Threat of Female Islamic Suicide Terrorists*, MSSI Thesis submitted to the Joint Military Intelligence College, July 2005), email interview follow-up, September 7, 2005.

49. Israeli, 85.

50. Israeli, 85, 86.

51. Cunningham, 183.

52. Israeli, 86–87.

53. Cunningham, 183.

54. Victor, 40, 41.

55. Victor, 43–46.

56. Victor, 47–48.

57. Victor, 48.

58. Victor, 50.

59. Victor, 51.

60. Victor, 53.

61. Victor, 54.

62. Israel Defense Forces, "Inside the Circle of Terror- Palestinian Women as Terrorists," July 11, 2004. October 1, 2005, http://www1.idf.il/dover/site/mainpage.asp?sl=EN&id=7&docid=35064.EN.

63. Margot Dudkevitch, "Female Bomber: Attack Aimed at Youth," *The Jerusalem Post*. June 20, 2005. July 2, 2005, http://www.jpost.com/servlet/Satellite?pagename=JPost/JPArticle/ShowFull&cid=1119234009872; Manuela Dviri, "My Dream Was to Be a Suicide Bomber. I Wanted to Kill 20, 50 Jews. Yes, Even Babies,"

Telegraph, Tel Aviv, June 26, 2005. July 2, 2005, http://www.telegraph.co.uk/news/main.jhtml?xml=/news/2005/06/26/wmid26.xml.

64. Dudkevitch.

65. Dviri.

66. Dviri.

67. Dviri.

68. Dviri.

69. Dudkevitch.

70. Dviri.

71. Dviri.

72. Victor, 258.

73. Dviri.

74. "Women on the Edge of Destruction," Cageprisoners.com, July 2, 2005. July 9, 2005, http://www.cageprisoners.com/articles.php?id=5186.

75. "Women on the Edge of Destruction."

76. "Women on the Edge of Destruction."

77. "Women on the Edge of Destruction."

78. "Women on the Edge of Destruction."

79. Dviri.

80. Dviri.

Chapter 8

1. Jennifer Hardwick, email, September 12, 2005.

2. Yoram Schweitzer, "Suicide Terrorism: Development & Characteristics," April 21, 2000. April 15, 2005, http://www.ict.org.il/articles/articledet.cfm?articleid=112.

3. Schweitzer, "Development & Characteristics."

4. National Commission on Terrorist Attacks upon the United States, *The 9/11 Commission Report: Final Report of the National Commission on Terrorist Attacks Upon the United States*, New York: W.W. Norton, 2004, 363–364.

5. Intelligencer Editorial Board, "Global Struggle: War No More," *Seattle Post*, July 28, 2005. July 29, 2005, http://seattlepi.nwsource.com/opinion/234205_wared.html.

6. Intelligencer Editorial Board.

7. Larry Johnson, "Former CIA Man Says Bush Not Happy Over New Terror Language," Raw Story Media, Inc., August 2, 2005. Oct. 4, 2005, http://rawstory.com/news/2005/Former_CIA_man_says_Bush_not_happy_over_new_terror_la_0802.html.

8. Laurie Goodstein, "Muslim Leaders Confront Terror Threat Within Islam," *New York Times*, September 2, 2005. September 2, 2005, http://www.nytimes.com/2005/09/02/national/nationalspecial3/02muslims.html?th=&adxnnl=1&emc=th&adxnnlx=1125684055-GC+GTs7828J+YcvEoMQI4Q.

9. U.S. Patriot Act, USA Patriot Act FOIA Page, HR 3162 RDS, 107th Congress, 1st Session, H. R. 3162, in the Senate of the United States, Received October 24, 2001. September 4, 2005, http://www.epic.org/privacy/terrorism/hr3162.html.

10. National Commission on Terrorist Attacks upon the United States, *The 9/11 Commission Report*, 395.

11. U.S. Department of State, Bureau of Public Affairs, Counterterrorism Office, "U.S. Counterterrorism Policy," n.d. July 16, 2005, http://www.state.gov/s/ct/.

12. U.S. Department of State, "U.S. Counterterrorism Policy."

13. Declan McCullagh, CNET News.com, "Bush signs Homeland Security Bill," ZDNet, November 25, 2002. July 17, 2005, http://news.zdnet.com/2100-1009_22-975305.html.

14. U.S. Department of Homeland Security, "Transcript of Secretary of Homeland Security Tom Ridge at the Launch of New Ready Campaign Public Service Advertisements," November 22, 2004. July 17, 2005, http://www.dhs.gov/dhspublic/interapp/speech/speech_0230.xml.

15. Hanley J. Harding, Jr. (Boca Raton, FL: *C/B/R/N: Chemical/Biological/Radiological/Nuclear Disaster Familiarization and Overview Manual*), March 2005.

16. Mariano-Florentino Cuellar, "Choosing Anti-Terror Targets by National Origin and Race," 6 *Harvard Latino Law Review* 9 (Spring, 2003).

17. Cuellar, 38.

18. Cuellar, 39.

19. Edmund L. Andrews, "Who Bears the Risks of Terror?" *New York Times*, July 10, 2005. July 10, 2005, http://www.nytimes.com/2005/07/10/business/yourmoney/10view.html?th&emc=th&oref=login.

20. Edmund L. Andrews.

21. Breaking News and Commentary from Citizens for Legitimate Government, July 31, 2005. August 2, 2005, http://www.legitgov.org/index.html#breaking_news.

22. MSNBC.com, "Congress Renews Patriot Act for One Month," December 22, 2005. December 26, 2005, http://www.msnbc.msn.com/id/10562008/.

23. Charles E. Grassley (R-IA), U.S. Senate, letter, Sept. 15, 2005.

24. Grassley, letter, Sept. 15, 2005.

25. Kristen Elizabeth Uhl, "Comment: the Freedom of Information Act Post-9/11: Balancing the Public's Right to Know, Critical Infrastructure Protection, and Homeland Security," 53 *American University Law Review* 261 (October 2003).

26. U.S. Department of Justice, *The Attorney General's Guidelines on General Crimes, Racketeering Enterprise and Terrorism Enterprise Investigations*, 22, 2002. July 17, 2005, http://www.usdoj.gov/olp/generalcrimes2.pdf.

27. Tom Lininger, "Sects, Lies, and Videotape: The Surveillance and Infiltration of Religious Groups," 89 *Iowa Law Review* n1 (April 2004).

28. Michael Ignatieff, "Book Review: What Is the Greatest Evil?: the Lesser Evil: Political Ethics in an Age of Terror," 118 *Harvard Law Review* 2134 (May 2005).

29. Leigh A. Kite, "Note: Red Flagging Civil Liberties and Due Process Rights of Airline Passengers: Will a Redesigned Capps II System Meet the Constitutional Challenge?" 61 *Washington and Lee Law Review* 1385 (Summer 2004).

30. Rear Admiral D.M. Williams, Jr., USN (Ret.), interview, May 16, 2005.

31. Williams, interview, May 16, 2005.

32. Williams, interview, May 16, 2005.

33. Williams, interview, May 16, 2005.

34. Williams, interview, May 16, 2005.

35. Williams, interview, May 16, 2005.

36. Peter Baker, "'New Stage' of Fear for Chechen Women Russian Forces Suspected in Abductions," *Washington Post*, October 19, 2004, A12. April 9, 2005, http://www.washingtonpost.com/wp-dyn/articles/A43296-2004Oct18.html?sub=AR.

37. Mariya Rasner, "'Black Widow' Fears Surround a Russian Verdict," *Women's eNews*, February 6, 2005. April 9, 2005, http://www.womensenews.org/article.cfm/dyn/aid/2175/context/cover/.

38. Rasner.

39. Williams, interview, May 16, 2005.

40. Barbara Ehrenreich, "A New Counterterrorism Strategy: Feminism," AlterNet.org, May 10, 2005. May 11, 2005, http://www.truthout.org/issues_05/051005WA.shtml.

41. Robert A. Pape in Patricia Wilson, "Religion, Suicide Terrorism Link Disputed in Book," *Reuters*, June 3, 2005. June 4, 2005, http://news.yahoo.com/news?tmpl=story&cid=578&e=6&u=/nm/20050603/ts_nm/security_terrorism_dc.

42. Robert A. Pape, "Al Qaeda's Smart Bombs," *New York Times*, July 9, 2005. July 9, 2005, http://www.nytimes.com/2005/07/09/opinion/09pape.html?ex=1121572800&en=7ebffbfaf30039a5&ei=5070&emc=etal.

43. Pape, "Al Qaeda's Smart Bombs."

44. Wesley K. Clark, "Al-qaeda Has Changed; Bush Strategy Also Needs to Shift," *USAToday.com*, July 10, 2005. July 12, 2005, http://www.usatoday.com/news/opinion/editorials/2005-07-10-london-clark_x.htm.

45. Clark.

46. Clark.

47. Pape, "Al Qaeda's Smart Bombs."

48. "The 11 March 2004 Madrid Train Bombings," Wikipedia, September 30, 2005. October 4, 2005, http://en.wikipedia.org/wiki/March_11,_2004_Madrid_attacks.

49. Pape, "Al Qaeda's Smart Bombs."

50. Scott Atran, "Mishandling Suicide Terrorism," *The Washington Quarterly*, Summer 2004, 83. May 26, 2005, http://www.twq.com/04summer/docs/04summer_atran.pdf.

51. Preston Taran, "Martyrdom," Arabic Media Internet Network, June 1, 2005. June 22, 2005, http://www.amin.org/eng/uncat/2005/june/june1.html.

52. Taran.

53. Atran, 83.

54. Atran, 83.

55. Atran, 84.

56. "Counter-Terrorism: Keep Them Dumb and Radicalized," News About Counter-Terrorism Operations at StrategyPage.com's How to Make War, 1998–2005. July 13, 2005, http://www.strategypage.com//fyeo/howtomakewar/default.asp?target=htterr.

57. "Counter-Terrorism: Keep Them Dumb and Radicalized."

58. Atran, 86.

59. Debra D. Zedalis, *Female Suicide Bombers* (Carlisle, PA: Strategic Studies Institute, U.S. Army War College), June 2004, 12–13. April 2, 2005, http://www.carlisle.army.mil/ssi/pdffiles/00373.pdf.

60. Atran, 80.

61. Susan B. Glasser, "Review May Shift Terror Policies: U.S. Is Expected to Look Beyond Al Qaeda," *Washington Post*, May 29, 2005, A01. October 4, 2005, http://www.washingtonpost.com/wp-dyn/content/article/2005/05/28/AR2005052801171.html.

62. Zedalis, 12–13.

63. Yoram Schweitzer, "Suicide Bombings The Ultimate Weapon?" August 7, 2001. April 15, 2005, http://www.ict.org.il/articles/articledet.cfm?articleid=373.

64. Atran, 70.

65. Atran, 71–72.

66. U.S. Department of State, Bureau of Public Affairs, Counterterrorism Office, Counterterrorism Finance Unit, n.d. July 16, 2005, http://www.state.gov/s/ct/terfin/. *See also* U.S. Department of State, Bureau of Public Affairs, Bureau of Economic and Business Affairs, "Money Laundering and Terrorist Financing in the Middle East and South Asia," July 13, 2005. July 16, 2005, http://www.state.gov/e/eb/rls/rm/2005/49564.htm.

67. Williams, Jr., interview, May 16, 2005.

68. Williams, Jr., interview, May 16, 2005.

69. Corporal Ray Youngblut, USA (Ret.), 45th Division Infantry, Thunderbird, interview, Sept. 12, 2005.

70. Williams, Jr., interview, May 16, 2005.

71. Williams, Jr., interview, May 16, 2005.

72. Hardwick, email, Sept. 9, 2005.

73. Associated Press, "Former September 11 Panel: U.S. Unready for Next Terror Attack." *Courier* (Iowa), December 5, 2005, A1, A5.

74. Jessica Stern, "When Bombers Are Women," *Washington Post*, Dec. 18, 2003, 1A, 35 in Zedalis, 1.

75. Stern, 35 in Zedalis, 1.

76. Lisa, Kruger, *Gender and Terrorism: Motivations of Female Terrorists*, MSSI thesis, Joint Military Intelligence College, July 2005, abstract.

Chapter 9

1. Heather A. Andrews, *Veiled Jihad: The Threat of Female Islamic Suicide Terrorists*, master of science, strategic intelligence thesis, Joint Military Intelligence College, July 2005, 1.

2. "Suspect Retells Beslan's Horror; Leader Blew Up Female Bombers After They Balked at Taking Children Hostage, Court Told," Associated Press, *The Record* (Kitchener-Waterloo, Ontario), June 1, 2005, Final Ed., A7.

3. Basel Saleh, "Palestinian Suicide Attacks Revisited," *Peace Magazine* 21, no. 2, April 1, 2005, p. n/a.

4. Naim Ateek, "Suicide Bombers: What Is Theologically and Morally Wrong with Suicide Bombings? A Palestinian Christian Perspective," Sabeel Ecumenical Liberation Theology Center, Document No. 1 (2003) in Basel Saleh, "Palestinian Suicide Attacks Revisited," *Peace Magazine* 21, no. 2, April 1, 2005, p. n/a.

5. Emile Durkheim, *Suicide: A Study in Sociology*, translated by John A. Spaulding and George Simpson, George Simpson (ed.) (New York: The Free Press), 1897/1996, 14, 305–306.

6. Lisa Kruger, *Gender and Terrorism: Motivations of Female Terrorists*, master of science, strategic intelligence thesis, Joint Military Intelligence College, July 2005, 31.

7. Rosemarie Skaine, *Women at War: Gender Issues of Americans in Combat*, Jefferson, N.C.: McFarland, 1999, 16.

8. Skaine, *Women at War*, 164.

9. Mia Bloom, *Dying to Kill: The Allure of Suicide Terror* (New York: Columbia University Press), 2005, 162.

10. V.G. Julie Rajan, "Essay: Subversive Visibility and Political Agency: The Case of Palestinian Female Suicide Bombers," *To Kill, to Die: Feminist Contestations on Gender and Political Violence*, March 2004, 13.

11. Rajan, 13.

12. Raphael Israeli, "Palestinian Women: The Quest for a Voice in the Public Square through 'Islamikaze Martyrdom,'" *Terrorism and Political Violence*, 16, no. 1 (Spring 2004), 67.

13. Clara Beyler, "Messengers of Death Female Suicide Bombers," International Policy Institute for Counter-Terrorism, February 12, 2003. April 10, 2005, http:www.ict.org.il/articles/articledet.cfm?articleid=470.

14. Yoram Schweitzer, "Female Suicide Bombers for God," No. 88, October 9, 2003. June 6, 2005, www.tau.ac.il/jcss/tanotes/TAUnotes88.doc.

15. Israeli, 66.

16. Jefferson D. Reynolds, "Collateral Damage on the 21st Century Battlefield: Enemy Exploitation of the Law of Armed Conflict, and the Struggle for a Moral High Ground," 56 *Air Force Law Review* 75 (2005).

17. Reynolds, 76.

18. Reynolds, n321.

19. Israeli, 93.

20. Beyler, "Messengers."

21. Skaine, *Women at War*, 19.

22. Linda Grant De Pauw in Skaine, *Women at War*, 19.

23. Linda Grant De Pauw in Skaine, 18–19.

24. Skaine, *Women at War*, 13.

25. Skaine, *Women at War*, Ch. 5.

26. Adam Brookes, "U.S. Rejects Ban on Women in Combat," BBC News, May 19, 2005. July 1, 2005, http://news.bbc.co.uk/2/hi/americas/4560847.stm.

27. Kruger, *Gender and Terrorism*, 84.

28. Kruger, email interview, September 21, 2005.

29. Discovery Channel, "Suicide Bombers: Cult of Death," September 10, 2005.

30. Kruger, *Gender and Terrorism*, 26.

31. Andrews, *Veiled Jihad*, 1.

Notes to the Tables

Table 4.1

a. Mohammed Daraghmeh, "In Search of Stealthier Suicide Attackers, Islamic Jihad Encourages Women," Associated Press, May 31, 2003. June 22, 2005, http://sfgate.com/cgi-bin/article.cgi?file=/news/archive/2003/05/31/international1634EDT0609.DTL.

b. Daraghmeh.

c. Luca Ricolfi (Paolo Campana), "Suicide Missions in the Palestinian Area: A New Database," 2004. August 2, 2005, http://www.prio.no/cscw/pdf/micro/techniqes/suicide_missions.pdf; Palestine Facts: Israel 1967–1991 Terrorist Attacks 1970S, 2005. September 12, 2005, http://www.palestinefacts.org/pf_1967to1991_terrorism_1970s.php.

d. Majeda Al-Batsh, "Mystery Surrounds Palestinian Woman Suicide Bomber," Agence France Presse, January 28, 2002, Sec.: International. News; Clara Beyler, "Chronology of Suicide Bombings Carried out by Women," International Policy Institute for Counter-Terrorism, February 12, 2003. April 15, 2005, http://www.ict.org.il/; Robert A. Pape, *Dying to Win: The Strategic Logic of Suicide Terrorism*, New York: Random House, 2005, 138; Yoram Schweitzer, "Female Suicide Bombers for God," No. 88, October 9, 2003. June 6, 2005, www.tau.ac.il/jcss/tanotes/TAUnotes88.doc; Debra D. Zedalis, *Female Suicide Bombers*, Carlisle, PA: Strategic Studies Institute, U.S. Army War College, June 2004, 5. April 2, 2005, http://www.carlisle.army.mil/ssi/pdffiles/00373.pdf.

e. Ricolfi.

f. Pape, *Dying to Win*, 212.

g. For photo see SSNP.com, Syrian Social Nationalist Party, Gallery, "Our Martyrs," 1977. September 13, 2005, http://www.ssnp.com/new/gallery/shouhada_en.htm.

h. Beyler, "Chronology"; Ricolfi.

i. Pape, *Dying to Win*, 205.

j. Beyler, "Chronology,"; Ricolfi.

k. Beyler, "Chronology."

l. For photo see SSNP.com.; Pape, 206.

m. Pape, *Dying to Win*, 205.

n. Beyler, "Chronology"; Ricolfi; Zedalis, 5.

o. Beyler, "Chronology."

p. Beyler, "Chronology."

Table 4.2

a. Debra D. Zedalis, *Female Suicide Bombers*, Carlisle, PA: Strategic Studies Institute, U.S. Army War College, June 2004, 4. April 2, 2005, http://www.carlisle.army.mil/ssi/pdffiles/00373.pdf.

b. Clara Beyler, "Chronology of Suicide Bombings Carried Out by Women," International Policy Institute for Counter-Terrorism, February 12, 2003. April 15, 2005, http://www.ict.org.il/; Zedalis, 4.

c. Zedalis, 4.

d. Beyler, "Chronology"; Zedalis, 4.

e. Beyler, "Chronology"; Zedalis, 5.

f. Beyler, "Chronology"; Zedalis, 5.

g. Beyler, "Chronology"; Zedalis, 3.

h. Beyler, "Chronology."

i. Zedalis, 5.

j. Beyler, "Chronology."

k. U.S. Department of State, Counterterrorism Office. *Patterns of Global Terrorism 2003*, April 2004, 56. April 28, 2005, http://www.state.gov/s/ct/rls/pgtrpt/2003/.

Table 5.1

a. Isaac Kfir, "Commentary — A Blow to the Peace Process," International Center for Terrorism (ICT) — Terrorism and Counter-Terrorism, August 14, 2005. August 16, 2005, http://www.ict.org.il/spotlight/comment.cfm?id=1108; Robert A. Pape, *Dying to Win: The Strategic Logic of Suicide Terrorism* (New York: Random

House), 2005, 226–227; U.S. Department of State, Bureau of Public Affairs, Office of the Historian, "Significant Terrorist Incidents, 1961–2003: A Brief Chronology," March 2004. April 17, 2005, http://www.state.gov/r/pa/ho/pubs/fs/5902.htm.

b. "Sri Lanka Database — Suicide Attacks by the LTTE," 2001. September 17, 2005, http://www.satp.org/satporgtp/countries/shrilanka/database/data_suicide_killings.htm.

c. Clara Beyler, "Messengers of Death: Female Suicide Bombers," International Policy Institute for Counter-Terrorism, February 12, 2003. April 10, 2005, http://www.ict.org.il/articles/articledet.cfm?articleid=470; Pape, 226.

d. K.T. Rajasingham, "Sri Lanka: the Untold Story: Rajiv Gandhi's Assassination, Asia Times, 1995–2005. July 23, 2005, http://www.lankalibrary.com/pol/rajiv.htm.

e. Pape, *Dying to Win*, 226–227.
f. "Sri Lanka Database."
g. "Sri Lanka Database."
h. "Sri Lanka Database."
i. "Sri Lanka Database."
j. "Sri Lanka Database."
k. "Sri Lanka Database."
l. "Sri Lanka Database."
m. "Sri Lanka Database."
n. "Sri Lanka Database."
o. "Sri Lanka Database."

p. Heather A. Andrews, *Veiled Jihad: The Threat of Female Islamic Suicide Terrorists*, master of science, strategic intelligence thesis, Joint Military Intelligence College, July 2005, 134; *AsiaNow*, "Suspected Suicide Bomber Kills at Least 11 in Sri Lanka," January 5, 2000. May 24, 2005, http://archives.cnn.com/2000/ASIANOW/south/01/05/sri.lanka.explosion/index.html; "Sri Lanka Database."

q. Andrews, *Veiled Jihad*, 134; *AsiaNow*, "Suspected"; "Sri Lanka Database."

r. Andrews, *Veiled Jihad*, 134; *AsiaNow*, "Suspected"; "Sri Lanka Database."

s. Andrews, *Veiled Jihad*, 134–135; "Sri Lanka Database."

Table 6.1

a. Clara Beyler, "Messengers of Death: Female Suicide Bombers," International Policy Institute for Counter-Terrorism, February 12, 2003. April 10, 2005, http://www.ict.org.il/articles/articledet.cfm?articleid=470; Chris Kline and Mark Franchetti, "The Woman Behind the Mask," *Sunday Times* (London), November 3, 2002, Sec.: Features; News Review, 1.; Debra D. Zedalis, *Female Suicide Bombers*, Carlisle,

PA: Strategic Studies Institute, U.S. Army War College, June 2004, 2. April 2, 2005, http://www.carlisle.army.mil/ssi/pdffiles/00373.pdf.

b. Clara Beyler, "Chronology of Suicide Bombings Carried Out by Women," International Policy Institute for Counter-Terrorism, February 12, 2003. April 15, 2005, http://www.ict.org.il/.

c. Mainat Abdulajewa, "Why They Murder: About the Chechen Terrorism," September 3, 2004. July 23, 2005, http://www.tamera.org/english/aktuelltext/News/whytheykill.html; Robert A. Pape, *Dying to Win: The Strategic Logic of Suicide Terrorism* (New York: Random House), 2005, 212.

d. Answers.com, "Tell Me About: Female Suicide Bomber," Information from *Wikipedia*, March 13, 2005. April 16, 2005, http://www.answers.com/topic/female-suicide-bomber.

e. Mariya Rasner, "'Black Widow' Fears Surround a Russian Verdict," *Women's eNews*, February 6, 2005. April 9, 2005, http://www.womensenews.org/article.cfm/dyn/aid/2175/context/cover/.

f. Beyler, "Chronology"; Pape, *Dying to Win*, 212; Zedalis, 5.

g. Center for Nonproliferation Studies (CNS), "Moscow Theater Hostage Crisis: Incapacitants and Chemical Warfare," November 4, 2002. September 19, 2005, http://cns.miis.edu/pubs/week/021110b.htm; Viv Groskop, "Chechnya's Deadly 'Black Widows'..." *New Statesman*, Vol. 133 Issue 4704 (September 6, 2004): 32(2); Radio Free Europe/Radio Liberty, "Factbox: Major Terrorist Incidents Tied to Russian-Chechen War," September 6, 2004. June 27, 2005, http://rfe.rferl.org/featuresarticle/2004/09/d981dd2d-8b08-41ff-a2e2-ada25338093c.html.

h. Brian Handwerk, "Female Suicide Bombers: Dying to Kill," National Geographic Channel, December 13, 2004. April 3, 2005, http://news.nationalgeographic.com/news/2004/12/1213_041213_tv_suicide_bombers.html.

i. Vadim Rechkalov "Psychology of Chechen Woman Suicide Bombers Pondered," *Global News Wire*, August 5, 2003.

j. Anne Speckhard, Nadejda Tarabrina, Valery Krasnov and Khapta Akmedova, "Research Note: Observations of Suicidal Terrorists in Action," *Terrorism and Political Violence*, 16, no. 2 (Summer 2004), 309.

k. Clara Beyler, "Female Suicide Bombers An Update," International Policy Institute for Counter-Terrorism, March 7, 2004. April 15, 2005, http://www.ict.org.il/.

Notes to the Tables

l. MILNET, "Brief Chronology of Russian Terrorism 1/1/1990 to 9/02/2004," August 28, 2005, http://www.milnet.com/Russian-Terror ism.html.

m. "Basayev Takes Responsibility for Znamenskoye Explosion and Death of Gazimago-madov," *Chechen Times*, May 19, 2003, News. August 28, 2005, http://www.chechentimes. org/en/news/?id=8718; MILNET.

n. Answers.com.

o. Zedalis, 3.

p. Beyler, "Update"; CBS News, "Truck Bomb Kills Dozens in Chechnya," May 13, 2003. August 28, 2005, http://www.cbsnews.com/stories/ 2003/05/13/world/main553581.html; Christoph Reuter, *My Life Is a Weapon: A Modern History of Suicide Bombing*, translated by Helena Ragg-Kirkby (Princeton, N.J.: Princeton University Press), 2004, 151.

q. Answers.com; Beyler, "Update"; CNN. com, "Woman Kills 17 in Russia Bus Blast," June 5, 2003. May 24, 2005, http://www.cnn. com/2003/WORLD/europe/06/05/russia.bus/ index.html; Norwegian Institute of International Affairs, Centre for Russian Studies Database, "Chronology of Events: a Wave of Terror Hits Russia — an Overview of the Most Important Terrorist Acts 1995–2004," August 31, 2004. April 16, 2005, http://www.nupi.no/cgi-win/Russland/krono.exe?6224; Reuter, 151; United Nations Office for the Coordination of Humanitarian Affairs (OCHA) in the Russian Federation United, "Russian Media Review for 15.05.2003," *RIA Novosti*, May 15, 2003. August 28, 2005, http://www.ocha.ru/public. php?_act=new&_op=view&_ti=7128; U.S. Department of State, Counterterrorism Office, *Patterns of Global Terrorism 2003*, April 2004. April 28, 2005, http://www.state.gov/s/ct/rls/ pgtrpt/2003/.

r. Beyler, "Update"; Zaur Farniyev (Kommersant), "One Life Sentence for 19 Lives — Court Hands Down Sentences in Mozdok Bombing Case," *Current Digest of the Post-Soviet Press* 57, no. 11, Sec.: The Russian Federation — North Caucasus (April 13, 2005); Reuter, 151.

s. David E. Kaplan, "Tangled Roots of an Atrocity (Chechen Terrorism, Russia)," *U.S. News & World Report* 137, Issue 9, September 20, 2004, p. 28; Reuter, 151.

t. CNN.com, "Woman Kills."

u. Beyler, "Update."

v. Beyler, "Update"; U.S. Dept. of State, *Patterns of Global Terrorism 2003*, 37.

w. CNN.com, "Two Moscow Concert Bombers Kill 14," July 5, 2003. May 24, 2005, http://

www.cnn.com/2003/WORLD/europe/07/05/ russia.blast/index.html.

x. Groskop.

y. MILNET.

z. Beyler, "Update"; Pape, *Dying to Win*, 212.

aa. Answers.com.

bb. Beyler, "Update."

cc. Beyler, "Update"; *RIA Novosti*, "Reference: Terrorist Attacks in Moscow in 1999–2004," September 1, 2004, ACC-NO: 4791672; U.S. Department of State, Bureau of Public Affairs, Office of the Historian, "Significant Terrorist Incidents, 1961–2003: A Brief Chronology," March 2004. April 17, 2005, http://www.state. gov/r/pa/ho/pubs/fs/5902.htm; U.S. Department of State, *Patterns of Global Terrorism 2003*; Zedalis, 4, 5.

dd. Groskop.

ee. Groskop.

ff. CNN.com, "'Bribe' Got Bomber on Russian Jet," September 15, 2004, International, Ed. May 24, 2005, http://www.cnn.com/2004/ WORLD/europe/09/15/russia.planecrash/index. html; Norwegian Institute of International Affairs, Centre for Russian Studies Database; Rasner.

gg. CNN.com, "Moscow Suicide Bomber Kills 9," August 31, 2004 International, Ed. May 24, 2005, http://www.cnn.com/2004/ WORLD/europe/08/31/russia.carblast/index. html; UPI NewsTrack (Moscow), "FSB: Woman Responsible for Car Bomb," August 31, 2004 pNA.

hh. "Beslan School Hostage Crisis," *Wikipedia*, September 25, 2005. September 30, 2005, http://en.wikipedia.org/wiki/Beslan_ school_massacre; Diplomat News Service, "The Beslan Attack & Qaeda Link," Vol. 61 Issue 11. September 13, 2004; John Kampfner, *New Statesman*, Vol. 133 Issue 4705, September 13, 2004, p. 10(4); "Suspect Retells Beslan's Horror; Leader Blew Up Female Bombers After They Balked at Taking Children Hostage, Court Told," Associated Press, *Toronto Star Newspapers, Ltd., The Record* (Kitchener-Waterloo, Ontario), June 1, 2005, Final Ed., Sec. Front, A7.

Table 6.2

a. Sergei Gulyayev, "Woman Who Tried to Blow Up Commandant's Office Identified," *TASS*, December 20, 2000; Debra D. Zedalis, *Female Suicide Bombers* (Carlisle, PA: Strategic Studies Institute, U.S. Army War College), June 2004, 6. April 2, 2005, http://www.carlisle. army.mil/ssi/pdffiles/00373.pdf.

b. Stephen Mulvey, "Russia's Suicide Bomb Nightmare," BBC News Online, February 6, 2004. September 19, 2005, http://news.bbc.co.uk/1/hi/world/europe/3020231.stm.

c. Richard Beeston, "Black Widow Suicide Bombers Are Extremists' Worst Weapon," *The Times* (London), September 3, 2004, Sec.: Overseas news, 4; Clara Beyler, "Female Suicide Bombers an Update," International Policy Institute for Counter-Terrorism, March 7, 2004. April 15, 2005, http://www.ict.org.il/; *RIA Novosti*, "Reference: Terrorist Attacks in Moscow in 1999–2004," September 1, 2004, ACC-NO: 4791672; Zedalis, 6.

d. Mia Bloom, *Dying to Kill: The Allure of Suicide Terror* (New York: Columbia University Press), 2005, 145.

Table 7.1

a. Mohammed Daraghmeh, "In Search of Stealthier Suicide Attackers, Islamic Jihad Encourages Women," Associated Press, May 31, 2003. June 22, 2005, http://sfgate.com/cgi-bin/article.cgi?file=/news/archive/2003/05/31/international1634EDT0609.DTL.

b. BBC News, Middle East, "Israel's History of Bomb Blasts," February 25, 2005. June 4, 2005, http://news.bbc.co.uk/1/hi/world/middle_east/1197051.stm.

c. Majeda Al-Batsh, "Mystery Surrounds Palestinian Woman Suicide Bomber," *Agence France Presse*, January 28, 2002, Sec.: International. News; Wafa Amr, "Palestinian Women Play Role in Fighting Occupation," Palestine, *Aman Daily News*, January 29, 2002. August 7, 2005, http://www.amanjordan.org/english/daily_news/wmview.php?ArtID=27; Karla J. Cunningham, "Cross-Regional Trends in Female Terrorism," Studies in Conflict and Terrorism 26, Issue 3 (May-June 2003): 182; BBC Worldwide Monitoring (Source: Voice of Palestine, Ramallah), "Palestinian Radio Says Israeli Shelling of Jenin Continues," September 14, 2001; Israel Ministry of Foreign Affairs, "The Role of Palestinian Women in Suicide Terrorism (Communicated by Israeli security sources)," January 30, 2003. August 29, 2005, http://www.mfa.gov.il/MFA/MFAArchive/2000_2009/2003/1/The+Role+of+Palestinian+Women+in+Suicide+Terrorism.htm; Erica Silverman, "Jordanian Citizens in Israeli Prisons," *Al-Bawaba*, July 23, 2005.

d. Clara Beyler, "Chronology of Suicide Bombings Carried Out by Women," International Policy Institute for Counter-Terrorism, February 12, 2003. April 15, 2005, http://www.

ict.org.il/; Council on Foreign Relations, "Terrorism: Q & A: Al-Aqsa Martyrs Brigades," 2004. April 14, 2005, http://cfrterrorism.org/groups/alaqsa.html; Cunningham, 183, 184; Hilla Dayan, "Theories of Gender and Nationalism," work in progress. May 13, 2005, http://www.fhk.eur.nl/personal/zuidhof/Hilla_files/Nationalism%20Engendered.doc; Israel Defense Forces, "Major Palestinian Terrorist Attacks Since September 2000," February 25, 2004; Israel Defense Forces, "Main Terrorist Attacks against Israeli Civilians and IDF Soldiers since the Onset of Ebb and Flow," June 30, 2005, http://www1.idf.il/SIP_STORAGE/DOVER/files/7/32367.doc; Ministry Foreign Relations, Israel, "Suicide and Other Bombing Attacks in Israel Since the Declaration of Principles (September 1993)," *MFR Newsletter*, 2004. June 30, 2005, http://www.mfa.gov.il/MFA/Terrorism-+Obstacle+to+Peace/Palestinian+terror+since+2000/Suicide%20and%20Other%20Bombing%20Attacks%20in%20Israel%20Since; State of Israel, Ministry of Foreign Relations, "Facts About Israel: 2000–2004 — Major Terror Attacks," November 2, 2000. April 16, 2005, http://www.mfa.gov.il/MFA/Facts+About+Israel/Israel+in+Maps/2000-2004-+Major+Terror+Attacks.htm; U.S. Department of State, Counterterrorism Office, *Country Reports on Terrorism, 2004*, April 2005, "Terrorist Group Profiles," "Al-Aqsa Martyrs Brigade," U.S. Navy, May 10, 2005. June 23, 2005, http://library.nps.navy.mil/home/tgp/aqsa.htm; Barbara Victor, *Army of Roses: Inside the World of Palestinian Women Suicide Bombers* (Emmaus, PA: Rodale), 2003, 4–5, 20; Debra D. Zedalis, *Female Suicide Bombers*, Carlisle, PA: Strategic Studies Institute, U.S. Army War College, June 2004. April 2, 2005, http://www.carlisle.army.mil/ssi/pdffiles/00373.pdf.

e. Al-Batsh.

f. Beyler, "Chronology"; Luca Ricolfi (Paolo Campana), "Suicide Missions in the Palestinian Area: A New Database," 2004. August 2, 2005, http://www.prio.no/cscw/pdf/micro/techniqes/suicide_missions.pdf.

g. Beyler, "Chronology"; Cunningham, 184; Ricolfi.

h. Libby Copeland, "Female Suicide Bombers: The New Factor in Mideast's Deadly Equation," *Washington Post*, April 27, 2002, C01. July 11, 2005, http://amenusa.org/fembombers.htm.

i. Answers.com, "Tell Me About: Female Suicide Bomber," Information from *Wikipedia*, March 13, 2005. April 16, 2005, http://www.answers.com/topic/female-suicide-bomber; Beyler, "Chronology"; Cunningham, 184; Ashley M. Heher, "Female Suicide Bombers an Extension of an Old Tradition," *Cox News Service*, Sec.: Washington, General News, April 28, 2002; Israel Defense Forces, "Major Attacks Since September 2000"; Israel Defense Forces, "Main Terrorist Attacks Since the Onset"; V.G. Julie Rajan, "Essay: Subversive Visibility and Political Agency: The Case of Palestinian Female Suicide Bombers," *To Kill, to Die: Feminist Contestations on Gender and Political Violence*, March 2004, 12; Ricolfi; U.S. Department of State, Bureau of Public Affairs, Office of the Historian, "Significant Terrorist Incidents, 1961–2003: A Brief Chronology," March 2004, fig. 90. April 17, 2005, http://www.state.gov/r/pa/ho/pubs/fs/5902.htm.

j. Israel Ministry of Foreign Affairs, "The Role of Palestinian Women."

k. Clara Beyler, "Female Suicide Bombers An Update," International Policy Institute for Counter-Terrorism, March 7, 2004. April 15, 2005, http://www.ict.org.il/; Daraghmeh; Yoni Fighel, International Center for Terrorism (ICT), "Palestinian Islamic Jihad and Female Suicide Bombers," October 6, 2003. July 7, 2005, http://www.ict.org.il/; Ricolfi; U.S. Department of State, "Significant Terrorist Incidents, 1961–2003"; Zedalis, 4.

l. James Taranto, "Best of the Web Today," *WSJ.com Opinion Journal*, June 3, 2002. September 19, 2005, http://www.opinionjournal.com/best/?id=110001794; TruthNews, "Female Bomber Disgusted by Fatah Handlers," May 31, 2002. June 22, 2005, http://truthnews.com/world/2002060103.htm.

m. U.S. Department of State, Counterterrorism Office, *Patterns of Global Terrorism 2003*, April 2004, 62. April 28, 2005, http://www.state.gov/s/ct/rls/pgtrpt/2003/.

n. Beyler, "Update"; Fighel; Israel Defense Forces, "Major ... Attacks 2000"; Israel Defense Forces, "Main Terrorist Attacks Since the Onset"; Ministry Foreign Relations, Israel, "Attacks Since the Declaration of Principles"; Robert A. Pape, *Dying to Win: The Strategic Logic of Suicide Terrorism* (New York: Random House), 2005, 212; Ricolfi.

o. Ministry Foreign Relations, Israel, "Attacks Since the Declaration of Principles"; State of Israel, Ministry of Foreign Relations, "Facts About Israel"; Zedalis, 4, 5.

p. BBC News, Middle East, "Hamas Woman Bomber Kills Israelis," January 14, 2004. June 4, 2005, http://news.bbc.co.uk/2/hi/middle_east/3395973.stm.

q. CNN.com, "A Female Bomber Kills 2 Policemen in Jerusalem," September 22, 2004, International, Ed. May 24, 2005, http://www.cnn.com/2004/WORLD/meast/09/22/mideast/index.html; Ministry Foreign Relations, Israel, "Attacks Since the Declaration of Principles.";
Mitch Potter, "Female Bomber Kills 2 Israeli Border Guards," *The Toronto Star*, September 23, 2004, Sec., News, A06.

Table 7.2

a. Majeda Al-Batsh, "Mystery Surrounds Palestinian Woman Suicide Bomber," *Agence France Presse*, January 28, 2002, Sec.: International. News; Karla J. Cunningham, "Cross-Regional Trends in Female Terrorism," *Studies in Conflict and Terrorism* 26, I. 3 (May–June 2003):182.

b. Cunningham, 182; Yoni Fighel, "Palestinian Islamic Jihad and Female Suicide Bombers," International Center for Terrorism & Counter-Terrorism (ICT), October 6, 2003. July 7, 2005, http://www.ict.org.il/.

c. Cunningham, 182; Israel Ministry of Foreign Affairs, "The Role of Palestinian Women in Suicide Terrorism (Communicated by Israeli security sources)," January 30, 2003. August 29, 2005, http://www.mfa.gov.il/MFA/MFA Archive/2000_2009/2003/1/The+Role+of+Palestinian+Women+in+Suicide+Terrorism.htm.

d. Israel Ministry of Foreign Affairs, "The Role of Palestinian Women."

e. Manuela Dviri, "My Dream Was to Be a Suicide Bomber. I Wanted to Kill 20, 50 Jews. Yes, Even Babies," *Telegraph*, Tel Aviv, June 26, 2005. July 2, 2005, http://www.telegraph.co.uk/news/main.jhtml?xml=/news/2005/06/26/wmid26.xml; Israel Ministry of Foreign Affairs, "The Role of Palestinian Women"; Cageprisoners.com, "Women on the Edge of Destruction," July 2, 2005. July 9, 2005, http://www.cageprisoners.com/articles.php?id=5186.

f. Clara Beyler, "Chronology of Suicide Bombings Carried Out by Women," International Policy Institute for Counter-Terrorism, February 12, 2003. April 15, 2005, http://www.ict.org.il/; Israel Ministry of Foreign Affairs, "The Role of Palestinian Women"; Barbara Victor, *Army of Roses: Inside the World of Palestinian Women Suicide Bombers* (Emmaus, PA): Rodale, 2003, 259; Debra D. Zedalis, *Female Suicide Bombers*, Carlisle, PA: Strategic Studies Institute, U.S. Army War College, June 2004, 6. April 2, 2005, http://www.carlisle.army.mil/ssi/pdffiles/00373.pdf.

g. TruthNews, "Female Bomber Disgusted By Fatah Handlers," May 31, 2002. June 22,

2005, http://truthnews.com/world/2002060103.htm.

h. Beyler, "Chronology"; *TruthNews*; Zedalis, 6.

i. Beyler, "Chronology"; *TruthNews*.

j. Celean Jacobson, "Palestinian Woman Tells of Changing Her Mind, Calling Off Planned Suicide Attack," Associated Press, May 30, 2002. September 22, 2005, http://www.papillonsartpalace.com/palestiWn.htm.

k. Victor, 260.

l. Beyler, "Chronology"; Zedalis, 6.

m. Beyler, "Chronology"; Zedalis, 6.

n. Raphael Israeli, "Palestinian Women: The Quest for a Voice in the Public Square through 'Islamikaze Martyrdom,'" *Terrorism and Political Violence*, 16, no. 1 (Spring 2004), 84; Victor, 258–259.

o. Kalfaisms, "One Suicide Bomber Captured — Search for Second Bomber Called Off," October 20, 2004. June 22, 2005, http://www.thekalfafamily.com/one_suicide_bomber_captured.htm; "Terrorists and Militants in Haaretz," Tutti i diritti riservati, *Paravia Bruno Mondadori* Editori, October 20, 2004. July 4, 2005, http://www.pbmstoria.it/fonti1865.

p. Center for Special Studies (C.S.S), Intelligence and Terrorism Information Center, "Bi-weekly Summary Data on Palestinian Terrorism Since the Sharm El-sheikh Summit," June 16–30, 2005. July 4, 2005, http://www.intelligence.org.il/eng/pa_t_e/t30june_05.htm; Margot Dudkevitch, "Female Bomber: Attack Aimed at Youth," *The Jerusalem Post*. June 20, 2005. July 2, 2005, http://www.jpost.com/servlet/Satellite?pagename=JPost/JPArticle/ShowFull&cid=1119234009872.

q. Dviri.

r. Shaul Kimhi and Shemuel Even, "Who Are the Palestinian Suicide Bombers," *Terrorism and Political Violence*, 16, no. 4 (Winter 2004), 818.

s. Cageprisoners.com.

t. Cageprisoners.com.

u. Cageprisoners.com.

v. Cageprisoners.com.

w. Cageprisoners.com.

Bibliography

Abu Ramadan, Saud. "Muslim Women Can Be Martyrs Too," United Press International, provided by COMTEX. January 15, 2004, pNA. April 7, 2005, http://www.comtex news.com.

Abdulajewa, Mainat. "Why They Murder: About the Chechen Terrorism," September 3, 2004. July 23, 2005, http://www.tamera.org/english/aktuelltext/News/whytheykill. html.

Al-Batsh, Majeda. "Mystery Surrounds Palestinian Woman Suicide Bomber," *Agence France Presse*, January 28, 2002.

Alahmad, Nida. "Response to Birgit Langenberger," *To Kill, to Die: Feminist Contestations on Gender and Political Violence* (March 2004). 5–6.

Amr, Wafa. "Palestinian Women Play Role in Fighting Occupation," *Aman Daily News*, January 29, 2002. August 7, 2005, http://www.amanjordan.org/english/daily_news/ wmview.php?ArtID=27.

Andrews, Edmund L. "Who Bears the Risks of Terror?" *New York Times*, July 10, 2005. July 10, 2005, http://www.nytimes.com/2005/07/10/business/yourmoney/10view. html?th&emc=th&oref=login.

Andrews, Heather A. Email interview, August 29, 2005; follow-up, September 7, 2005.

_____. *Veiled Jihad: The Threat of Female Islamic Suicide Terrorists*, master of science, strategic intelligence thesis, Joint Military Intelligence College, July 2005.

Answers.com. "Tell Me About: Female Suicide Bomber," Information from *Wikipedia*, March 13, 2005. April 16, 2005, http://www.answers.com/topic/female-suicide-bomber.

AsiaNow. "Six Dead in Sri Lanka Blast," January 5, 2000. August 20, 2005, http://archives. cnn.com/2000/ASIANOW/south/01/04/sri.lanka.explosion.01/.

_____. "Suspected Suicide Bomber Kills at Least 11 in Sri Lanka," January 5, 2000. May 24, 2005, http://archives.cnn.com/2000/ASIANOW/south/01/05/sri.lanka.explo sion/index.html.

Associated Press. "Female Bombers Kill 27 in Iraq." *Courier* (Iowa), December 6, 2005, B1.

_____. "Former September 11 Panel: U.S. Unready for Next Terror Attack." *Courier* (Iowa), December 5, 2005, A1, A5.

_____. "Iraqi Woman Admits on TV to Jordan Attack." *Courier* (Iowa), A1.

Atran, Scott. "Mishandling Suicide Terrorism." *The Washington Quarterly* (Summer 2004). May 26, 2005, http://www.twq.com/04summer/docs/04summer_atran.pdf.

Ateek, Naim. "Suicide Bombers: What Is Theologically and Morally Wrong with Suicide Bombings? A Palestinian Christian Perspective." Sabeel Ecumenical Liberation Theology Center, Document No. 1 (2003), in Basel Saleh, "Palestinian Suicide Attacks Revisited," *Peace Magazine* 21, no. 2 (April 1, 2005), p. n/a.

Baker, Peter. "'New Stage' of Fear for Chechen Women Russian Forces Suspected in Abduc-

tions," *Washington Post.* October 19, 2004, A12. April 9, 2005, http://www.washing
tonpost.com/wp-dyn/articles/A43296-2004Oct18.html?sub=AR.

BBC News. "Hamas Woman Bomber Kills Israelis," January 14, 2004. June 4, 2005, http://
news.bbc.co.uk/2/hi/middle_east/3395973.stm.

_____. "Iraq Says Women Killed Troops," April 5, 2003. June 5, 2005, http://news.bbc.
co.uk/2/hi/middle_east/2917107.stm.

_____. "Israel's History of Bomb Blasts," February 25, 2005. June 4, 2005, http://news.
bbc.co.uk/1/hi/world/middle_east/1197051.stm.

BBC Worldwide Monitoring (Source: Voice of Palestine, Ramallah). "Palestinian Radio Says
Israeli Shelling of Jenin Continues," September 14, 2001.

Beeston, Richard. "Black Widow Suicide Bombers Are Extremists' Worst Weapon." *The
Times* (London). September 3, 2004, Sec.: Overseas news, 4.

Berry, Jessica. "Fury Over Hijacker's Visit to Britain," *Telegraph Network*, May 27, 2002.
July 4, 2005, http://www.portal.telegraph.co.uk/news/main.jhtml?xml=%2Fnews%
2F2002%2F05%2F27%2Fnpflp27.xml.

Beshara, Adel. "Antun Sa'adeh and the Struggle for Syrian National Independence (1904–
1949)," *Syrian Social Nationalist Party* (no date). June 6, 2005, http://www.geocities.
com/CapitolHill/Lobby/3577/adel_bechara2.html.

"Beslan School Hostage Crisis." *Wikipedia*, September 25, 2005. September 30, 2005,
http://en.wikipedia.org/wiki/Beslan_school_massacre.

Beyler, Clara. "Chronology of Suicide Bombings Carried Out by Women," International
Policy Institute for Counter-Terrorism, February 12, 2003. April 15, 2005, http://www.
ict.org.il/.

_____. "Female Suicide Bombers: An Update," International Policy Institute for Counter-
Terrorism, March 7, 2004. April 15, 2005, http://www.ict.org.il/.

_____. "Messengers of Death: Female Suicide Bombers," International Policy Institute for
Counter-Terrorism, February 12, 2003. April 10, 2005, http://www.ict.org.il/articles/
articledet.cfm?articleid=470.

bin Laden, Osama. "American Imperialism Motivates Suicide Bombers." In Lauri S. Friedman (ed.), *What Motivates Suicide Bombers?* San Diego: Greenhaven, 2005.

_____. "Text of Fatwah Urging Jihad Against Americans." *al-Quds al-'Arabi* February 23,
1998, in Lauri S. Friedman (ed.), *What Motivates Suicide Bombers?* San Diego: Greenhaven, 2005.

Bloom, Mia. *Dying to Kill: The Allure of Suicide Terror*, New York: Columbia Univ. Press, 2005.

Bobbitt, Philip. "Facing Jihad, Recalling the Blitz," *New York Times*, July 10, 2005. July 10,
2005, http://www.nytimes.com/2005/07/10/opinion/10bobbitt.html?th&emc=th.

Borger, Julian. "Rice Changed Terrorism Report," *The Guardian*, April 23, 2005. April 23,
2005, http://www.guardian.co.uk/usa/story/0,12271,1468541,00.html.

Breaking News and Commentary from Citizens for Legitimate Government. July 31, 2005.
August 2, 2005, http://www.legitgov.org/index.html#breaking_news.

Brookes, Adam. "U.S. Rejects Ban on Women in Combat," BBC News, May 19, 2005. July
1, 2005, http://news.bbc.co.uk/2/hi/americas/4560847.stm.

Bush, George W. Address before a Joint Session of the Congress on the State of the Union,
40 Weekly Comp. Pres. Doc. 94, 97 (January 20, 2004) in Richard A. Falk, "Agora:
ICJ Advisory Opinion on Construction of a Wall in the Occupied Palestinian Territory: Toward Authoritativeness: the ICJ Ruling on Israel's Security Wall," 99, n43
American Journal International Law 50 (January 2005).

_____. Address, Islamic Center of Washington, D.C., September 17, 2001, in Lauri S. Fried-
man (ed.), *What Motivates Suicide Bombers?* San Diego: Greenhaven, 2005.

Cageprisoners.com. "Women on the Edge of Destruction," July 2, 2005. July 9, 2005,
http://www.cageprisoners.com/articles.php?id=5186.

Bibliography

CBS News. "Truck Bomb Kills Dozens in Chechnya," May 13, 2003. August 28, 2005, http://www.cbsnews.com/stories/2003/05/13/world/main553581.shtml.

Center for Nonproliferation Studies. "Moscow Theater Hostage Crisis: Incapacitants and Chemical Warfare," November 4, 2002. September 19, 2005, http://cns.miis.edu/pubs/week/02110b.htm.

Center for Special Studies, Intelligence and Terrorism Information Center. "Bi-weekly Summary Data on Palestinian Terrorism since the Sharm El-sheikh Summit," June 16–30, 2005. July 4, 2005, http://www.intelligence.org.il/eng/pa_t_e/t30june_05.htm.

_____. "News of the Israeli-Palestinian Conflict: The End of an Era," September 1–15, 2005, 1. October 1, 2005, http://www.intelligence.org.il/eng/eng_n/pdf/t15sep_05.pdf.

_____. "Newsletter: Escalation of Palestinian Terrorism After the Disengagement," September 28, 2005. www.intelligence.org.il.

_____. "Newsletter: The Hamas-associated Al-Mustaqbal Research Center Presents Another Study," September 28, 2005. www.intelligence.org.il.

Charter of Allah: the Platform of the Islamic Resistance Movement (Hamas). Translated and annotated by Raphael Israeli, Harry Truman Research Institute, The Hebrew University, Jerusalem, Israel. "The Role of Muslim Women," Articles 17, 18, n.d. July 2, 2005, http://www.fas.org/irp/world/para/docs/880818.htm.

Chechen Times. "Basayev Takes Responsibility for Znamenskoye Explosion and Death of Gazimagomadov." May 19, 2003. August 28, 2005, http://www.chechentimes.org/en/news/?id=8718.

Clark, Wesley K. "Al-Qaeda Has Changed; Bush Strategy Also Needs to Shift," *USAToday.com,* July 10, 2005. July 12, 2005, http://www.usatoday.com/news/opinion/editorials/2005-07-10-london-clark_x.htm.

CNN.com. "Basayev: Russia's Most Wanted Man," September 8, 2004. October 5, 2005, http://edition.cnn.com/2004/WORLD/europe/09/08/russia.basayev/.

_____. "Belgian Paper IDs 'Suicide Bomber,'" December 1, 2005, International Ed. December 17, 2005, http://www.cnn.com/2005/WORLD/europe/12/01/belgium.iraq/index.html.

_____. "'Bribe' Got Bomber on Russian Jet," September 15, 2004, International Ed. May 24, 2005, http://www.cnn.com/2004/WORLD/europe/09/15/russia.planecrash/index.html.

_____. "EU Moves to Curb Terror Funding," July 12, 2005. July 14, 2005, http://www.cnn.com/2005/WORLD/europe/07/12/terror.funds.reut/index.html.

_____. "A Female Bomber Kills 2 Policemen in Jerusalem," September 22, 2004, International, Ed. May 24, 2005, http://www.cnn.com/2004/WORLD/meast/09/22/mideast/index.html.

_____. "Group Pleads for Release of Hostages; Suicide Bombers Kill Dozens in Iraq," December 6, 2005. December 18, 2005, http://www.cnn.com/2005/WORLD/meast/12/06/iraq.main/?section=cnn_topstories.

_____. "Moscow Suicide Bomber Kills 9," August 31, 2004, International, Ed. May 24, 2005, http://www.cnn.com/2004/WORLD/europe/08/31/russia.carblast/index.html.

_____. "Two Moscow Concert Bombers Kill 14," July 5, 2003. May 24, 2005, http://www.cnn.com/2003/WORLD/europe/07/05/russia.blast/index.html.

_____. "Woman Kills 17 in Russia Bus Blast," June 5, 2003. May 24, 2005, http://www.cnn.com/2003/WORLD/europe/06/05/russia.bus/index.html.

CNN Headline News. July 15, 2005.

Concord Learning Systems. "Russian History (Summary): The Russian Revolution and The Soviet Union, 200 B.C.–2000 A.D." Concord, N.C.: 1998–2003. May 20, 2005, http://www.laughtergenealogy.com/bin/histprof/misc/russia.html.

Bibliography

Conn, Tracy L. "Book Review: *When Women Kill: Questions of Agency and Subjectivity* by Belinda Morrissey, London: Routledge, 2003, p. 213," 27 *Harvard Women's Law Journal* 285 (Spring 2004).

Copeland, Libby. "Female Suicide Bombers: The New Factor in Mideast's Deadly Equation," *Washington Post*, April 27, 2002, C01. July 11, 2005, http://amenusa.org/fem bombers.htm.

Council on Foreign Relations. "Terrorism: Q & A: Al-Aqsa Martyrs Brigades," 2004. April 14, 2005, http://cfrterrorism.org/groups/alaqsa.html.

_____. "Terrorism Q & A: Do Women Ever Become Suicide Terrorists," 2005. April 15, 2005, http://cfrterrorism.org/terrorism/suicide2.html.

_____. "Terrorism: Q & A: Hezbollah (Lebanon, Islamists)," 2002. July 23, 2005, http://cfrterrorism.org/groups/hezbollah.html.

_____. "Terrorism Q & A: Is Suicide Terrorism Becoming More Common?" 2005. May 25, 2005, http://www.cfr.org/reg_issues.php?id=13||||1.

_____. "Terrorism: Q & A: Syria," 2004. July 23, 2005, http://www.cfrterrorism.org/spon sors/syria.html.

_____. "Terrorism: Q & A: Types of Terrorism," 2004. July 23, 2005, http://www.cfrter rorism.org/terrorism/types2.html.

"Counter-Terrorism: Keep Them Dumb and Radicalized." News About Counter-Terrorism Operations at StrategyPage.com's How to Make War, 1998–2005. July 13, 2005, http://www.strategypage.com/fyeo/howtomakewar/default.asp?target=htterr.

Cuellar, Mariano-Florentino. "Article: Choosing Anti-Terror Targets by National Origin and Race," 6 *Harvard Latino Law Review* 9 (Spring 2003).

Cunningham, Karla J. "Cross-Regional Trends in Female Terrorism," *Studies in Conflict and Terrorism* 26, Issue 3 (May–June 2003): 171–195.

Daraghmeh, Mohammed. "In Search of Stealthier Suicide Attackers, Islamic Jihad Encourages Women," Associated Press, May 31, 2003. June 22, 2005, http://sfgate.com/cgi-bin/article.cgi?file=/news/archive/2003/05/31/international634EDT0609.DTL.

David, Peter. "Islam Advocates Suicide Terrorism." In Lauri S. Friedman (ed.), *What Motivates Suicide Bombers?* San Diego: Greenhaven, 2005.

Dayan, Hilla. "Poisoned Cats and Angels of Death: Israeli and Palestinian Combatant Women." *To Kill, to Die*, 9–12.

_____. "Theories of Gender and Nationalism," work in progress. May 13, 2005, http://www.fhk.eur.nl/personal/zuidhof/Hilla_files/Nationalism%20Engendered.doc.

Dickey, Christopher. "Women of Al Qaeda." *Newsweek*, U.S. Ed., December 12, 2005, 26.

Diplomat News Service. "The Beslan Attack & Qaeda Link," Vol. 61 Issue 11. September 13, 2004.

Discovery Channel. "Suicide Bombers: Cult of Death." September 10, 2005.

Doroquez, David B. "The Israeli-Lebanon Conflict: Past and Present," 2003. September 10, 2005, http://www.doroquez.com/arts/documents/rsoc03.pdf.

Dudkevitch, Margot. "Female Bomber: Attack Aimed at Youth," *Jerusalem Post*. June 20, 2005. July 2, 2005, http://www.jpost.com/servlet/Satellite?pagename=JPost/JPArticle/ShowFull&cid=1119234009872.

Durkheim, Emile. *Suicide: A Study in Sociology*, translated by John A. Spaulding and George Simpson, George Simpson (ed.). New York: Free Press, 1897/1996.

Dviri, Manuela. "My Dream Was to Be a Suicide Bomber. I Wanted to Kill 20, 50 Jews. Yes, Even Babies," *Telegraph*, June 26, 2005. July 2, 2005, http://www.telegraph.co.uk/news/main.jhtml?xml=/news/2005/06/26/wmid26.xml.

"11 March 2004 Madrid Train Bombings." Wikipedia, September 30, 2005. October 4, 2005, http://en.wikipedia.org/wiki/March_11,_2004_Madrid_attacks.

Falk, Richard A. "Agora: ICJ Advisory Opinion on Construction of a Wall in the Occupied

Bibliography

Palestinian Territory: Toward Authoritativeness: the ICJ Ruling on Israel's Security Wall," 99 *American Journal International Law* 42 (January 2005).

Farniyev, Zaur. "One Life Sentence for 19 Lives — Court Hands down Sentences in Mozdok Bombing Case," *Current Digest of the Post-Soviet Press* 57, no. 11, Sec.: The Russian Federation — North Caucasus (April 13, 2005).

Fighel, Yoni. "Palestinian Islamic Jihad and Female Suicide Bombers," International Policy Institute for Counter-Terrorism, October 6, 2003. July 7, 2005, http://www.ict.org.il/.

Flash Points: World Conflicts. "Turkey-Kurdistan Conflict Briefing," no date. September 14, 2005, http://www.flashpoints.info/countries-conflicts/Turkey-Kurdistan-web/Turkey-Kurdistan_briefing.html.

Friedman, Lauri S. (ed.). *What Motivates Suicide Bombers?* San Diego: Greenhaven, 2005.

Ganor, Boaz. "Defining Terrorism: Is One Man's Terrorist Another Man's Freedom Fighter?" International Policy Institute for Counter-Terrorism, June 25, 2001. April 29, 2005, http://www.ict.org.il/.

Gardner, Simon, and Arjuna Wickramasinghe. "Sri Lanka Minister's Killing Sparks Civil War Fears," August 13, 2005. August 13, 2005, http://today.reuters.com/news/News Article.aspx?type=topNews&storyID=uri:2005-08-13T153939Z_01_DIT305931_RTRIDST_0_NEWS-SRILANKA-DC.XML&pageNumber=0&summit=.

_____. "Top Sri Lanka Minister Shot Dead, Tigers Blamed," August 13, 2005. August 13, 2005, http://thestar.com.my/news/story.asp?file=/2005/8/13/worldupdates/2005-08-13T163104Z_01_NOOTR_RTRJONC_0_-212571-2&sec=Worldupdates.

Garwood, Paul. "U.S. Military Released Iraqi of Same Name as One of Amman Hotel Bombers." *NC Times*, November 14, 2005. December 18, 2005, http://www.nctimes.com/articles/2005/11/15/military/111405195034.txt.

Glasser, Susan B. "Review May Shift Terror Policies: U.S. Is Expected to Look Beyond Al Qaeda," *Washington Post*, May 29, 2005, A01. October 4, 2005, http://www.washingtonpost.com/wp-dyn/content/article/2005/05/28/AR2005052801171.html.

Goodstein, Laurie. "Muslim Leaders Confront Terror Threat Within Islam," *New York Times*, September 2, 2005. September 2, 2005, http://www.nytimes.com/2005/09/02/national/nationalspecial3/02muslims.html?th=&adxnnl=1&emc=th&adxnnlx=1125684055-GC+GTs7828J+YcvEoMQI4Q.

Grassley, U.S. Senator Charles E. Letter, September 15, 2005.

Groskop, Viv. "Chechnya's Deadly 'Black Widows,'" *New Statesman* Vol. 133 Issue 4704 (September 6, 2004): 32(2).

Gulyayev, Sergei. "Woman Who Tried to Blow Up Commandant's Office Identified," *TASS* December 20, 2000.

Hammami, Rema, and Salim Tamari. "Anatomy of Another Rebellion," *Middle East Report 217* (Winter 2000). August 9, 2005, http://www.merip.org/mer/mer217/217_hammami-tamari.html.

Handwerk, Brian. "Female Suicide Bombers: Dying to Kill," National Geographic Channel, December 13, 2004. April 3, 2005, http://news.nationalgeographic.com/news/2004/12/1213_041213_tv_suicide_bombers.html.

Harding, Hanley J., Jr. Aurora Protection Specialists, Boca Raton, FL: *C/B/R/N: Chemical/Biological/Radiological/Nuclear Disaster Familiarization and Overview Manual*, March 2005.

_____. Email, "Personal Theory on the Psycho-sociology of Muslim Women Suicide Bombers," May 14, 2005.

_____. Boca Raton, FL: "Thoughts on Muslim Extremists and Terrorism." Aurora Protection Specialists A.L.E.T.A. (Advanced Law Enforcement Training Academy), Special Response Team Anti-Terrorism Training Curriculum, 2005.

Hardwick, Jennifer. Terrorism Research Center Emails, September 9, 12, 2005.

Hathout, Hasan. *Reading the Muslim* Mind. Plainfield, IN: American Trust, 1995.

Bibliography

Hathout, Maher. "What Happens After We Die?," *Larry King Live*, CNN, April 14, 2005.

Healing, Raven. "Chechnya After Aslan Maskhadov: Assassination of the Rebel President Signals Escalation in North Caucasus," *World War 4 Report*, April 10, 2005. October 5, 2005, http://WW4Report.com.

Heher, Ashley M. "Female Suicide Bombers an Extension of an Old Tradition," *Cox News Service*, April 28, 2002.

Hoagland, Jim. "The True War: Within, and for, Islam," *Washington Post*, July 14, 2005, A25.

"How Terrorists Train in Cyberspace." *The Washington Post* in *The Courier* (Waterloo-Cedar Falls, Iowa), August 7, 2005, A8.

Howard, Michael, and Ewen MacAskill. "Female Suicide Bomber Kills Six in Iraqi City Declared Free of Terrorists: New Tactics on Two Fronts: First Woman to Detonate Bomb Since 2003; Invasion 30 Wounded as They Queue to Join Army." *The Guardian* (London), September 29, 2005, S. International, 13.

Huly, Lt Gen Jan C. "Terrorist Bombing of the Marine Barracks, Beirut, Lebanon." *Henderson Hall News*, October 23, 2003. May 24, 2005, http://www.arlingtoncemetery.net/terror.htm.

Human Rights Watch, Russia. "Last Seen...: Continued 'Disappearances' in Chechnya," 14, no. 3 (D) (April 2002). April 9, 2005, http://hrw.org/reports/2002/russchech02/.

Hussain, Zahid, and Jay Solomon. "Al Qaeda's Changing Face," *Far Eastern Economic Review*, 167, Issue 34 (August 26, 2004): 20–21.

Ignatieff, Michael. "Book Review: What Is the Greatest Evil?: the Lesser Evil: Political Ethics in an Age of Terror," 118 *Harvard Law Review* 2134 (May 2005).

Intelligencer Editorial Board. "Global Struggle: War No More," *Seattle Post*, July 28, 2005. July 29, 2005, http://seattlepi.nwsource.com/opinion/234205_wared.html.

Israel Defense Forces. "Inside the Circle of Terror — Palestinian Women as Terrorists," July 11, 2004. October 1, 2005, http://www1.idf.il/dover/site/mainpage.asp?sl=EN&id=7&docid=35064.EN.

_____. "Main Terrorist Attacks against Israeli Civilians and IDF Soldiers since the Onset of Ebb and Flow," 2000–2003. June 30, 2005, http://www1.idf.il/SIP_STORAGE/DOVER/files/7/32367.doc.

_____. "Major Palestinian Terrorist Attacks Since September 2000," February 25, 2004. www1.idf.il.

Israel Ministry of Foreign Affairs. "The Role of Palestinian Women in Suicide Terrorism (Communicated by Israeli Security Sources)," January 30, 2003. August 29, 2005, http://www.mfa.gov.il/MFA/MFAArchive/2000_2009/2003/1/The+Role+of+Palestinian+Women+in+Suicide+Terrorism.htm.

_____. "Suicide and Other Bombing Attacks in Israel Since the Declaration of Principles (September 1993)," *MFR Newsletter*, 2004. June 30, 2005, http://www.mfa.gov.il/MFA/Terrorism-+Obstacle+to+Peace/Palestinian+terror+since+2000/Suicide%20and%20Other%20Bombing%20Attacks%20in%20Israel%20Since.

Israel-Palestine Liberation Organization Agreement: 1993. The Avalon Project, Yale Law School, August 9, 2005. August 9, 2005, http://www.yale.edu/lawweb/avalon/mideast/isrplo.htm.

"Israeli-Palestinian Conflict." *Wikipedia Encyclopedia*, August 1, 2005. August 2, 2005, http://en.wikipedia.org/wiki/Israeli-Palestinian_conflict.

Israel Security Agency. "Summary of Terrorist Activity 2004," January 5, 2005. April 15, 2005, http://www.mfa.gov.il/MFA/MFAArchive/2000_2009/2005/Summary%20of%20Terrorist%20Activity%202004.

Israeli, Raphael. "Palestinian Women: The Quest for a Voice in the Public Square through 'Islamikaze Martyrdom.'" *Terrorism and Political Violence*, 16, no. 1 (Spring 2004), 66–96.

Bibliography

_____. "The Promise of an Afterlife Motivates Suicide Bombers." In Lauri S. Friedman (ed.), *What Motivates Suicide Bombers?* San Diego: Greenhaven, 2005.

Jacob, Jabin T. "Suicide Bombers: A New Front Opens in Iraq." Article no. 1165, Institute of Peace and Conflict Studies, New Delhi, India, September 29, 2003. July 11, 2005, http://www.ipcs.org/ipcs/kashmirLevel2.jsp?action=showView&kValue=1174&subCatID=1022&mod=g.

Jacobson, Celean. "Palestinian Woman Tells of Changing Her Mind, Calling Off Planned Suicide Attack," Associated Press, May 30, 2002. September 22, 2005, http://www.papillonsartpalace.com/palestiWn.htm.

Jayamaha, Dilshika. "Partners in Arms: LTTE Women Fighters and the Changing Face of the Sri Lankan Civil War," 2004, 16. October 3, 2005, http://www.jjay.cuny.edu/terrorism/womencombatants.pdf.

Johnson, David. "Major Players in the Lebanese Conflict: The Governments, Militias, and Countries Involved." All Infoplease, 2000–2005. September 10, 2005, http://www.infoplease.com/spot/lebanon1.html.

_____, and Borgna Brunner. "Timeline of Key Events in Chechnya, 1830–2004," 2005. September 30, 2005, http://www.infoplease.com/spot/chechnyatime1.html.

Johnson, Larry. "Former CIA Man Says Bush Not Happy over New Terror Language." Raw Story Media, August 2, 2005. October 4, 2005, http://rawstory.com/news/2005/Former_CIA_man_says_Bush_not_happy_over_new_terror_la_0802.html.

Jurist. "Terrorism Law and Policy: World Anti-terrorism Laws," 2003. July 14, 2005, http://jurist.law.pitt.edu/terrorism/terrorism3a.htm.

Kalfaisms. "One Suicide Bomber Captured — Search For Second Bomber Called Off," October 20, 2004. June 22, 2005, http://www.thekalfafamily.com/one_suicide_bomber_captured.htm.

Kampfner, John. "A President Craves Understanding: "Would You Like It If People Who Shoot Children in the Back Come to Power, Anywhere on This Planet?" Vladimir Putin Gives Our Political Editor a Homily, Over Tea and Fruit Cake." *New Statesman* 133, Issue 4705, September 13, 2004, p. 10(4).

Kaplan, David E. "Tangled Roots of an Atrocity (Chechen Terrorism, Russia)," *U.S. News & World Report* Vol. 137, Issue 9, September 20, 2004, p. 28.

Kfir, Isaac. "Commentary — A Blow to the Peace Process," International Policy Institute for Counter-Terrorism, August 14, 2005. August 16, 2005, http://www.ict.org.il/spotlight/comment.cfm?id=1108.

Kimhi, Shaul, and Shemuel Even. "Who Are the Palestinian Suicide Bombers," *Terrorism and Political Violence*, 16, no. 4 (Winter 2004), 815–840.

Kite, Leigh A. "Note: Red Flagging Civil Liberties and Due Process Rights of Airline Passengers: Will a Redesigned CAPPS II System Meet the Constitutional Challenge?" 61 *Washington and Lee Law Review* 1385 (Summer 2004).

Kline, Chris, and Mark Franchetti. "The Woman Behind the Mask," *Sunday Times* (London). November 3, 2002, Sec. Features; News Review, 1.

Kruger, Lisa. Email interview, September 16, 21, 2005.

_____. *Gender and Terrorism: Motivations of Female Terrorists.* Master of science, strategic intelligence thesis, Joint Military Intelligence College, July 2005.

Kuttab, Daoud. "The Two Intifadas: Differing Shades of Resistance," Palestine Center and The Jerusalem Fund, Information Brief No. 66, February 8, 2001. August 9, 2005, http://www.thejerusalemfund.org/images/informationbrief.php?ID=53.

Langenberger, Birgit. "Women's Political Violence — A Case of Emancipation?" *To Kill, to Die, Feminist Contestations on Gender and Political Violence*, March 2004, 4–5.

"Lebanese Civil War." *Wikipedia*, January 13, 2005. October 2, 2005, http://en.wikipedia.org/wiki/Lebanese_Civil_War.

Bibliography

Lester, David, Bijou Yang and Mark Lindsay. "Suicide Bombers: Are Psychological Profiles Possible?" *Studies in Conflict and Terrorism* 27, no. 4 (July-August 2004): 283–295.

Ling, Lisa. "Female Suicide Bombers: Dying to Kill," National Geographic Channel, December 13, 2004.

Lininger, Tom. "Sects, Lies, and Videotape: The Surveillance and Infiltration of Religious Groups," 89 *Iowa Law Review* 1201 (April 2004).

Lippman, Matthew. "Essay: The New Terrorism and International Law," 10 *Tulsa Journal of Comparative and International Law* 297 (Spring, 2003).

Lopez Jr., Sgt. Melvin. "Terrorist Bombing of the Marine Barracks, Beirut, Lebanon," *Henderson Hall News*, October 23, 2003. May 24, 2005, http://www.arlingtoncemetery.net/terror.htm.

MacDonald, Neil. "Three Days to the Brink," *The Magazine*, October 12, 2000. October 5, 2005, http://www.cbc.ca/news/background/middleeast/threedays.html.

Marcus, Itamar. "Palestinian Authority TV Portrays Palestinian Martyrdom as a Christian Ideal." Palestinian Media Watch (see permissions) May 30, 2002. August 3, 2005, http://www.israel-wat.com/p4_eng.htm.

McCullagh, Declan. "Bush Signs Homeland Security Bill," CNET News.com, ZDNet, November 25, 2002. July 17, 2005, http://news.zdnet.com/2100-1009_22-975305.html.

McDonald, Mark. "Chechnya's Eerie Rebels: Black Widows," *Gazette* (Montreal, Quebec), Source: Knight Ridder Newspapers, October 24, 2003, Final Ed., Sec. News; A4.

Medetsky, Anatoly. "Counting on FSB's Bombing Testimony," *Moscow Times*, April 5, 2004, Sec.: No. 2894.

MILNET. "Brief Chronology of Russian Terrorism 1/1/1990 to 9/02/2004," August 28, 2005, http://www.milnet.com/Russian-Terrorism.html.

Morrissey, Belinda. *When Women Kill: Questions of Agency and Subjectivity.* London: Routledge, 2003.

Moscow Times. "24 Years Sought for Would-Be Bomber." April 7, 2004, Sec.: No. 2896.

MosNews.com. "Chechen Rebels Acknowledge Maskhadov's Death, Vow to Fight On." March 9, 2005. October 5, 2005, http://www.mosnews.com/news/2005/03/09/chechreaction.shtml.

MSNBC.com. "Congress Renews Patriot Act for One Month," December 22, 2005. December 26, 2005, http://www.msnbc.msn.com/id/10562008/.

Mulvey, Stephen. "Russia's Suicide Bomb Nightmare," BBC News Online, February 6, 2004. September 19, 2005, http://news.bbc.co.uk/1/hi/world/europe/3020231.stm.

Murphy, Kim. "Chechen Women Are Increasingly Recruited to Become Suicide Bombers." In Lauri S. Friedman (ed.), *What Motivates Suicide Bombers?* San Diego: Greenhaven, 2005.

National Commission on Terrorist Attacks upon the United States. *The 9/11 Commission Report: Final Report of the National Commission on Terrorist Attacks Upon the United States.* New York: W.W. Norton, 2004.

Nirenstein, Fiamma. "Anti-Semitism Motivates Suicide Bombers." In Lauri S. Friedman (ed.), *What Motivates Suicide Bombers?* San Diego: Greenhaven, 2005.

Norwegian Institute of International Affairs, Centre for Russian Studies Database. "Chronology of Events: A Wave of Terror Hits Russia—an Overview of the Most Important Terrorist Acts 1995-2004," August 31, 2004. April 16, 2005, http://www.nupi.no/cgi-win/Russland/krono.exe?6224.

Palestine Facts: Israel 1967–1991 Terrorist Attacks 1970s, 2005. September 12, 2005, http://www.palestinefacts.org/pf_1967to1991_terrorism_1970s.php.

Palestinian Media Watch, translator. "The Beat of the Words," Palestinian Authority Television, May 30, 2002, screening of clip on May 5, 2002. August 3, 2005, http://www.israel-wat.com/p4_eng.htm.

Bibliography

Pape, Robert A. "Al Qaeda's Smart Bombs," *New York Times*, July 9, 2005. July 9, 2005, http://www.nytimes.com/2005/07/09/opinion/09pape.html?ex=1121572800&en=7ebffbfaf30039a5&ei=5070&emc=etal.

_____. *Dying to Win: The Strategic Logic of Suicide Terrorism*. New York: Random House, 2005.

_____, in Patricia Wilson. "Religion, Suicide Terrorism Link Disputed in Book." *Reuters*, June 3, 2005. June 4, 2005, http://news.yahoo.com/news?tmpl=story&cid=578&e=6&u=/nm/20050603/ts_nm/security_terrorism_dc.

_____. "Nationalism Motivates Suicide Terrorists." In Lauri S. Friedman (ed.), *What Motivates Suicide Bombers?* San Diego: Greenhaven, 2005.

Parfitt, Tom. "Meet Black Fatima — She Programmes Women to Kill," London: *Sunday Telegraph*, July 20, 2003, 28.

"Peace Deal in Sri Lanka." *BBC News*, February 21, 2002. October 4, 2004, http://news.bbc.co.uk/1/hi/world/south_asia/1833230.stm.

Pedahzur, Ami, Arie Perliger and Leonard Weinbergy. "Altruism and Fatalism: the Characteristics of Palestinian Suicide Terrorists," *Deviant Behavior* 24, no. 4 (July-August 2003): 405–423.

Perry, Tom, and Edmund Blair. "Three Killed, Seven Injured in Two Cairo Attacks," April 30, 2005. May 1, 2005, http://www.reuters.com/newsArticle.jhtml?type=topNews&storyID=8351898.

Philp, Catherine and Rana Sabbagh-Gargour. "Husband and Wife Suicide Team 'Behind Jordan Bomb,'" TimesOnline, November 12, 2005. December 19, 2005, http://www.timesonline.co.uk/article/0,,251-1869041,00.html.

Pipes, Daniel. "Despair and Hopelessness Do Not Motivate Suicide Bombers." In Lauri S. Friedman (ed.), *What Motivates Suicide Bombers?* San Diego: Greenhaven, 2005.

Potter, Mitch. "Female Bomber Kills 2 Israeli Border Guards," *The Toronto Star*, September 23, 2004, A06.

"Profiles: Russia's Most Wanted." BBC News, September 8, 2004. October 5, 2005, http://news.bbc.co.uk/1/hi/world/europe/3637126.stm.

Prusher, Ilene R. "Despair and Hopelessness Motivate Suicide Bombers." In Lauri S. Friedman (ed.), *What Motivates Suicide Bombers?* San Diego: Greenhaven, 2005.

Radio Free Europe/Radio Liberty. "Factbox: Major Terrorist Incidents Tied to Russian-Chechen War," September 6, 2004. June 27, 2005, http://rfe.rferl.org/featuresarticle/2004/09/d981dd2d-8b08-41ff-a2e2-ada25338093c.html.

Rajan, V.G. Julie. "Essay: Subversive Visibility and Political Agency: The Case of Palestinian Female Suicide Bombers," *To Kill, to Die*, 12–13.

Rajasingham, K.T. "Sri Lanka: the Untold Story: Rajiv Gandhi's Assassination, Asia Times, 1995–2005. July 23, 2005, http://www.lankalibrary.com/pol/rajiv.htm.

Rasner, Mariya. "'Black Widow' Fears Surround a Russian Verdict." *Women's eNews*, February 6, 2005. April 9, 2005, http://www.womensenews.org/article.cfm/dyn/aid/2175/context/cover/.

Rechkalov, Vadim. "Psychology of Chechen Woman Suicide Bombers Pondered," *Global News Wire*, August 5, 2003.

Renke, Wayne N. "Special Issue Globalization and the Law: Book Review: Why Terrorism Works: Understanding the Threat, Responding to the Challenge, Alan M. Dershowitz," 41 *Alberta Law Review* 771 (December 2003).

Reuter, Christoph. *My Life Is a Weapon: A Modern History of Suicide Bombing*, translated by Helena Ragg-Kirkby. New Jersey: Princeton University Press, 2004.

Reuters. "Iraq Woman Bomber Kills Army Recruits in Tal Afar," *New York Times*, September 28, 2005.

Reynolds, Jefferson D. "Collateral Damage on the 21st Century Battlefield: Enemy Exploita-

Bibliography

tion of the Law of Armed Conflict, and the Struggle for a Moral High Ground," 56 *Air Force Law Review* 1 (2005).

RIA Novosti. "Reference: Terrorist Attacks in Moscow in 1999–2004," September 1, 2004, ACC-NO: 4791672.

Ricolfi, Luca (Paolo Campana). "Suicide Missions in the Palestinian Area: A New Database," 2004. August 2, 2005, http://www.prio.no/cscw/pdf/micro/techniqes/suicide_missions.pdf.

Ritzer, George, and Douglas J. Goodman. *Sociological Theory, 6th ed.* Boston: McGraw-Hill, 2004.

Roberts, Bob. "Gulf War 2: Forces Mystery: Women Suicide Bombers," *The Mirror*, April 5, 2003, 2.

Rose, Jacqueline. "Deadly Embrace: Book Reviews: *My Life Is a Weapon: A Modern History of Suicide Bombing* by Christoph Reuter, trans. Helena Ragg-Kirkby, and *Army of Roses: Inside the World of Palestinian Women Suicide Bombers* by Barbara Victor," *London Review of Books*, 26 no. 21, November 4, 2004. April 9, 2005, http://www.lrb.co.uk/v26/n21/rose01_.html.

Saleh, Basel. "Palestinian Suicide Attacks Revisited," *Peace Magazine* 21, no. 2, April 1, 2005, p. n/a.

Schweitzer, Yoram. "Female Suicide Bombers for God." No. 88, October 9, 2003. June 6, 2005, www.tau.ac.il/jcss/tanotes/TAUnotes88.doc.

_____. "Suicide Bombings: The Ultimate Weapon?" ICT, August 7, 2001. April 15, 2005, http://www.ict.org.il/articles/articledet.cfm?articleid=373.

_____. "Suicide Terrorism: Development & Characteristics." ICT, April 21, 2000. April 15, 2005, http://www.ict.org.il/articles/articledet.cfm?articleid=112.

"Second Chechen War." *Wikipedia Encyclopedia*, August 1, 2005. August 2, 2005, http://en.wikipedia.org/wiki/Second_Chechen_War.

Shah, Anup. "Crisis in Chechnya," globalissues.org, September 4, 2004. October 5, 2005, http://www.globalissues.org/Geopolitics/Chechnya.asp.

Shemin, Stephanie. "Wrongheadedness of Female Suicide Bombers," *Chicago Tribune*, Op-Ed, June 18, 2002. July 2, 2005, http://www.cfr.org/pub4621/stephanie_shemin/wrong headedness_of_female_suicide_bombers.php.

Silverman, Erica. "Jordanian Citizens in Israeli Prisons," *Al-Bawaba*, July 23, 2005.

Skaine, Rosemarie. "Neither Afghan Nor Islam," "Symposium on September 11, 2001: Terrorism, Islam and the West." *Ethnicities* 2, Issue 2 (June 2002): 142–144.

_____. *Women at War: Gender Issues of Americans in Combat*, Jefferson, N.C.: McFarland, 1999.

_____. *The Women of Afghanistan Under the Taliban*, Jefferson, N.C.: McFarland, 2002.

Smith Craig S. "Raised as Catholic in Belgium, She Died as a Muslim Bomber." *New York Times*, December 6, 2005. December 17, 2005, http://www.nytimes.com/2005/12/06/international/europe/06brussels.html?ex=1134968400&en=bcc647f73eedbcdb&ei=5070.

Speckhard, Anne, Nadejda Tarabrina, Valery Krasnov and Khapta Akmedova. "Research Note: Observations of Suicidal Terrorists in Action," *Terrorism and Political Violence*, 16, no. 2 (Summer 2004), 305–327.

Speulda, Nicole, and Mary McIntosh. "Global Gender Gaps," Pew Research Center for the People and the Press Commentary, May 13, 2004. August 22, 2005, http://pew global.org/commentary/print.php?AnalysisID=90.

Spinner, Jackie. "Female Suicide Bomber Attacks U.S. Military Post." *The Washington Post*, September 29, 2005, A16. December 23, 2005, washingtonpost.com.

"Sri Lanka Database — Suicide Attacks by the LTTE." 2001. September 17, 2005, http://www.satp.org/satporgtp/countries/shrilanka/database/data_suicide_killings.htm.

Bibliography

SSNP.com. Syrian Social Nationalist Party, Gallery, "Our Martyrs," 1977. September 13, 2005, http://www.ssnp.com/new/gallery/shouhada_en.htm.

State of Israel, Ministry of Foreign Relations. "Facts About Israel: 2000–2004 — Major Terror Attacks," November 2, 2000. April 16, 2005, http://www.mfa.gov.il/MFA/Facts+About+Israel/Israel+in+Maps/2000-2004-+Major+Terror+Attacks.htm.

"Suspect Retells Beslan's Horror; Leader Blew Up Female Bombers After They Balked at Taking Children Hostage, Court Told." Associated Press in *The Record* (Kitchener-Waterloo, Ontario), June 1, 2005, A7.

Taran, Preston. "Martyrdom," Arabic Media Internet Network, June 1, 2005. June 22, 2005, http://www.amin.org/eng/uncat/2005/june/june1.html.

Taranto, James. "Best of the Web Today," *WSJ.com Opinion Journal*, June 3, 2002. September 19, 2005, http://www.opinionjournal.com/best/?id=110001794.

Tavernise, Sabrina. "Suicide Blast by Woman in Iraq Kills 8 Others; 57 Are Hurt," *New York Times*, September 29, 2005.

"Terror 2005: Learning How to Be a Killer on the Net." *Irish Independent*, July 23, 2005.

"Terrorists and Militants in Haaretz." Tutti i diritti riservati, *Paravia Bruno Mondadori* Editori, October 20, 2004. July 4, 2005, http://www.pbmstoria.it/fonti1865.

Thompson, Paul. "Abridged 9/11 Timeline," n.d. September 26, 2005, http://billstclair.com/911timeline/main/timelineshort.html.

Timmerman, Kenneth R. "Children Are Indoctrinated to Become Suicide Bombers." In Lauri S. Friedman (ed.), *What Motivates Suicide Bombers?* San Diego: Greenhaven, 2005.

Trevelyan, Mark. "Terrorist Bank Deals Seen as Impossible to Spot," *Reuters*, September 29, 2005. September 29, 2005, http://today.reuters.com/news/NewsArticle.aspx?type=topNews&storyID=uri:2005-09-29T133403Z_01_BAU948325_RTRUKOC_0_US-SECURITY-FINANCE.xml.

TruthNews. "Female Bomber Disgusted by Fatah Handlers," May 31, 2002. June 22, 2005, http://truthnews.com/world/2002060103.htm.

Uhl, Kristen Elizabeth. "Comment: the Freedom of Information Act Post–9/11: Balancing the Public's Right to Know, Critical Infrastructure Protection, and Homeland Security," 53 *American University Law Review* 261 (October 2003).

United Nations News Centre. "Annan Announces New Initiative to Bridge Gap Between Islamic, Western Worlds," July 14, 2005. July 15, 2005, http://www.un.org/apps/news/story.asp?NewsID.

United Nations Office for the Coordination of Humanitarian Affairs in the Russian Federation United. "Russian Media Review for 15.05.2003," RIA Novosti, May 15, 2003. August 28, 2005, http://www.ocha.ru/public.php?_act=new&_op=view&_ti=7128.

United Nations Office on Drugs and Crime. "Conventions Against Terrorism," 2005. July 15, 2005, http://www.unodc.org/unodc/en/terrorism_conventions.html.

_____. "Implementing International Action Against Terrorism," 2005. July 14, 2005, http://www.unodc.org/unodc/en/terrorism.html.

_____. "Overview — Conventions Against Terrorism," 2005. July 15, 2005, http://www.unodc.org/unodc/en/terrorism_convention_overview.html.

UPI NewsTrack. "FSB: Woman Responsible for Car Bomb," August 31, 2004, pNA.

U.S. Department of Homeland Security. "Transcript of Secretary of Homeland Security Tom Ridge at the Launch of New Ready Campaign Public Service Advertisements," November 22, 2004. July 17, 2005, http://www.dhs.gov/dhspublic/interapp/speech/speech_0230.xml.

U.S. Department of Justice. *The Attorney General's Guidelines on General Crimes, Racketeering Enterprise and Terrorism Enterprise Investigations*, 22, 2002. July 17, 2005, http://www.usdoj.gov/olp/generalcrimes2.pdf.

Bibliography

U.S. Department of State, Bureau of Democracy. "Human Rights, and Labor Turkey Country Report on Human Rights Practices for 1998," February 26, 1998. September 22, 2005, http://www.hri.org/docs/USSD-Rights/1998/Turkey.html.

U.S. Department of State, Bureau of Public Affairs, Bureau of Economic and Business Affairs. "Money Laundering and Terrorist Financing in the Middle East and South Asia," July 13, 2005. July 16, 2005 http://www.state.gov/e/eb/rls/rm/2005/49564.htm.

U.S. Department of State, Bureau of Public Affairs, Counterterrorism Office, Counterterrorism, Finance Unit. n.d. July 16, 2005, http://www.state.gov/s/ct/terfin/.

U.S. Department of State Bureau of Public Affairs, Counterterrorism Office. "U.S. Counterterrorism Policy," n.d. July 16, 2005, http://www.state.gov/s/ct/.

U.S. Department of State, Bureau of Public Affairs, Office of the Historian. "Significant Terrorist Incidents, 1961–2003: A Brief Chronology," March 2004. April 17, 2005, http://www.state.gov/r/pa/ho/pubs/fs/5902.htm.

U.S. Department of State, Counterterrorism Office. *Country Reports on Terrorism, 2004*, Chapter 6 Terrorist Groups, April 27, 2005. June 7, 2005, http://www.state.gov/s/ct/rls/45394.htm.

_____. *Country Reports on Terrorism, 2004*, April 2005, "Terrorist Group Profiles," "Al-Aqsa Martyrs Brigade," U.S. Navy, May 10, 2005. June 23, 2005, http://library.nps.navy.mil/home/tgp/aqsa.htm.

_____. *Country Reports on Terrorism, 2004*, April 2005, "Terrorist Group Profiles," "Al-Qaeda," U.S. Navy, May 11, 2005. June 24, 2005, http://library.nps.navy.mil/home/tgp/qaida.htm.

_____. *Country Reports on Terrorism, 2004*, April 2005, "Terrorist Group Profiles," "Hamas," U.S. Navy, May 11, 2005. June 24, 2005,http://library.nps.navy.mil/home/tgp/hamas.htm.

_____. *Country Reports on Terrorism, 2004*, April 2005, "Terrorist Group Profiles," "Kongra-Gel (KGK)," U.S. Navy, May 11, 2005. June 24, 2005, http://library.nps.navy.mil/home/tgp/kurds.htm.

_____. *Country Reports on Terrorism, 2004*. April 2005. "Terrorist Group Profiles," "Tanzim Qa'idat al-Jihad fi Bilad al-Rafidayn (QJBR)," U.S. Navy, May 11, 2005. June 24, 2005, http://library.nps.navy.mil/home/tgp/qjbr.htm. .

_____. *Patterns of Global Terrorism 2003*, April 2004. April 28, 2005, http://www.state.gov/s/ct/rls/pgtrpt/2003/.

U.S. Patriot Act. USA Patriot Act FOIA Page, HR 3162 RDS, 107th Congress, 1st Session, H. R. 3162, in the Senate of the United States, Received October 24, 2001. September 4, 2005, http://www.epic.org/privacy/terrorism/hr3162.html.

Usher, Graham. "Palestinian Women, the Intifada and the State of Independence: an Interview with Rita Giacaman," *Race and Class* 34, no. 3 (January-March 1993): 31 (13).

Uzzell, Lawrence. "Profile of a Female Suicide Bomber," *Chechnya Weekly*, 5, i. 6, (February 11, 2004).

Victor, Barbara. *Army of Roses: Inside the World of Palestinian Women Suicide Bombers.* Emmaus, PA: Rodale, 2003.

Viner, Katharine. "I Made the Ring from a Bullet and the Pin of a Hand Grenade," *The Guardian*, January 26, 2001. September 10, 2005, http://www.mqm.com/EnglishNews/Jan-2001/leilakhalid.htm.

Wadhams, Nick. "U.S. Seeks to Firm Up Terrorist Sanctions," Associated Press in *Guardian Unlimited*, July 14, 2005. July 14, 2005, http://www.guardian.co.uk/worldlatest/story/0,1280,-5139772,00.html.

Williams, Jr., Rear Admiral D.M., USN (Ret.). Former Commander, Naval Investigative Service Command, interview, May 16, 2005.

Bibliography

Wong, Edward. "Bombers Kill at Least 36 at Baghdad Police Academy." NYTimes.com News, December 6, 2005. December 18, 2005, http://www.nytimes.com/2005/12/06/international/middleeast/06cnd-iraq.html?ex=1135054800&en=6e369be2d930de44&ei=5070.

_____. "Rebels Dressed as Women Attack Iraqi Police Station," *New York Times*, November 5, 2005. November 5, 2005, http://www.nytimes.com/2005/11/05/international/middleeast/05iraq.html?ex=113185800.

"Worlds Apart: The Roots of Regional Conflicts Sri Lanka: The Price of Reconciliation." *Britannica.com*, 1999. August 2, 2005, http://www.britannica.com/worldsapart/5_timeline_print.html.

Youngblut, Corporal Ray, (Ret.), 45th Division Infantry (Thunderbird). Interview, September 12, 2005.

Zedalis, Debra D. *Female Suicide Bombers*. Carlisle PA: Strategic Studies Institute, U.S. Army War College, June 2004. April 2, 2005, http://www.carlisle.army.mil/ssi/pdffiles/00373.pdf.

Index

Index

Index

Index

globe 151
glory 8, 18
goal 3, 8, 14, 16, 22, 34, 44, 48, 61, 70, 74, 87, 133, 151, 159
God 8, 13, 16–18, 54, 127
governance 22
government 41
Grand Hyatt hotel 56
Grassley (R-IA), Charles E. 153
Greater Syria 23
Grebenskaya, Chechnya 115
Green Zone 54
grievance 17
Groskop, Viv 41, 100, 109, 116–117
Gross, Max vii
Gross, Nasrine 36
group 9, 23, 25–26, 29
groupthink 34, 171
Grozny, Chechnya, Russia 97, 99–101, 104, 115
Guantanamo Bay, Cuba 154
guerrilla 10, 56, 103, 111, 118
guerrilla war 10, 51
Gular, Otas 81–82

Ha'ayin, Israel 129
Hadarim detention center, south Israel 126
Hadera 141
Hadith 15
Haditha Dam 54
Haifa, Israel 76, 129
Hamamra, Tauriya 46, 143
Hamangoda, Brig. Anand 90
Hamas 4, 9, 28, 36–37, 39, 40, 49, 53, 75, 81–82, 94, 122–124, 126–127, 130–131, 133, 135, 145–146, 148, 150
Hamdan, Abir 141
Hamidah, Al Taher 78
hand grenade 59, 88, 144
handler 4, 30, 44, 46–47, 118
Haram esh Sharif 122
Harb, Kharib Ibtisam 77, 79
Harding, Hanley J., Jr. vii, 16, 44
Hardwick, Jennifer vii, 7, 150, 164
Harkat el-Mukawma el Islamiya or "The Islamic Resistance Movement" see Hamas
Harkat ul-Mujahedeen 21, 23
harm 64
Hashaika 141
Hashash, Haula 145
Hashishiyun 8
Hassan, Norma Abu 49, 79
Hathout, Maher 17
Hatzbaya, Lebanon 78
Heathrow Airport 76
heaven 15
Hebrew University, Jerusalem, Israel 11

Heher, Ashley M.
hero/heroine 38, 137, 170
heroism 9, 139
Hezbollah 9, 23, 49, 74–76, 79, 87, 122, 124, 147
hijacker 7, 58, 60, 72
hijacking 13, 59, 60, 65, 69, 74, 76–77
Hindu 85
history 21
Hoagland, Jim 72
Holy Land 16
holy war 16, 36, 146, 148; see also jihad
homeland 14, 85
homemaker 43
honor 1, 16, 21, 36, 41, 48, 134
hospital 56
hostages 65, 97, 103, 108, 111–113, 152
Hotari, Saeed 94
Hudaybiah treaty 43
Huly, Lt Gen Jan C. USMC 9
human bombs 32, 81
human rights 4–5, 68, 86, 98, 157–158, 162; watch 5, 157
human values 151
humanity 72
humiliation 21, 33, 41, 160
husband 19, 41, 51
Hussein, Saddam 54, 137

ideal 13
identity 33, 87
ideology 21, 131, 159
IDF see Israeli Defense Forces
Idris, Mabrook 138
Idris, Wafa 53, 125–126, 132, 134–139
Igor (handler) alias Ruslan 118
Ilankai Thamil Arasu Kadchi 94
illiteracy 20, 51
Imperial Roman world 8
imperialism 12, 15
imprisonment 145–146, 157
incidence/incident 11, 12
independence 32, 41, 85, 88, 97–98, 116–117, 124
India 8, 11, 67, 85, 89
Indian National Army 50, 62
India's Prime Minster 51, 89
individual 1–3, 11, 13, 18, 21, 33–35, 38, 64–65, 87, 133
indoctrination 18, 21, 37–38, 44–46
Indonesia 158
inequality 31, 170
infidelity 134
infidels 14, 54
information 1
injury 64, 90
injustice 21, 31

218

Index

Index

Palestinian-Israeli conflict 1, 4, 27, 121, 124–125, 140, 168
Palestinian Islamic Jihad (PIJ) 4, 27, 40, 43, 49, 53, 75, 123–124, 128–129, 140–141, 145, 150
Palestinian Liberation Organization (PLO) 36, 59, 73
Palestinian Media Watch 13
Palestinian refugee 73
Paley, Cass viii
Pape, Robert A. 2–3, 11–12, 14, 20–21, 25–26, 41–42, 48–50, 74, 76, 94–95, 158–159
paradise 14–15, 33, 97, 139, 148
paramilitary commanders 98
Parfitt, Tom 47
Parti Populaire Syrien (PPS) see Syrian Socialist National Party
Partiya Karkeren Kurdistan (PKK) see Kurdistan Workers Party
Party of God 74; see also Hezbollah
passivity 39
patriarchal society 10, 33, 48
Patriot Act 152, 153
patriotism 139
Patterns of Global Terrorism, 2004 12
peace 59, 96, 98, 148; agreement 138; process 151; treaty 41
Pedahzur, Ami 27
Pennsylvania 7
Pentagon 12
perpetrator 7, 10, 60, 166
Persian Gulf 158
Persian Gulf War 70
Pew Global Attitudes Project 31
phenomena 7
Philippine Islands 9
photographs 49
PIJ see Palestinian Islamic Jihad
Pipes, Daniel 18
pistols 109
PKK see Kurdistan Workers Party
plastic explosives 65
Plato 7, 24
poetry 13
police 43, 47, 52–53, 56, 81, 82, 83, 88, 90–91, 109, 115, 119, 122, 130, 136, 140–141, 144, 158, 166
Polichik, Irena 129
Popular Front for the Liberation of Palestine 58–59, 75–76, 125
population 31, 38, 61, 150, 170
poverty 18, 20, 87
Powell, Colin 48, 128
power 3, 8, 13, 16, 18, 38–39, 45, 48, 61, 134, 151, 167, 168
Prabhakaran, Velupillai 85, 86, 87

practice 2
predestined life 32
prejudice 3, 48
Primadasa, President Ranaginghe (Sri Lanka) 87
prime minister 51, 92
prisons 81, 115, 125, 144, 146, 149
prisoner abuse 154
prisoner of war 155
privacy concerns 153
Prokhladny Air Force base, Russia 105
propaganda 17
Prophet Muhammad 15, 19, 43
prophets 19, 43
prototypes 29
Prusher, Ilene R. 38
psyche 26
public opinion 31, 131
public morale 60
publicity 61
Puli Padai (Tigers Army) 94
punishment 36, 64, 134
purification 33
Pushkin Square 120
Putin, Vladimir 98

Qa'idat al-Jihad fi Bilad al-Rafidayn (QJBR) 22, 23
Quda, Faris 38
Qur'an 16, 37, 129; see also Koran

Rabi, Ashraf 62
Rabiya, Shireen 143
race 153
Radio Free Europe/Radio Liberty 111
Radisson SAS hotel 56
Rahum, Ofir
Rajan, V. G. Julie 38–40, 48, 131, 167, 168
Rajaratnam, A. 94
Rajaratnam, Thenmuli see Dhanu
Ramadi, Iraq 56
Ramallah, West Bank 127, 131–132, 139, 144
Ramla, Israel 126
rape 86–87, 120, 167
Razawi, Ayman 125,141
recruitment 4, 20, 29, 42, 44, 57
Red Crescent 126, 135, 139
reform 13
refugees 73, 98, 121
Regional Arab Convention for the Suppression of Terrorism 67
religion 3, 9, 12–14, 16–18, 21, 23, 29, 32, 36, 39–41, 45, 49, 66, 81, 87, 94, 103, 115, 127, 129, 135, 137, 146, 148, 154, 160, 168
remote control 108
Renke, Wayne N. 65
repression 20

222

Index

Index